Shubhanku Kochar and Neepa Sarkar (eds.)

Pastoral and Anti-Pastoral
Representation of City and Village in Literature

Shubhanku Kochar and Neepa Sarkar (eds.)

PASTORAL AND ANTI-PASTORAL
Representation of City and Village in Literature

Bibliografische Information der Deutschen Nationalbibliothek
Die Deutsche Nationalbibliothek verzeichnet diese Publikation in der Deutschen Nationalbibliografie; detaillierte bibliografische Daten sind im Internet über http://dnb.d-nb.de abrufbar.

Bibliographic information published by the Deutsche Nationalbibliothek
The Deutsche Nationalbibliothek lists this publication in the Deutsche Nationalbibliografie; detailed bibliographic data are available on the Internet at http://dnb.d-nb.de.

Cover graphic: 22562396 © Oumjeab | Dreamstime.com

ISBN (Print): 978-3-8382-1904-2
ISBN (E-Book [PDF]): 978-3-8382-7904-6
© *ibidem*-Verlag, Hannover • Stuttgart 2024
Alle Rechte vorbehalten

Das Werk einschließlich aller seiner Teile ist urheberrechtlich geschützt. Jede Verwertung außerhalb der engen Grenzen des Urheberrechtsgesetzes ist ohne Zustimmung des Verlages unzulässig und strafbar. Dies gilt insbesondere für Vervielfältigungen, Übersetzungen, Mikroverfilmungen und elektronische Speicherformen sowie die Einspeicherung und Verarbeitung in elektronischen Systemen.

All rights reserved. No part of this publication may be reproduced, stored in or introduced into a retrieval system, or transmitted, in any form, or by any means (electronic, mechanical, photocopying, recording or otherwise) without the prior written permission of the publisher. Any person who commits any unauthorized act in relation to this publication may be liable to criminal prosecution and civil claims for damages.

Printed in the EU

Contents

Introduction
Shubhanku Kochar and Neepa Sarkar 7

1   Shunned Space Theory and Complex Pastoral Interpretation
    Barry Michael Cole 25

2   The Urbanized Pastoral in the Novels of Thomas Hal Phillips
    Kelvin Beliele 45

3   Culture, Identity, Diaspora and Displacement in Monica Ali's
    Brick Lane
    Pavlína Flajšarová 61

4   The London Underground in Neil Gaiman's *Neverwhere*
    Marie Berndt 75

5   Casteism and Countryside: A Literary Scrutiny
    M. Anjum Khan 97

6   Romantic Ireland's 'Dead and Gone': Reading the Antipastoral in Donal Ryan's *The Spinning Heart*.
    Christa de Brún 115

7   Artificial Nature in 19th Century France: the Buttes Chaumont Park and Landscape Art
    Costanza Bergo 133

8   'Schrödinger's Pedestrian':(ab)history & the (ab)pastoral in Miéville's *The City & The City*
    Nancy Ciccone 149

9   Irish Protestant Poets and the Dichotomy of Urban Belfast and Rural West
    J.R. Sackett 167

10 Jamaica Kincaid's *Among Flowers: A Walk in the Himalayas* as a Black Pastoral
    Dorottya Mozes 187

11 Urban Pastoral and Collective Memory in Penelope Lively's *City of the Mind*
    Pei Zhang 209

12 Paradise to Paradise Lost: Transforming Rural scape in Bibhutibhusan Bandyopadhay's *Aranyak*
    Roshni Subba 227

13 P(i)e(a)ce in Pastoral
    Pulkita Anand 243

14 Pastoral Paradoxes: A Study of Ankush Saikia's *The Forest Beneath the Mountains*
    Pronami Bhattacharyya 259

15 Dystopian Landscapes, Urban and Rural, of the Spanish Generation of 1898
    Mark DeStephano 277

16 Between Retreats and Returns: The Elusive Homeland in Temsula Ao's *These Hills Called Home*
    Dharmendra K. Baruah 301

17 The Pastoral as History and Myth: 'Professorial' Travail in Freya Stark's Ionian Quest
    Abhishek Chatterjee 317

Introduction

I

The terms Pastoral and anti-Pastoral are as old as human acts of creativity. Their usage might have been discovered late, but their presence has been there since the beginning of human habitation. Therefore, what we intend to offer through this collection of essays is a social history and not simply a literary history as it has been already provided by various scholars in other books. All the observations in the following pages are based on trends and patterns visible in literature across ages and places. To explain our point of view, we intend to start with three creative narratives. They are our creations and have not been taken from anywhere. Readers are free to contextualize them in their local context.

1

It was early morning in April. The Sun had just begun to broom away the thick shield of darkness. One could observe the layer of sluggishness still clinging to everything. Everyone looked drowsy and inactive. A gentle, but consistent wind was blowing. One could also hear the mild, yet clear rustling of the leaves. A youthful shepherd was leading his cattle on a steep hill. He was playing a pipe and singing and his herd was marching behind him as if he was leading a trained army into a battlefield. Behind his group, another shepherd of his age was also leading his cattle. He was also playing the pipe and singing and his herd, also, was following him like a well-disciplined army. There was a pattern in their movement and they were following a unified and regular method. It seemed that years of practice had given them absolute control over their movement. They were climbing the hill to provide their animals with fresh grass softened by last night's dew. Before them, their ancestors had been doing the same thing.

After climbing and singing for half an hour, they arrived on a smooth ground which was surrounded by trees and grass from three sides. Both the shepherds went to their favourite tree and sat down after scanning the entire ground. Their cattle started munching the grass as if nothing existed for them which was of more importance. Both the shepherds, feeling relaxed and satisfied, took again to playing their pipes. Their eyes were unblinkingly staring beneath the hill from where they had come. Suddenly, they stopped playing as they noticed a group of women climbing the hill. They looked at each other with excitement and anticipation. They remained silent and focused, whereas, their herd kept eating and frolicking. After some time, the group passed them by and they continued staring at them. When the group was about to turn towards the left lane which led the women to the nearest spring, two girls who were walking in the rear, turned back and winked at them. Within seconds, the women disappeared and the shepherd started to sing again.

When the Sun had become hot and sultry, when their cattle had finished their first round of eating, when they had just stopped singing, they again heard the sound of songs this time intertwined with sounds of bangles and anklets. The same group of women who were now climbing down were carrying their buckets and pots full of water. They again held on to their place. They again were mesmerized and frozen in anticipation, they noticed that the entire group was looking jollier and more vibrant. As soon as the group had passed them and was about to disappear behind the thick foliage, they noticed that the same women who were in the rear in the morning and were again walking behind as always were now giving them smiles. They got up and waved their pipes to acknowledge the receipt of their coded exchange.

2

When the sharpness of the sun began to give way to the mildness of the moon and the sweetness of the stars, the entire village came out in groups. They were all happy and relaxed. They were all jumping with joy. They were all clad in their best attire. They were all going towards the village play-ground. They had just finished planting this year's crops, now they will be waiting and guarding their fields until harvest. Nobody was thinking about the days of hard work and patience that would be their future for the next six months. Whatever will happen will happen tomorrow, today was their day and they knew that after this day, they would again be gathering only after the harvest. They knew that all the weddings and yearly social and religious rituals would take place after the harvest. They knew that a bumper crop would be required to carry out all the rituals both social and religious. Today was their day and they were happy about that.

Soon the playground was inundated with people. They were huddled there in their age groups. Elders with elders, young with young, children with children, men with men and women with women. As soon as the drummer entered with his assistants, they welcomed him with loud and penetrating cheers. Within seconds, the drummer climbed on the temporary stage that was made only in the morning for him and his assistants. When the drummer had adjusted his drums and his assistants had taken their place, there was another loud cheer from the crowd which indicated their restlessness. Sensing the urgency, the drummer started his music. He began, first gently and very soon picked the pace. The entire village responded with equal gusto. They danced away their cares. They jumped, sang, shouted, screamed, ran and surpassed each bet. Neither the drummer got up before midnight, nor did the villagers begin going back before midnight.

3

It was 9 a.m. and he was driving his car to the office. He was not able to focus on the road, his mind was flooded with numerous conflicts. His daughter was not well, she had a high fever for the last three days. Despite proper medication given by the best doctors, it was not subsiding but he had to leave her with servants back home. He had to reach the Taj International Hotel to meet one of the international clients. His boss had informed him in the morning that if he did not go and crack the deal which was to bring millions of U.S.Ds. to his company, he might be demoted. This was very serious as it would mean less money and public ignominy. He had been divorced only last month and his younger daughter was given to his wife for custody. He was supposed to pay for her expenses along with the huge sum that he had already given as compensation to his wife. He got wedded fifteen years back when he had just arrived in the city. He had high hopes and he had begun well. Very soon, he was in his dream job he had been selected from the campus. He received a furnished flat and a big and expensive car to begin with. His job required him to be on the move all the time and as a result, he had visited half of the world as a senior executive officer. His wardrobe and his entire house were full of different knick-knacks that he had picked up during his visits. His wife was also working as a senior executive in another international firm whom he had met during an official dinner in a five-star hotel. They immediately fell in love and after a courtship of six months were married. In the beginning, all was well, his wife was not required to be on the move all the time and she would wait for the nicest presents that he would bring. In the early days, she would also travel with him, but later, children came one by one. His parents and her parents used to live in their villages and could not adjust themselves to their fast-paced life. Servants came and went and the waits became longer and longer. When he was home, she would be busy with her official and social work and when she was home, he was flying now to this country and now to that country. He had no idea about the school and class that his daughters were studying in; he could never remember his daughter's birthday or his wedding anniversary. His parents were now dead and as a single child, he did not have any siblings. His cousins were always interested only in his money and gifts. Yes, he had very good friends, but they were friends and they could not replace his parents or his own family. They could only advise him sometimes they would stand with him, but most of the time, they also had their own family to look after. Today, he was badly missing his childhood home in the village with his parents. Yes, life was hard back then, things were tough, he had to walk for half an hour to and from school, and there was hardly any day with electricity for two hours, but things were fine. He had his parents to take care of him, he had very good friends and they, together, would run and jump as if they were the undisputed kings of whatever they looked at.

Human society began its first social encounter in and around forests. Over time, small groups of men and women emerged and began moving in search of greener pastures. As time went by, agriculture came into existence, life became stable and predictable. When our ancestors began to settle near rivers and started cultivating the land, first with hands and later with stone and iron tools, depending on the stage of evolution they were in, they gave birth to the idea of a small, but reliable system of exchange named as village.

These villages were initially small and had a common way of life. People would participate in subsistent farming and their needs were limited and their desires were none. In the beginning, all would farm and raise cattle. As land, water and animals were the only sources of their livelihood, they began with songs and stories eulogizing the qualities of land, water and animals. So much so that, they began linking forces and elements of nature with something more sublime and greater; chiefly God, as their life and death depended upon it. However, this should not be concluded that all was well then and there was a perfect utopia. Life was more vulnerable back then. People would die because of heavy storms or snake bites. When floods would visit, they would sweep away the entire settlement. Life was dependent upon the cycle of rain. If it would rain in time and would rain as much as crops and people wanted, all was fine and people would sing and dance giving birth to the idea of pastoral literature, but if it would rain more than required or if it failed to come resulting in famine, people would still sing, hoping for the good times to return. This time their songs and stories would remind people of the time when cattle were dying and there was neither grass nor trees to shelter and comfort, this probably gave birth to the idea of anti-pastoral. What we are trying to argue is that both pastoral and anti-pastoral have been there from the beginning and have been coexisting. They are an integral part of our evolution story; they have been there for ages and have been defining our mood and approach towards our surroundings. Their meaning depends upon the context and time in which they have been set. Human imagination is based on human experience. We as a human society have created both Heaven and Hell as narrative and counter-narrative.

For example, the concept of Paradise across cultures is, nothing but an example of a pastoral or idealized community with perfect peace and harmony whereas the concept of Hell across cultures represents dystopia, violence and an anti-pastoral landscape where there is neither harmony nor unity, where no one wants to either retreat for relaxation or from where no one returns with wisdom, as it happens in almost all great works of pastoral literature. The concept of joy and harmony is not place-bound, but it depends upon the context. For illustration, white Americans, most of the time in American history particularly before the First World War, had a comfortable life and had land, money and slaves, as cheap labour. On the other hand, for African Americans, for the same period in history, life in the rural South was full of violence, lynching, rapes, murders and segregation. For the African American community, life in American villages throughout the eighteenth and nineteenth centuries was never pastoral.

Likewise, for the Dalit community living in Indian villages in the last one thousand years, have faced inadequate and inferior ways of social and economic living. For the so-called high-born communities, Indian villages have been always the land of joy and mirth as they had all the means of living life to the fullest. Unlike, the upper cast communities, life for the lower caste communities in Indian villages has always been full of torture, neglect and insult. Quite contrary to this, the life of lower caste communities in Indian cities has been manageable but demanding as far as discrimination is concerned.

In the three narratives written above, Pastoral and Anti-Pastoral coexist side by side. In the first story of two youthful shepherds, everything seems happy as they go on about their daily lives. Their lady loves also reciprocate in the very manner that they want them to. There is neither any dearth nor lack of any kind, but one should not be carried away with this. Their life is full of hard work and drudgery. They have to get up very early each morning in all seasons. They have to stay the entire day out with their cattle as guards. There is no concept of a holiday for them. For their beloveds also, life is not easy. They have to climb up and down the mountain daily for water. They are not supposed to neglect their duty for even a single day. Both lovers can only meet each other when everyone else is sleeping as it is a close-knit society. They cannot indulge in open courtship. They use pipes, bangles, anklets and songs to make their hardships endurable. Likewise, in the second narrative also, everything looks golden and musical. People are having fun and this is the perfect case of pastoral life. One should not forget that this is ephemeral, once the dance is danced, once people get up the next day, their life will be as demanding as that of a city dweller. They will be guarding and waiting for the coming six months and if it does not rain in the desired quantity, they will not be able to celebrate the post-harvest festivals. If rain fails, they might also have a year of famine. Similarly, the third narrative is also a meeting ground of pastoral and anti-pastoral. Though it is set in the city, there is disintegration and fragmentation in life and relationships. There is pollution and traffic jams, but still, it is a success story. The protagonist is a winner in his way, how many individuals can first find a dream job in time and how many can visit so many countries in such a short duration? He has everything in the city, a well-paying job, a big house, expensive cars, servants and other material comforts. Yes, his married life is not successful and his wife and one daughter are not living with him, but this can happen even in the countryside. Happiness and sorrow do not depend upon the city and village alone. People could be both happy and sad anywhere.

Pastoral and anti-pastoral stance depends upon experience. Where the experience of a particular group is good, it is hailed as pastoral whereas if the experience is otherwise, it is talked of as anti-pastoral. It is not uncommon to find friction, cheating, violence and bad practices in the village. Likewise, it is not impossible to encounter good people, love, humanity, respect and reliable and responsible communities in the cities. One should not forget that our great ancestors who laid the foundation of the city in the first place were themselves villagers in the first place and people who settled from nomadic communities into stable agricultural communities were not villagers by birth. Both villages and cities are the result of human mobility and the desire to create something better than what is available at present.

In modern times, especially after the growth of capitalism, the line has furthered blurred between cities and villages. These days it is very common to come across farmhouses, resorts, retreat houses and national parks for the conservation of birds and animals on the outskirts of towns. These places create an illusion of pastoral experience. They try to put an experience or a way of life in a fixed bracket. They have a fixed formula where they try to recreate an exotic worldview which is linear and predictable. For these commercial enterprises, pastoral experience is the result of living in huts, drinking cow milk and sleeping on mud floors. These projects try to capture an entire system of village economy in simple metaphors. Likewise, villages of the twenty-first century are not what they used to be a hundred years back. Those villages which are situated near cities or in other words, where cities have expanded beyond control, they have converted nearby villages into small towns. These villages now look like towns with modern paraphernalia.

In the final analysis, both pastoral and anti-pastoral are, but realities lived by individuals and groups in various contexts. When villages were more populated and were the centre of life and economy, one finds the production of pastoral literature in abundance with harmony and equilibrium as a whole mark of village life. Similarly, when cities became the centre of life and power, one finds art also replicating this shift in terms of talking about cities. As far as Pastoral and anti-Pastoral are concerned, one finds that they are a result of one's exchange with one's setting and reality. For some, the same village is paradise and for some it is pandemonium. Likewise, the same city is a source of joy for one and a source of grief for another. Both Pastoral and anti-Pastoral are, but two sides of the same coin.

II

Pastoral as a concept has had varied interpretative meanings over the centuries. Often seen as an idyllic space that oscillated between the productive (farmlands, teeming forests) and the unproductive (wasteland, moors), pastoral was an alternate space away from the reality of the mainstream world but affected by it. It was categorized as a less powerful and 'innocent' place as compared to the industrial cities of enterprise and activity of the twentieth century. Pastoral in the literary world has a long history of being the natural retreat away from the cruelty and ravages of time and the mechanized 'productive' urban world. Various scholarly interpretations of the concept of the pastoral have been published over the last fifty years; the most notable works being Jonathan Bates's *Romantic Ecology: Wordsworth and the Environmental* Tradition (1991), Terry Gifford's *Pastoral* (1999) and *The Cambridge Companion to Literature and the Environment*, ed. by Louise Westling (2014).

The 19th century in the Western world saw a lot of novels that brought out the effects of industrialization on nature and people and simultaneously established the pastoral as a childlike space, thereby appositioning it along with the city. Such constructions became immensely popular in novels like Heidi (1881) by Johanna Spyri and The Swiss Family Robinson (1812) by John David Wyss. However, it was the pioneering vision of Charles Dickens that brought out the problems of the industrial urban space on humans in his novels and Hardy's novels showed the effects of human greed and corruption on the idyllic pastoral.

This binary power structure was carried forward in projects of colonization and invasion as evinced in the histories of native American civilization, South Asia, Africa and other erstwhile colonized civilizations. Until the medieval ages, nature was seen as dark, unknown, sinister and untamed; but with the Renaissance and its anthropocentric vision which extended to every phase of the human body, mind and external reality- nature too, came under its ambit and the effects of measuring, categorizing and domesticating nature can be seen in the various forms of landscape gardening and painting that emerged at that time. In the Indian context, harmony, ethics and cohabitation with nature were omnipresent as seen in the life and culture of tribal who believe in the peaceful symbiotic relationship with nature.

What makes this book different

The present volume of essays becomes important in today's context as this critical volume will help us decode further the need for environmental understanding and justice as well as interpret the concept of pastoral as it stands today. For ages, human habitations, ways of living and narration have been interlinked with the experiences of nature and its effects on life. Most of the studies in this area have focused on the idea of the pastoral and its dichotomous relationship with the urban. In the twentieth century, focus on the city gained much ground as concepts like 'flaneur' found representation in the works of Baudelaire and Walter Benjamin. Recent works to focus on the city as seen in *The Palgrave Handbook of Literature and the City*, ed. Jeremy Tambling (2017) and *Cities and Literature* by Malcolm Miles (2019).

Terry Gifford in his "Pastoral, Anti-Pastoral and Post-Pastoral as Reading Strategies" (42) looks at how the trope of anti-pastoral was brought in as a corrective measure to rid pastoral of its romantic and mythical eulogizations It is also true that connotations of the pastoral and anti-pastoral have always been riddled with ambivalences and ambiguities and scholars have noted the contradictions evident in these concepts. However, Raymond Williams tells us that pastoral often becomes a "myth functioning as a memory" for the general populace where the idea of rest, peace, tranquility and a simplistic life is often absent in the representation of the urban metropolitan life.

This volume of critical essays seeks to decipher the heterogeneity and plural effects of urban and rural spaces as well as negotiate the tenuous relationship between identity and belonging in postcolonial, global times. There have been several attempts in theorizing the idea of the pastoral in literature and Terry Gifford's *Pastoral* and Raymond William's *The Country and the City* help us look into the concept of the pastoral. However, in recent times, much work has concentrated on the idea of the city and its representation in literature without further adding to the concept of the pastoral. This book through its essays will look into complex pastoral and anti-pastoral interpretations and explore the ideas of belonging and identity in this critical narrative. Most of the chapters in this book deal with not-so-familiar texts, regions and authors and by bringing critical insight and enquiry into the approach of the above-mentioned concepts, hopes to contribute effectively to the field of ecocritical studies.

Summary

In Chapter One, "Shunned Space Theory and Complex Pastoral Interpretation", Barry Michael Cole theorizes "Shunned Spaces", regarding the antipastoral idea of nature. He argues that "Shunned Spaces" are those places that are outside the society. These spaces are reserved only for marginalized communities. These places are dirty and deprived of basic infrastructure. He further argues that people living in these spaces are more vulnerable to death and disease. For masses habiting the "Shunned Spaces", there is no concept of pastoral as green pasture. To illustrate his argument, Cole examines the works of African American novelist Jesmyn Ward. He demonstrates how in the writings of Ward; blacks suffer and disintegrate because they stay in "Shunned Spaces". Cole also includes novels by William Faulkner to highlight how even white writers present blacks living in "Shunned Spaces" which complicates their concept of pastoral. Kelvin Beliele, in Chapter Two, "The Urbanized Pastoral in the Novels of Thomas Hal Phillips", questions the binary opposition between pastoral and anti-pastoral. He challenges the representation of pastoral as calm, beautiful and ideal vis- a vis the city as corrupt, negative and hostile. He argues that these binaries are artificially constructed and circulated. He cites the novels of American novelist Thomas Hal Phillips to illustrate how these divisions are blurred and faded into one another. He demonstrates how in the fiction of Phillips, almost all the crimes and disasters transpire in villages whereas, the city provides a haven to those who are escaping the harshness of the villages. Thus, Beliele breaks the static codification of rural life as happy and fulfilling in contrast to city life which is often presented as monstrous.

Pavlina in Chapter Three," Culture, Identity, Diaspora and Displacement in Monica Ali's *Brick Lane* ", theorizes the idea of

Pastoral and anti-Pastoral concerning Bangladesh and England. She brings in the concepts of Memory and Culture to problematize the notion of home and host nation. In a case study of Monica Ali's *Brick Lane*, she postulates how the characters in this novel keep shuttling between a pastoral setting in Bangladesh and an anti-pastoral setting in England. Here, the home is perceived as idyllic, golden and beautiful by the migrant community from Bangladesh whereas the same community finds it difficult to adjust to a multicultural society chiefly in England where to exist and to be accepted is both a struggle and challenge. Ali paints vividly the trials of the Bangladeshi community by presenting a cultural clash which is further complicated by individual and collective memory and, as a result, the distinction between Pastoral, anti-Pastoral and post-Pastoral blurs. Marie Berndt in Chapter Four," The London Underground in Neil Gaiman's *Neverwhere*", argues how the imagined underground of London provides an escape from reality. The underground here is conceptualized as pastoral as it is contrary to London which is both fast and furious. For Berndt, the underground takes the readers to the past which is medieval and golden. Berndt also brings in the terms like Complicated Pastoral and Sentimental Pastoral which makes the chapter more interesting. Anjum Khan in Chapter Five, "Casteism and Countryside: A Literary Scrutiny", blasts the myth of pastoralism about Bama's *Karukku* and Imayam's *Beasts of Burden*. She presents a counternarrative of the village being a place of beauty and harmony. She opined that such a description of village life is one-sided as leaves out Dalits from consideration. For her, the village, no doubt, offers an untainted paradise for upper-caste people, but for lower-caste people, it is hell. She demonstrates through her selected texts how Dalits are subjected to countless tortures in the countryside which punctures the idea of pastoralism and gives birth to anti-pastoral for them.

In Chapter Six, "Romantic Ireland's 'Dead and Gone': Reading the Anti-Pastoral in Donal Ryan's *The Spinning Heart*", Christa Brun examines the concept of anti-pastoral regarding Irish literature in general and the *Spinning Heart* in particular. She remarks that Irish literature recording village life is usually pastoral. One finds purity, innocence, calmness, beauty, harmony and unspoiled landscapes as prominent features of Irish rural literature. She states that Ryan in The *Spinning Heart* subverts this myth of Arcadia and a rural utopia. She continues that Ryan's village is anti-pastoral it punctures the popular narrative of the village being calm and comforting. Ryan presents the village life as full of tears, troubles, tensions, unemployment, and misery. Here, people are migrating to urban settings to find hope and jobs. She concludes that Ryan has taken the backdrop of the Irish recession of 2008 to debunk the myth of the village as paradise thereby breaking the pastoral tradition to give birth to anti-pastoral tradition.

Costanza Bergo in Chapter Seven, "Artificial Nature in 19th Century France: the Buttes Chaumont Park and Landscape Art", argues how this park in particular and other urbanized parks in general along with landscape paintings of the time are highly political. Bergo maintains that because of rapid industrialization and urbanization, the cities in general and France, in particular, became heavily populated. There was dirt, dust, noise, waste, sickness, death and unemployment all around. People had come from villages in quest of jobs and wages. There was a class divide as well. To handle the possibility of a potential revolt, the French administration started building parks with new tactics. These parks like the landscape paintings of the time gave an artificial pastoral experience to both rich and poor. These spaces provided a place of relief and escape to both classes at the same time, thus becoming tools of political and social stability. These parks catered for the need for pastoral experience for both classes by offering exotic and utopian images of nature as one finds in fairy tales. Nancy Ciccone in Chapter Eight, "Schrodinger's Pedestrian: (ab)history and the (ab) Pastoral in Mieville's *The City in the City*", gives an interesting dimension to the concept of pastoral and anti-pastoral. She argues that in the above-mentioned novel, one finds the city in its most alive form. There is concrete, heavy population, pollution, industries and crime. These cities can be more fitted with the idea of anti-pastoral as they are opposite of the ideas associated with pastoral. She asserts that within these cities, one may encounter seeds of pastoral like a tree here, an open ground there, a bird, etc. She concludes that pastoral, for these modern cities, is a thing of the past, it may be there in the books, stories and imagination, but in the real world, it is not to be found. These cities are the new anti-pastoral remnants of what was there a long time back as pure pastoral if it was there!

J.R. Sackett in Chapter Nine," Irish Protestant Poets and the Dichotomy of Urban Belfast and Rural West", argues that Irish identity is not easy to define in the poetry of Louis MacNeice and Michael Longley. Sackett theorizes that in Ireland, place, culture, religion and identity are interlinked. There is a categorical division between the urban and industrial North and the calm and idyllic West. Sackett analyses the poems of MacNeice and Longley to assert how these poets' shuttle from noisy Belfast to the serene West to come to terms with the question of identity. They present Belfast as polluted, industrialized, dull, protestant, British and a place of crime and sin, whereas the West is represented as pastoral, beautiful, bucolic, rural and catholic hence more Irish. Sackett concludes that the question of identity is complex in Ireland because of cultural nationalism, settler colonialism and political, religious and geographical partition as the poetry of MacNeice and Longley reflect and as a result, the idea of pastoral concerning Ireland becomes fraught with multiple threads of necessity and compulsion for various set of groups.

Dorottya Mozes in Chapter Ten," Jamaica Kincaid's *Among Flowers: A Walk in the Himalayas* as a Black Pastoral", theorizes the concept of 'Black Pastoral'. She argues that *Among Flowers* is a travelogue with a difference. She opines that Kincaid has blasted the conventional and Western notion of a travelogue by perpetuating the idea of black ecology thereby giving birth to 'Black Pastoral'. A Black Pastoral, as Mozes continues is one where the conventional features of a pastoral like domination, control, the assertion by men over nature and objectification of nature are all subverted here. Mozes further postulates that here the central protagonist is a black woman whose experience is otherwise limited by racism at home, she does not destroy or dominate nature but rather respects and reveres both nature and the natives of the Himalayas. Mozes concludes that by introducing a black woman as a central figure, Kincaid has debunked all the set practices of a mainstream Western Pastoral and given birth to 'Black Pastoral'.

Pei Zhang, in Chapter Eleven," Urban Pastoral and Collective Memory in Penelope Lively's *City of the Mind*", explores the concept of Urban Pastoral regarding Collective Memory. Zhang argues that it is possible to connect the city with the pastoral. Historically, pastoral is only connected with the countryside. Every time, the city is rebuilt or renovated, it hides the past which stays in collective memory. She further remarks that one remembers a city with nostalgia if he/she is familiar with its past. Citing from *City of the Mind*, Zhang concludes that as in the novel, London is rebuilt in the nineties with glass and metal, it eliminates what it is to be in the past, but the narrator fondly remembers the London of the past with its gardens, rivers, streets, poverty and pollution, thereby giving birth to the notion of Urban Pastoral. Roshni Subba in Chapter Twelve, "Paradise to Paradise Lost Transforming Rural Scape in Bibhutibhusan Bandyopadhyay's *Aranyak*", points out how a serene and calm pastoral is disturbed and distorted by the idea of growth and development which gives birth to anti-pastoral. Subba argues that how Bandyopadhyay was ahead of his time when he foresaw the ill impacts of urbanization and commercialization. She takes a conventional stance when she equates rural with paradise thereby with pastoral and city with wickedness and anti-pastoral. She states that it is high time that we understand the sanctity of nature and start respecting her, otherwise it will be too late. She concludes that the world needs more rural paradises where people respect each other, instead of industrialized cities where people doubt and hate each other.

Pulkita Anand in Chapter Thirteen," P(i)e(a)ce in Pastoral ", argues that pastoral and anti-pastoral can coexist together. She analyses Anukrti Upadhyay's *Bhaunri* to justify her claim. She provides the history of the term pastoral regarding European literature which contextualizes pastoral in Indian literature in a global context. She demonstrates how each character can symbolize both simplicity and complexity to establish the presence of pastoral and anti-pastoral. She further links the binaries of village and city with growing environmental debates to prove how returning to pastoral can solve eco-crises. Pronami Bhattacharyya in chapter Fourteen," Pastoral Paradoxes: A Study of Ankush Saikia's *The Forest Beneath the Mountains"*, postulates that the world has gone far from a serene and calm place and has entered into what she remarks as a Dark Pastoral. She defines Dark Pastoral as a place where the lush greenery of the past has been invaded by development-related projects. She links this phenomenon with Colonialism. She argues concerning the *Forest Beneath the Mountain* and how modern Assam has eliminated the remnants of what it used to be just 100 years back. It was full of trees and forests where elephants could roam freely, but in the 21st century, it has been stripped of all its beauty. With this, as she continues, the harmony between man and animals has also vanished. She concludes that if one wants to negate this Dark Pastoral, one has to embrace the concept of Post-Pastoral.

Mark DeStephano in Chapter Fifteen," Dystopian Landscapes Urban and Rural of the Spanish Generation of 1898", theorizes a new angle on Pastoral and anti-Pastoral. He opines that the writers of the late 1890s and the first two decades of the 1900s are critical of both rural and urban. They do not find harmony either in the villages or in the cities. After Spain was defeated by America in 1898, as DeStephano puts it, Spain was a God-forsaken country. He points out that at the same time, other European cities like London, Paris and Berlin were thriving both materially and intellectually, but Madrid was declining culturally and intellectually. The writers of the time tried their best to heal Spain by presenting dystopian landscapes of both rural and urban centres. DeStephano concludes that both villages and cities of that time were anti-pastoral as there was crime, profligacy, corruption, wickedness and bankruptcy rampant everywhere which are the characteristics of anti-Pastoral and the writers of the generation did their best by exposing and criticizing that.

Dharmendra Baruah in Chapter Sixteen, "Between Retreats and Returns: The Elusive Homeland in Temsula Ao's *These Hills Called Home*", deploys the two defining features of Pastoral literature chiefly: Retreat and Return to bring forth how post-colonial literature engages with the traditional idea of pastoral, but with a difference. He argues how *These Hills Called Home* is set against the troubled questions of the identity of the Naga community in the Indian Northeast and conflict within and with larger forces of the

Indian state. Still, as Baruah puts it, there is a contrast between rural simplicity and urban shrewdness. He opines that Temsula Ao has utilized the trope of Retreat and Return to comment on the divide between village and city and to theorize how a conflict-ravaged zone can also work as a place of retreat and nostalgic return to homeland for some.

Abhishek Chatterjee in Chapter Seventeen," The Pastoral as History and Myth: 'Professorial' Travail in Freya Starks's Ionian Quest", links the idea of pastoral with travel writing. He argues how Stark being a women traveller breaks and reshapes both the content and form of travel writing. Chatterjee points out how Stark through her travels among the ruins of Ionia, reconstructs the past which was both golden and pastoral. For this, as Chatterjee relates, Stark has to crisscross the realm of history, myth, art and philosophy. Chatterjee concludes that Stark also critiques the idea of modern travel with its connection with tourism and focuses on the pastoral side of Stark's travelogue which is the result of intellectual engagement with the past and present.

Shunned Space Theory and Complex Pastoral Interpretation

African American literature emphasizes the importance of community in resisting oppression from the larger, mostly White society. I argue that Shunned Space Theory offers a new, holistic lens into African American literature that highlights the identity formation of individual characters within communities marked by scarcity, political exclusion, and periodic invasion. By definition, shunned spaces consist of land and resources the larger society deems undesirable or unfit for its direct occupation, thereby setting the difficult stage for identity formation for any marginalized group forced to live within them. Shunned Space Theory is an actionable[1] term with ongoing significance that can be applied to virtually any venue within which marginalized communities take root, flourish, and/or collectively perish. Although Shunned Space Theory is portable to the experience of almost any marginalized group, the focus of my research is on African American literature's placement of environment, characters, and community in context with each other and the larger, predominantly White society. Although this theoretical framework applies to many authors from a broad variety of genres, this writing focuses on interpreting its role in works by Mississippi author Jesmyn Ward, who writes about her own experience within shunned space during the early 21st century.

Criteria for Determining Shunned Space

Despite limitations imposed by scarcity, political exclusion, and violence, shunned spaces are deployed in African American literature to allow marginalized individuals to maintain personal and communal identities. I argue that shunned spaces must meet most, if not all, of the following criteria:

---

1 I define shunned spaces as *actionable* in that they evidence creation by the larger society and force marginalized residents to innovate cultural responses to produce enduring communities.

1. Exist either historically or in the present and are found within either a fictional landscape or an actual place. Shunned spaces can be adjacent to the dominant society or entirely separated from it.
2. Are overwhelmingly populated by a marginalized group (at least 75%).[2]
3. Endure violence, both external and internal, out of proportion to the general population.
4. Are sufficiently populated to permit communal identification framed by religious practice, oral and written narratives, a common sense of history, and community purpose.[3]
5. Possess third-space venues[4] in which individuals codify and rehearse a distinctive cultural perspective unique to each shunned space. In African American shunned spaces, churches typically fill a third-space role by converting the symbolic aspects of religion and place into a stage within which freedom from persecution is rehearsed and enacted.
6. Generate original, ingenious responses to scarcity, including oral and written narratives that convey a sense of communal identity.
7. Facilitate the formation of internal hierarchies that permit some degree of self-government.

---

[2] I choose 75% to emphasize that shunned spaces are not simply racially integrated, but overwhelmingly populated by historically marginalized individuals.

[3] In *The Negro's Church* (1969), Benjamin Elijah Mays and Joseph William Nicholson argue that the church serves as the primary venue "through which the masses of the Negro race [received] adult education" throughout Jim Crow (58).

[4] Yu-sien Lin interprets Bhabha's original definition of third space in a manner that fits my discussion. Lin had described the third space as a new productive space in which the historical dimensions and identities of cultures are challenged when two cultures meet. When white Christianity is joined with marginalized spaces, the result is a rejection of oppression and a call for freedom.

8. Are intermittently stripped of land and other resources by the dominant culture, thereby ensuring scarcity.[5&6]

Shunned space is visually interpreted as follows:

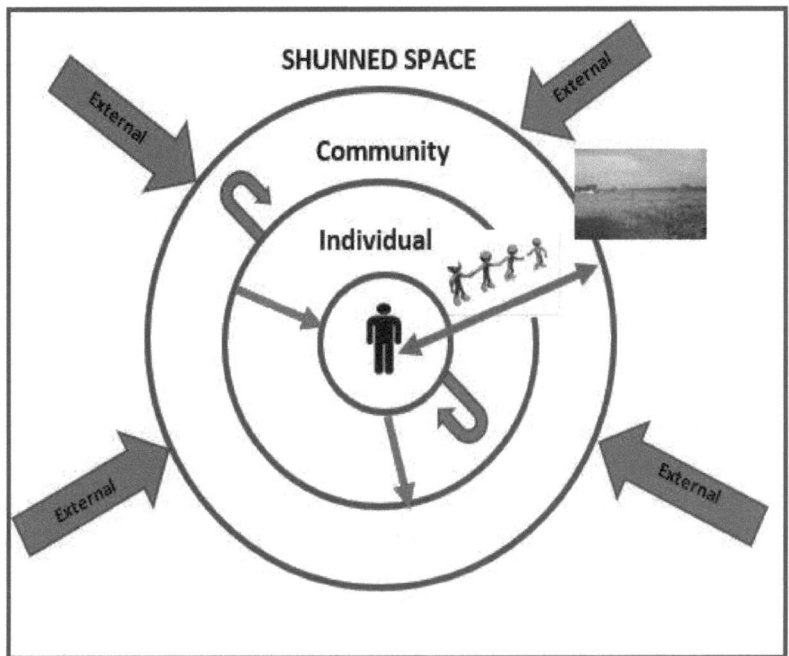

Figure 1

The visual components of shunned spaces are imperative for understanding such venues. I have therefore developed the generic diagram presented above for representing relationships between individuals, communities, and external forces at a glance. The individual is the innermost circle and is contained within the community, which is surrounded by the landscape of the shunned space.

---

5   NPR's Steve Inskeep explores an excellent example. The Osage Native American tribe in Oklahoma suffered the appropriation of their oil wealth to white "guardians," who confiscated much of the treasure in 1921, converting a community marked by enormous wealth into an impoverished enclave

6   Dr. Azita Amiri addresses the healthcare scarcity of Uniontown's residents by revealing that the town has only one doctor and the nearest hospital is over thirty miles away A toxic waste dump almost certainly contributes to the town's inability to access basic medical services.

The external force from the larger, predominantly White society is at least partly repelled by the shunned space, offering a relatively safe zone within which community and individual identity take root. (However, shunned spaces are not immunized from external invasion and aggression.) Additionally, the interrelationships between the individual, community, and the landscape are indicated by the two-pointed blue arrow. Three red, interior arrows directed from the individual to the community and vice versa indicate conflict between and among citizens of shunned space.

I argue that Ward illustrates the endemic racism, feminine empowerment, and environmental degradation of shunned space in *Men We Reaped: A Memoir*, *Salvage the Bones*, and *Sing, Unburied, Sing* to varying degrees. As a holistic endeavour, examining these writings from the perspective of shunned space involves a great deal of interplay among all these categories. They blend such that the whole is more than the sum of the parts. For example, the impact of Hurricane Katrina presented in *Salvage the Bones* underscores how scarcity and political exclusion leave shunned spaces especially vulnerable to the environmentally destructive forces of natural disasters. Furthermore, the role of feminist empowerment in the novel is complicated by the fact that Esch, its female protagonist, although young and susceptible to male dominance, eventually rises to bring a modicum of healing to her family. *Men We Reaped: A Memoir* documents Ward's journey through the personal loss of five young Black men from her hometown of DeLisle, Mississippi. Having grown up in a shunned space, Ward is intrinsically aware of the challenges facing its inhabitants, and how those problems sometimes claim the lives of young people.

Although the tide of demographic shift is set squarely against a continuation of binary trends as immigrants enter the United States from all corners of the world, the South possesses many counterexamples such as DeLisle, Mississippi and Uniontown, Alabama. I resist the notion that such a shift away from a binary population is universal. Instead, I insist that shunned spaces remain outliers to the prevailing theme of multicultural transformation and retain populations that are overwhelmingly minority, marginalized, and culturally innovative. The writings of Jesmyn Ward therefore address the lingering significance of shunned space through the lenses of race, gender, and ecology. Although each of these subjects opens windows into an extraordinary variety of analyses that would easily fill a volume, I explore each subject to introduce the analytical possibilities for referencing shunned space in African American literature. Ward politically invests shunned spaces with a multitude of visual reminders that America's flirtation with racial apartheid has not yet ended. Like other writers, Ward anchors her writing both on place and moment.

The imagination of a writer depends on her environment and draws its referents from both historical and present facts. In his 2017 book titled *The Multitemporal Contemporary: Colson Whitehead's Presents*, Daniel Grausam addresses the link between literature, historical truth, and current events. Concerning Colson Whitehead's Pulitzer Prizewinning novel titled *The Underground Railroad*, Grausam writes:

> Whitehead's more conventionally set novels might be said to provide the figurative prehistory of the discordant now of his speculative works, and they do so by returning to the ruptures engendered by neoliberalism (125).

Ward features shunned space as a failure of neoliberalism's efforts to fuse America's racial fractures via economic opportunity. Both the economic scarcity and political exclusion experienced by residents of DeLisle and Bois Sauvage demonstrate that the nation has a long way to go in granting equal access to its extraordinary abundance.

As Ward's depiction of a wolf demonstrates, space itself can take on the properties of a non-human character, reflected both in her novels and in her memoir. Given the impact of history, shunned space is layered, just as human characters are layered. It experiences upheavals in the form of storms and human-induced catastrophes. A resonance therefore exists between human characters and the surrounding spaces in which they live, flourish, suffer, die, and forge the bonds of community. Kate Soper writes in "Feminism and Ecology: Realism and Rhetoric in the Discourses of Nature (1995)" that "representations of nature and the concepts and symbolisms we bring to it have very definite political effects" (312). Nature symbolically infuses the music and narratives of shunned space residents, echoing their demands for equality and liberation from external invasion and marginalization.

Men We Reaped: A Memoir emphasizes the historical and prevailing role of racism in shaping the experience of shunned space residents. Ward's memoir also mentions several examples of the unexpected spiritual role of automobiles in providing sanctuary for young people. However, I contend that the sanctuary offered by the community that evolves within shunned space is the most important incubator of identity for the inhabitants of DeLisle and Bois Sauvage. Ward's memoir relates her struggle with racialized systems that caused the deaths of so many young Black men in and around DeLisle, Mississippi.[7] Perhaps the binary nature of shunned space reinforces the notion of "us vs. them" implicit within racist assumptions by placing two segregated population groups in such proximity. Individuals from shunned spaces who cross into the more privileged White enclaves therefore invite all of the racialized assumptions that have accumulated over generations. Young Ward is therefore greeted with suspicion and racialized assumptions when she attends a predominantly White private school (2).

Shunned spaces are often binary, combining otherwise opposite characteristics. For instance, DeLisle, Mississippi and its surrounding, predominantly Black districts are both sanctuary and predator for Ward, offering comfort, family, and community on one hand while simultaneously fostering mortal danger on the other. The residents of her shunned space provide a home that both nurtures and predates. However, as illustrated earlier in Figure 1, the external, largely White society that has created shunned space bears significant responsibility for many of its lingering challenges. Ward

---

7   On the other hand, *Sing, Unburied, Sing* manifests the psychological and spiritual scars of historical racism embedded in the land and communities of shunned spaces. Environmental degradation and feminism are not emphasized as strongly as we will see in Ward's memoir or *Salvage the Bones*. However, they do significantly influence the novel's shunned space and provide insight into distinguishing Bois Sauvage from similar venues such as prisons disproportionately allocated for marginalized groups.

experiences the small, mostly Black community of her childhood as a place violated by systemic oppression extending back centuries; but she simultaneously finds the strength to grieve the immense loss within or near its borders. Her loss is achingly apparent in *Men We Reaped: A Memoir* as she mourns what seems to be an endless succession of young men vanishing from her life.

Ward's memoir also illustrates the vital role of women in her family given the absence of men. She states, "I have always thought of my family as something of a matriarchy since the women of my mother's side have held my nuclear family and my immediate family and my extended family together through so much" (83). Women in shunned spaces are often simultaneously forced to occupy the roles of caregivers and breadwinners. Ward summarizes the role of women in her family as follows:

> Like the women in my family before her, my mother knew the family was her burden to bear. She could not leave. So, she did what her mother did before her, what her sisters did, what her aunts did: she worked and set about the business of raising her children. She did not know it then, but she would be the sole financial provider for us until we reached adulthood. (131)

Ward's mother refuses to send the children to live permanently with other relatives and instead opts to battle the financial burden and raise them herself (131). Her steadfast determination illustrates feminine empowerment that evolves from a condition of necessity and survival. I argue that Ward seizes her mother's tenacity, pursues education, and pushes forward as a political writer.

Nerissa, Ward's sister, uses her physical appearance to negotiate a space for herself in a patriarchal society. At birth, she launches her first attack against masculine privilege by refusing to enter the world peacefully. Ward writes:

> [Mother] carried Nerissa to term, and my sister had been a hard birth. She'd been the heaviest of us all and had refused to descend the birth canal, so the doctors and nurses had to drive her out of my mother by taking their forearms and sweeping down my mother's stomach from rib cage to hip, and then grabbing Nerissa's head with forceps. She didn't want to leave me, my mother says. (55)

Forced from her mother's womb, Nerissa reluctantly entered a world of powerful masculine privilege and innovated a clever response that capitalized on her appearance and graceful personality. Ward writes: "[Rob's male friends] told [Nerissa] their secrets, and she kept them. Nerissa embodied femininity in the way she sat, legs crossed, toes painted and polished, a bundle of curves, and then sullied it with the way she cussed easily and made them laugh" (63). She is therefore a moving target for hetero-male attraction, confounding any easy interpretation of her intentions by responding to them in unexpected ways. Ward's description of her sister's sexual allure demonstrates an interpretation of sensuality as a political instrument, swaying like tree moss between lasciviousness and obscene language, depending on her whim.

Ward's memoir demonstrates that the South's racialized systems continue to kill young Black men in shunned spaces. The chapter headings read like tombstones. For example, the death of her dear friend Roger opens a view into a virtual cemetery cataloguing the author's accumulating grief:

Roger Eric Daniels III
Born: March 5, 1981
Died: June 3, 2004

Ward's memoir is therefore a cross between a cemetery and a living memorial for the young men swept away from her life. Table 1 seems to anaesthetize their deaths as presented below:

Table 1 Ward's List of Loss

Victim	Born	Died	Relationship to Jesmyn	Cause of Death
Roger Eric Daniels III	Mar. 5, 1981	June 3, 2004	Friend	Drug overdose
Demond Cook	May 15, 1972	Feb. 26, 2004	Friend	Murder
Charles Joseph Martin	May 5, 1983	Jan. 5, 2004	Friend	Auto accident
Ronald Wayne Lizana	Sept. 20, 1983	Dec. 16, 2002	Friend	Suicide
Joshua Adam Dedeaux	Oct. 27, 1980	Oct. 2, 2000	Brother	Killed by a white, drunk driver

Source: *Men We Reaped: A Memoir*

A glance at this list reveals an existential crisis for the inhabitants of DeLisle, especially young, Black men. Five young men living nearby in only four years have died of preventable causes ranging from drunk driving to murder. Hence, DeLisle serves as a superb example of a shunned space in which violence, both internal and external, is experienced far out of proportion to the general population.

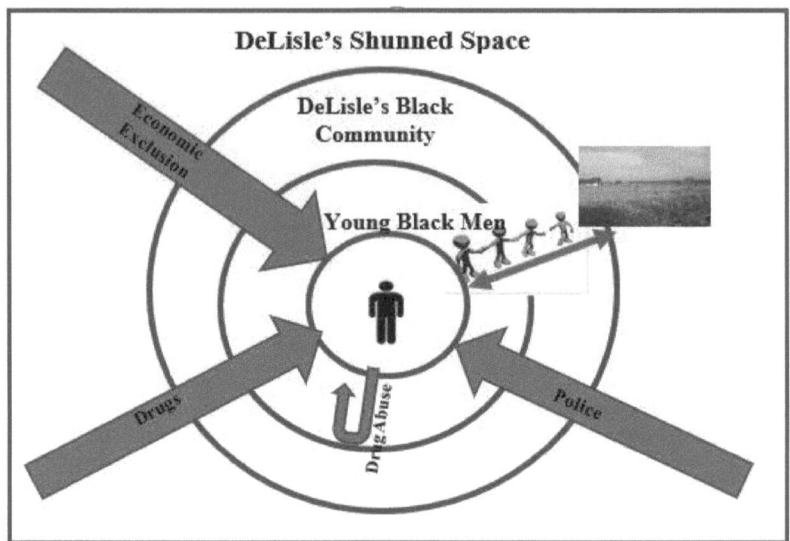

Figure 2

Almost all shunned spaces are pockmarked by the graves of marginalized individuals who die from sweltering oppression. Nevertheless, Ward's memoir is more than a series of lamentations: it is also a cry for her readers to confront the racialized system that has infected venues such as DeLisle. Each young man's story ripples outward in ways that not only engulf their shunned space but also the white community that surrounds it. At times, Ward's rage overwhelms her grief. She writes:

> But my ghosts were once people, and I cannot forget that. I cannot forget that when I am walking the streets of DeLisle, streets that seem even barer since Katrina...the only sound I hear is a tortured parrot that one of my cousins owns, a parrot that screams so loudly it sounds through the neighbourhood, a scream like a wounded child, from a cage so small the parrot's crest barely clears the top of the cage while its tail brushes the bottom...I wonder why silence is the sound of our subsumed rage, our accumulated grief. I decide this is not right, that I must give voice to this story. (8)

The voice Ward supplies to her rage is a scream—nothing less than a cry for political reform[8]— so that DeLisle and all other shunned spaces can eventually escape the cycle of senseless death.[9] Before she can accomplish this task, citing each lost life that ripples outward through the entire community, she must name the source of all that grief. She must find her bearings as a writer and as a feminist. I argue that Ward's father is one of the unlikely sources for her capacity to face the grief and social injustice afflicting DeLisle and other shunned spaces like it. *Men We Reaped: A Memoir* is primarily a story about young people, told by a young woman, in a shunned space that bears the marks of racialized poverty. Historically, young, marginalized African Americans have been closely tethered to the shunned spaces they call home—until the arrival of automobiles.

In Ward's writings, the environment delivers both elixirs and catastrophes to the residents of shunned space. By necessity, residents are intimately aware of every facet of their surroundings since scarcity imposes the need to use every scrap of resources available. As a result, a phenomenal array of folk remedies and natural cures have been identified in or near shunned space. However, scarcity can also lead to further environmental degradation as illustrated by the Pit in *Salvage the Bones* in which the land itself is commodified and sold by the truckload to glean money from whites. Guided by scarcity, shunned space resident's horde material that can poison the landscape. Natural disasters further complicate the toxic mix as illustrated by this passage detailing the impact of Hurricane Katrina:

---

8   In *Toni Morrison and the New Black: Reading God Help the Child,* Jaleel Akhtar highlights the abundant inconsistencies of any notion that America has achieved a "post-racial" consciousness. He writes, "The emergence of [a] new movement in view of persistent racism and police brutality shatters the illusion of a color-blind, post-racial United States…The nationwide protests, such as those in Ferguson, Missouri, have given added strength to the demands for justice and dealt a further blow to post-racial new black demands" (5).

9   In *Black Girl Dangerous* (2014), Mia McKenzie writes, "People who care about freedom, really care about it, more than their own comfort, more than their own ego, people who are ready to hear you, will hear you, even in your rage. Especially then" (163).

> It is the flailing wind that lashes like an extension cord used as a beating belt. It is the rain, which stings like stones, which drives into our eyes and bids them shut. It is the water, swirling and gathering and spreading on all sides, brown with an undercurrent of red to it, the clay of the Pit like a cut that won't stop leaking. It is the remains of the yard, the refrigerators and lawnmowers and the RV and mattresses, floating like a fleet. (230)

I argue that shunned spaces in Ward's writings offer excellent examples for discussing ecological resistance and "slow violence" committed against their marginalized inhabitants by the placement of toxic waste both within and outside their communities.

When toxicity is multiplied across all the yards in Bois Sauvage, tenuously holding rusted machinery and chemicals, the environment is poisoned for humans and all other living things in the area. As inhabitants of shunned space, Esch and her family are especially vulnerable since they lack the resources to escape the poisonous deluge. However, Esch's pregnancy makes her doubly susceptible to the poisons. Esch's family must trudge through the contaminated water, often with their bare feet.

Although *Salvage the Bones* primarily highlights the agency of male characters, I argue that Ward's feminist lens manifests as she describes her relationship with each of the men throughout her memoir and novels. In *Men We Reaped,* she laments their abrupt deaths as the product of social and historical forces at play long before they were born. Bois Sauvage, Ward's fictional equivalent of DeLisle, is the main setting for *Salvage the Bones* and *Sing, Unburied, Sing*, and Ward's feminism is quickly evident. Although she follows the lives and deaths of young men with excruciating detail, the motif of feminine empowerment is often evidenced by its absence. For example, Esch's mother posthumously surfaces in *Salvage the Bones* many times. Even China, a dog and the novel's only other female, embodies Ward's grief and anger. China eventually loses her puppies in the same manner that Ward loses young Black men in her hometown—one at a time. China, Ward, and even her brother Skeetah are powerless to prevent the unfolding tragedy. Although Ward does not address the long-term effects of *Salvage the Bones*, the pathological consequences are amplified for the shunned citizens of Bois Sauvage, who do not possess the financial wherewithal to start again away from the toxic water.[10]

Only when ecological disaster threatens to expand the resulting pool and swallow the remainder of his property does Esch's father stop selling clay to the white men (14). He attempts to reverse the damage to its aesthetics by adding fake coral and rocks, which reminds her of a dry fish tank. Hurricane Katrina multiplies the destruction, and her father realizes that his efforts to stem the hurricane's violence have been for nought. Ward writes that Esch is the only family member with the fortitude to survey the carnage in the storm's immediate aftermath:

> I scooted past Daddy, whose eyes were closed as he mumbled against his maimed hand and his good hand, which were folded like he was praying, past Randall, who still held Junior, who still had his hands over his eyes, to Skeetah...He looked like he wanted to jump. (237)

The storm inflicts another casualty by assaulting the masculine agency of Esch's father. For him, masculine prerogative centres on a man's hands, on his ability to shape the world around him to fit his will. With only one good hand, Esch's father is unable to give birth to anything new in the world. From the perspective of a controlling masculinity, he is therefore rendered barren.[11] Every male around Esch is paralyzed by the inability to reestablish dominion over his surroundings in the aftermath of Katrina. For a moment, as illustrated by the above passage, Esch recovers more quickly and is the only active agent in the family.

---

10   Ward's memoir offers an exception when her father is offered the opportunity to move to Oakland, California in the wake of Hurricane Camille. However, he eventually returned to DeLisle in response to homesickness described by Ward: "For all of us, the pull home is an inexorable thing" (17).

11   Nigel Edley identifies the role of hands and work for men whose masculinity is measured as a function of physical labor. He writes: "When I think of the word 'work,' for example, the images that immediately spring to mind are of manual labor: the physical practices of digging, lifting and carrying" (55-6). Without the ability to perform such labor, men such as Esch's father feel inept, as though they are failures as men.

During the storm, shunned space contracts for Esch's family, pressing on them with the force of the wind, rain, and memories. Feminism and emotions swirl in the mix as the battered inhabitants try to brace. Esch sees flashbacks of her mother, and Ward conveys these moments as a stream of consciousness. Skeetah observes that Esch resembles her mother, summoning the girl's grief in full force: "I don't know what to say, so I half grimace, and I shake my head. But Mama, mama is always here. See? I miss her so badly I have to swallow salt, imagine it running like lemon juice into the fresh cut that is my chest, feel it sting" (222). Esch's reference to lemon juice as medicine invokes the healing agency her dead mother provided. Through characters such as Esch, Ward demonstrates an authentic interpretation of her own experience within a shunned space. However, the insights of writers such as William Faulkner provide a perspective worth noting.

William Faulkner was an observer of shunned space, not a participant, and I argue that this fact both limits and expands his insight into these venues. In September 1956, Faulkner made a grand confession in a letter to *Ebony* titled "A Letter to the Leaders in the Negro Race"[12] in which he declared the limitations of white, privileged writers in attempting to comprehend the lives and vision of marginalized communities. Faulkner states: "It is easy enough to say glibly, 'If I were a Negro, I would do this or that.' But a white man can only imagine himself for a moment a Negro; he cannot be that man of another race and griefs and problems" (110). Faulkner's outsider status minimizes the currency of any contrived, first-person attempt to conjure a full rendering of the African American experience in shunned space. At first glance, this seems to contradict Faulkner's metanarrative of writing vivid portrayals of African American life throughout Mississippi during Jim Crow. That is the authentic power of expressing what one sees daily and feels in his or her gut as a result of direct participation in a marginalized community triumphs over even the most compassionate and insightful

---

12 The original title was "If I Were a Negro" (1956). Faulkner's decision to change the title underscores his ambivalence to represent fully the lives of African Americans in shunned spaces.

outsider's viewpoint.[13] Nevertheless, the circles of Faulkner's life often intersected shunned spaces reserved for many of Mississippi's most impoverished African Americans, especially Caroline "Mammy" Barr.[14]

Barr's influence on Faulkner extends back to his early childhood, and he credits her as one of his two mothers. In "In Praise of the Black Mother; An Unpublished Faulkner Letter on 'Mammy' Caroline Barr," Bart H. Welling describes the monumental role Barr played in Faulkner's formative years. He writes:

> His mammy by inheritance, Caroline Barr—a tiny, quick-tempered, stubborn woman who gave him the gift of environmental literacy and responsibility, schooled him in his family and the art of storytelling and kept nudging or shoving him back onto the straight and narrow until the end of her almost one hundred years of life—was black… To the curious duality of his upbringing, he owed a less obvious but equally powerful debt—this one as a novelist, and especially as one whose works resonate more and more in an age of rapidly blurring cultural boundaries. (541)

In other words, Barr brought shunned space with her, inside her, and shared the golden nuggets of wisdom her own childhood spaces taught her to Faulkner. In turn, the young novelist invested his work with Barr's palpable influence.

Although his privileged lens allowed him to focus on bits and pieces of Black lives and their communities swirling around him, Faulkner was a master at assembling the bigger picture from a torrent of smaller pieces. Moreover, even when all the pieces fit together like an elaborate jigsaw puzzle, Faulkner's image of shunned spaces is blurred around the edges. As a result, he never acquired the resolution found in the narratives of writers such as Jesmyn Ward and Richard Wright, whose firsthand accounts have

---

13 Faulkner descends from a long line of bankers, military officers, and businessmen.

14 Mammy Caroline Barr is perhaps the greatest example of how Faulkner's life intersected with a former resident of shunned space. He delivered her eulogy with unmistakable tenderness and respect: "I saw fidelity to a family which was not hers," he wrote, "devotion and love for people she had not borne" (117). Source: "Funeral Sermon for Mammy Caroline Barr" (February, 1940).

generated their authenticity. In this chapter, I use Shunned Space Theory to discuss three of Faulkner's novels: *Go Down, Moses* (1942), *Intruder in the Dust* (1948), and *The Reivers* (1962). Within *Go Down, Moses*, I focus primarily on the introduction titled "Was," which I feel deserves more attention than literary analysts have given thus far, even though it explores themes such as miscegenation, the trickster motif, and portability between shunned spaces. *Intruder in the Dust* illuminates the unbendable dignity of Lucas Beauchamp, a Black man falsely accused of murder, who refuses to buckle to Jim Crow laws and customs. Instead, he lives on a ten-acre plot in the centre of the white Beauchamp Plantation. Lucas Beauchamp's homestead is separate from larger shunned spaces near Jefferson, where he must travel to attend Church and mingle with other African Americans. Finally, I explore Faulkner's Pulitzer Prizewinning novel, *The Reivers*, which has been repeatedly castigated by critics for its overtly conciliatory attitude toward Jefferson's racialized society near the beginning of the 20th Century. However, I contend that Ned Beauchamp, the African American protagonist who eventually wins a horse race by stealth, offers the power of a trickster, a primary survival strategy in shunned space, to turn the tables on white privilege. Next, I argue that Ned decides to stay in place not only to assuage the area's white population but also because he, like many other residents of shunned space, including Jesmyn Ward, feels a strong pull toward home. I conclude this chapter with a discussion of Caroline Barr, Faulkner's "Mammy," who does not fit the stereotypical profile. Instead, she is, in many ways, the moral and spiritual centre of the Faulkner household. Her agency is illustrated by the difficulty she overcomes to visit her family in their shunned space near Sardis. Although Barr has no formal education, she is a brilliant storyteller who regales young William Faulkner with many tales that later influenced his fiction.

Despite his sensitivity to miscegenation and the disempowerment of Black women, Faulkner experiences the South in wildly differing ways from either Wright or Ward. His description of shunned spaces and their residents is also distinct. For Faulkner, the dilapidated plantations dotting the sweltering landscape of Northern Mississippi bear witness to the old stories he heard from uncles and grandparents about a glorious, Confederate past. His family, although defeated during the Civil War a couple of generations before him, views their connection to the land as dissoluble. Faulkner even posits his version of "White Man's Burden" in his 1955 "Address to the Southern Historical Association":

> We, the western white man who does believe that there exists individual freedom above and beyond this mere equality of slavedom [Communism], must teach the nonwhite peoples this while there is yet a little time left... We, America, have the best chance to do this because we can do it here, at home, without needing to send costly freedom expeditions into alien and inimical places already convinced that there is no such thing as freedom and liberty and equality in peace for all people, or we would practice it at home. (*Essays*, Faulkner, 148-9)

Faulkner's speech is rife with racialized language and ironic in that it declares that whites must instill the knowledge of individual human freedom for all nonwhites, even though many white Americans strongly resist any such egalitarian notions for African Americans and other minorities. Faulkner insists that "liberty and equality" will result in a successful model to be followed across the globe by de-marginalizing the residents of shunned spaces and breaking down political and economic barriers that enforce the scarcity in such spaces.

The speech is a strange departure from William Faulkner's usual decorum, and I argue that he cannot be broad-stroked as a racist and sent to the ash heap of history. His novels and other speeches contradict the racist sentiments raised in the Address to the Southern Historical Association. Even within the same speech, Faulkner writes:

> It is our white man's shame that in our present southern economy, the Negro must not have economic equality; our double shame that we fear giving him more social equality will jeopardize his present economic status; our triple shame that even then, to justify ourselves, we must becloud the issue with the purity of white blood... (*Essays* 150)

The above quote animates many of the African American characters in Faulkner's novels, and accounts for both the individual agency granted to them as well as the material obstacles placed in their way by Jim Crow limitations.

Although many readers and literary analysts may view Faulkner as the panacea to white racism in the Jim Crow South, he is conflicted over the role of Blacks in American society. I contend that his contrapuntal attitude toward race emerges from an incomplete understanding of shunned spaces and the cultural accomplishments they herald. In other words, by negotiating simultaneously with scarcity and political exclusion, Black Americans not only prove themselves equal to the task of American citizenship but of mentoring the larger, mostly white society about a myriad of accomplishments innate to shunned space. In Faulkner's fiction, the residents of shunned space illustrate their cultural accomplishment by resisting racialized oppression and by frequently turning the tables on their oppressors.

Erskine Peters, author of *William Faulkner: The Yoknapatawpha World and Black Being* (1983), addresses the fact that marginalized residents are fully aware of their oppressors' motives. He writes:

> What is apparent in these particular characters, moreover, is that Faulkner grants them a high sense of awareness of their relationship to the culture which they know is juggling them. They are not as submissive in their roles as some critics have held. One might say that while they are biding their time and eking out the best existence that they can for the moment, they are also manoeuvring whenever possible to gain control over their immediate situations. (189)

Peters rejects the notion that shunned space residents are childlike and pliable to white demands. It is important to note that "biding their time" is a luxury reserved for whites. Hence, African Americans remain vigilant for any option that presents itself to improve their lot. They are fully aware that they are confronted with a monolithic, racialized system that perennially imposes disadvantages on them as individuals and their communities. Blacks also comprehend the origin of such thinking, and it has everything to do with the force that holds together the monolithic structures of elite white power.

Future research into shunned space will confirm that such venues always materialize with an asymmetrical distribution of rights and privileges that advantage one group over another. Hence, shunned spaces are found throughout the world, and evidence of their existence punctuates human history and culture. Perhaps the creativity of shunned space is borne from necessity: the need to generate sufficient food stocks in scarcity-laden environments where the ground reluctantly yields to agriculture. Or, the creativity of shunned space originates from the human need to stand outside of a routine of unending labour and oppressive violence, and to allow the human soul to perceive itself in terms of a larger world, and to generate works of beauty, written or sculpted, or passed across generations from old lips to new ears. I propose that carefully studying the literature of shunned space brings to light the greatest proof of the full humanity of marginalized people. Shunned Space Theory opens a portal into marginalized communities that require literary analysts to celebrate the cultural achievement of these venues while deploring the racialized systems that created them. Equally important, it reminds those who merely visit such venues that scarcity, violence, and political exclusion are no match for the human spirit, and that shunned space represents an opportunity for the larger society to work with shunned residents to reverse the cumulative injustice it has created.

Works cited

Akhtar, Jaleel. *Toni Morrison and the New Black: Reading God Help the Child*. Routledge: Taylor & Francis Group, 2019.

Amiri, Azita. *Have They Been Forgotten?* Montogomery: Alabama Nurse, 2017.

Benston, Kimberly W. "Preface to a Twenty Volume Critical Note: For Amiri Note for Amiri, Ghost of the Future." *Callaloo. Vol. 37 Issue 3(2014): 480-482*.

Edley, Nigel. *Men and Masculinity: The Basics*. New York: Routledge, 2017.

Faulkner, William. "Funeral Sermon for Mammy Caroline Barr." Faulkner, William. *Essays, Speeches and Public Letters: William Faulkner*. Ed. James B Meriweather. New York: Random House, 1965. 117-118.

--- *Intruder in the Dust*. New York: Vantage, 2011.

--- *The Reivers*. New York: Vantage, 1962.

Grausman, Daniel. *The Multitemporal Contemporary: Colson Whitehead's Presents*. London: Palgrave Macmillan, 2017.

Lin, Yu-sien. "A third space for dialogues on creative pedagogy: Where hybridity becomes possible." *Thinking Skills and Creativity* (2014): 45-56.

Mays, Benjamin E. and Joseph William Nicholson. *The Negro's Church*. New York: Russell and Russell, 1969.

McKenzie, Mia. *Black Girl Dangerous*. Oakland: BGD Press, 2014.

Nixon, Robert. *Slow Violence and the Environmentalism of the Poor*. Cambridge: Harvard UP, 2011.

Peters, Erskine. *William Faulkner: The Yoknapatawpha World and Black Being*. Darby: Norwood Editions, 1983.

Soper, Kate. "Feminism and Ecology: Realism and Rhetoric in the Discourses of Nature". *Science, Technology, & Human Values, Vol. 20, No. 3(1995):311*.

Ward, Jesmyn. *Men We Reaped: A Memoir*. New York: Bloomsbury, 2013.

--- *Salvage the Bones*. New York: Bloomsbury, 2011.

--- *Sing, Unburied, Sing*. New York: Bloomsbury, 2017.

Welling, Bart H. "In Praise of the Black Mother; An Unpublished Faulkner Letter on "Mammy" Caroline Barr." *The Georgia Review*, Vol 55, No. 3 (2001): 536-542.

The Urbanized Pastoral in the Novels of Thomas Hal Phillips

Often, we are inclined to consider the rural as wholesome and calming and the urban as corrupt and debilitating. However, the two terms are not always in direct opposition but rather have ambiguous meanings. In viewing the novels of Thomas Hal Phillips, I will examine the rural/urban binary as a forced social construct and demonstrate that the characters and the narratives are much more flexible and mobile than any fixed ideas of pastoral life. The two terms, *pastoral* and *urban* now have increasingly indefinite meanings, and the emotional and intellectual weighting of these terms has shifted decidedly. Terry Gifford in *Pastoral* discusses different ideas of pastoral as a genre, a style, and finally a concept rather than a genre or a style: "pastoral is a historical form with a long tradition," "any literature that describes the country as providing implicit or explicit contrast to the urban," " 'pastoral' as pejorative, implying that the pastoral vision is too simplified and thus an idealisation of the reality of life in the country," and a fourth use of the term, "neutrally descriptive of literature concerned with a life of pastoral farming practices in raising grazing animals" (Gifford, 2020, pp. 1-2). All of these terms, at least loosely, can be applied to the novels of Thomas Hal Phillips.

Nancy Lindheim, in *The Virgilian Pastoral Tradition: from the Renaissance to the Modern Era*, agrees with Gifford that the idea of the pastoral is difficult to explain or control:

> One of the reasons pastoral has proved so hard to define is that it takes so many guises. Throughout its history 'pastoral' has been both noun and adjective, at times the whole substance, at other times a combining element in a compound that explores ideas only implicit in the original matrix. (136)

We can see these terms (pastoral, urban, rural, etc.) as having vague and shifting definitions, especially in the context of our current questioning of archaic binaries and opposites.

However, regardless of the ambiguities, a reader can easily assume, based on traditional wisdom, that a novel with a rural setting will rely on the historical ideas of the pastoral. Additionally, novels grounded in the culture of the southern United States can be expected to address the traditional values of that area. Thomas Hal Phillips's first five novels were published in the early 1950s, during the later years of the Jim Crow era and in the time that has become known as the Joe McCarthy/Red Scare years. Phillips's novels, at first blush, can be seen as pastoral and adhering to traditional beliefs and customs. His isolated northern Mississippi villages and farms usually provide comfort and shelter to the characters, and these rural settings afford an ultimate retreat from the hostile outside world. Yet, Phillips's characters are as complex and rural/urban as Phillips himself. He was a mix of the agricultural South and the academic non-South. He was born and raised near the small town of Kossuth, named after the nineteenth-century Hungarian activist Lajos Kossuth, in northeastern Mississippi. He served in the United States Navy, earned a master's degree in writing, taught at Southern Methodist University in Dallas, ventured into Mississippi politics working as his brother Rubel's campaign manager, and worked as a Hollywood screenwriter and producer, especially with director Robert Altman. After these varied experiences, he retired to Kossuth and is buried there. Phillips exemplified the urbanized rural in his life and his writings, stretching the themes of the pastoral and the anti-pastoral.

Terry Gifford, beyond his definitions of *pastoral*, also has indicated, "Pastoral's celebration of retreat is its strength and its inherent weakness. When retreat is an end in itself, pastoral is merely escapist" (49). For most of Phillips's characters, a retreat can be comforting solitude and withdrawal after a defeat or a dangerous encounter. For some of them, this retreat to the rural proves to be a failed escapism; these characters must eventually face themselves and the consequences of their actions. Therefore, rural settings can be as dangerous and threatening as any city.

Nonetheless, the idea of pastoral can still be seen as the tranquility of nature with pleasantly coexisting flora and fauna. The pastoral can still include a sense of looking back, longing for better times and places, based on the Virgilian pastoral and Virgil's own looking back. Virgil's *Georgics* depict the beauty of farm life. Book II begins with an homage to Bacchus, one of the major gods of the forests and countryside:

> Hactenus arvorum cultus et sidera caeli:
> nunc te, Bacche, canam, nec non silvestria tecum
> Virgulta et prolem tarde crescentis olivae. (136)
> Thus far the tillage of the fields and stars of heaven: now you, Bacchus, will I sing, and with you the forest saplings, and offspring of the slow-growing olive. (137)

In Book II, in addition to discussing types of soil, offering further prayers to the rural and forest deities, and extolling life in nature, Virgil, most of all, praises farmers:

> O fortunatos nimium, sua si bona norint,
> agricolas! quibus ipsa, procul discordibus armis,
> fundit humo facilem victum iustissima tellus. (168)
> O farmers, happy beyond measure could they but know their blessings! For them, far from the clash of arms, most righteous Earth, unbidden, pours forth from her soil an easy sustenance. (169)

He is looking back to the time when "before a godless race banqueted on slaughtered bullocks, such was the life golden Saturn lived on earth" (Virgil, 1999, p. 175). Virgil is looking back beyond his own time, even his epoch, to the time before Jupiter when Saturn ruled the world.

Among the strongest proponents of looking back to an idyllic time in the United States (i.e., an antebellum era), are the authors of *I'll Take My Stand: The South and the Agrarian Tradition*, originally published in 1930. They were known as the Twelve Southerners and the Vanderbilt Agrarians among other similar names. They had a strong belief in, and possibly a need for, a sense of the South being steadfastly agrarian, Protestant, and politically conservative. In their railings against the evils of Northern industry and manufacturing, they often praised the agricultural South in light of the necessity of the "peculiar institution" of slavery. The Agrarians believed in what can now be called a revisionist view of Southern history: the Civil War had been about economics and Northern aggression; slavery had been beneficial to all, including the slaves; segregation and a return to a rural economy (cotton and tobacco) was the solution to industrial, urban liberalism. Pastoral ideology was inherent in this historical and social stance. Life in the country was safe and nurturing, the races falling into their natural places just as the livestock and wild animals did.

According to this ideology, all the elements of business production need to be controlled by financially comfortable, educated white men while the Blacks fit into their natural place as subservient and inferior beings. This maudlin nostalgia looks to the Civil War as the destruction of Southern intellectual and social life by the North (also indirectly by the English). The poet and novelist Robert Penn Warren explains the natural place of African Americans in Southern life:

> In the past, the Southern negro [sic] has always been a creature of the small town and farm. That is where he still chiefly belongs, by temperament and capacity; there he has less the character of a 'problem' and more the status of a human being who is likely to find in agricultural and domestic pursuits the happiness that his good nature and easy ways incline him to as an ordinary function of his being." (260-261)

Even by educated and socially astute individuals, Blacks were thought to be better off in the country where they knew their place—Black women working as housekeepers and cooks, Black men working as drivers and farm hands—and were cared for by benevolent white Protestant men, making the Southern economy possible. It would seem that cotton and tobacco were valued as agrarian gods as Herman Clarence Nixon declares in his essay, "Whither Southern Economy?":

> The South's greatest activity is that of cotton-growing, and this agricultural pursuit is the basis for cotton-milling, the South's greatest manufacturing enterprise. One of the greatest agricultural productions, after cotton, is tobacco, and tobacco manufacturing. (179)

In keeping with the theme of the pastoral and the past, alongside Virgil, Frank Lawrence Owsley, in "The Irrepressible Conflict," contrasts the Greeks and Romans:

> The Greek tradition became partly grafted upon an Anglo-Saxon and Scotch tradition of life. However, it was the Romans of the early republic, before land speculators and corn laws had driven men from the soil to the city slums, who appealed most powerfully to the South. These Romans were brave, sometimes crude, but open and without guile—unlike the Greeks. They reeked of the soil. (70).

Owsley here, by implication, is contrasting the Greeks and the Northern urbanite industrialists with the less refined but honest and hard-working Southern rural agriculture population.

Owsley's brave and crude Romans resemble the farmers of Virgil's *Georgics* and its virtual paean to the bucolic existence, including religious life and closeness to the gods. Phillips's characters are often brave and crude, but not very religious. If they do identify as Christian, they mostly view the church and church activities as social events. In *Search for a Hero*, regarding the suicide of Don's girlfriend, William says, "Did you know the Catholics won't have anything to do with a person who commits suicide?" "I wanted to kill all the damned Catholics, the way they treated Meb. The Primitives wouldn't treat a-body like that. They take care of the dead. I don't believe a lot of things anymore." "Like in the Bible: *Let the dead bury the dead*. What the hell does that mean?" (Phillips, 1952, p. 299). William's skepticism is indicative of Phillips's generally agnostic beliefs.

However, in *The Golden Lie*, Phillips's second novel, the village of Old Shiloh is dominated by the strict and non-swerving dogma of the Primitive Church. At first, this seems to be a simple adherence to a life of prayer and meditation in a community of compassionate and spiritual people. Savanna Lloyd is introduced to the reader during her time of meditation immediately following a church meeting; "She always set aside a few minutes every day for meditation, and usually she chose late afternoon or dusk, a few minutes before Walter and Foster came in from the fields" (5). She seems to be bolstered and reassured by her religion and her church attendance.

The church building stands as the only white building in the town, an example of the isolation and elitism of the church and its members:

> Old Shiloh is at the foot of the mountains: its buildings are spread unevenly on a knoll like empty fruit jars grey with dust. Below the grey stores, in a rocky trough is the grey station house. The houses—all but one—are grey; the gin is grey; and the school is grey. The church is white. (3)

The "all but one" house, a yellow house, belongs to Walter Lloyd and his wife Savanna who holds the "highest woman office" in the Primitive Church. Walter has recently painted the house yellow, and Savanna opposes the colour yellow:

> The lingering odour of the new paint came through the south windows. It sickened her, for she had been told at the meeting that afternoon that yellow was the brightest sign of the sin of Adam. She would have Walter repaint the house immediately, or else she would never let him touch her body again. (5)

This is an indication of her selfish and socially skewed ideas about sex and physical affection. Savanna is not pleased with her husband or her marriage. In addition to her aversion to marital sex, she indulges her long-standing attraction to the sharecropper Roy Bynum, her extra-marital love interest (and sometimes sexual partner). Her religion does not bring her the peace which Virgil's Roman gods bring to his farmers and their families. Instead, she is nearly consumed by her sexual drives, selfishness, and bigotry. For example, when she was younger, on Sunday mornings, her father often slept late:

> She would slip under the covers beside him, lie deep in the curl of his lap and feel sorry for Laura piddling around in the cold kitchen. She would warm her hands against her father's thighs and think: Papa will not care, for I love him more than Laura does… I know I love him more… he never calls her 'Baby-doll.' His body was full of secrets that her hand unfolded. (191)

Her incestuous behaviour is not only sexual but also a means to be superior to her sister.

Savanna's son Foster treats Kirby (the eldest son of Tassie and Surrey, the Black employees of the Lloyds), nearly as a brother, including him and the white Ansel Stone in his close circle of best friends. Savanna objects, exhibiting her racial elitism. Foster and Kirby have hidden a victrola in the barn. "Kirby began to play blues and jazz records that Savanna would not allow in her house" (14). Also, "Foster deliberately took them [Kirby and Ansel] to the front door because he could smell food cooking and he thought that Savanna was in the kitchen. Kirby sat down at the piano and began to play" (19). Savanna confronts Foster concerning Kirby:

> Do you think it's very nice to keep bringing Kirby to the front door and putting him down at my piano as if he's a deacon?' 'I hadn't thought of it as nice or not nice.' 'You'd better think about it. (19)

The narrow-mindedness and hypocritical sanctimony of Savanna and her fellow church members contradict the surface appearance of the rural paradise. Instead, most of Old Shiloh's inhabitants are exposed as cold and materialistic beneath their veneer of spiritual austerity and nearly incessant talk of God and His Chosen. Walter Lloyd tells Savanna:

> What you stand for is not Christianity. I don't know what the hell it is but I know what it's not. All of you are full of the same thing. And all you want to do is shout and pray and thank God you're better. (86)

Roy Bynum eventually turns against the church and its mendacity. He discovers what he sees as "the golden lie" of the book's title and sets the church on fire because "he could not bear the thought of darkness moving away and leaving it there" (222). Later, upon returning home, he "saw the bright glow beyond the houses. He guessed it was like the sun coming up out of the ocean" (222). Setting the fire has been a redemptive and freeing action for Roy, allowing him to achieve a sense of peace and clarity which he did not find in the local religion. Later, he steals the donations which have been raised for rebuilding the church. He has stolen the money to "buy back" the unusually large head of Daddy Moe, Kirby's grandfather, from Dr. David Moss. Dr Moss had surgically straightened Kirby's legs *pro bono*. In exchange for the surgery, Daddy Moe had agreed that Dr. Moss could have Daddy Moe's head for scientific research. Ironically, Roy's criminal acts are a kind of penance and redemption, rather than what the church condemns as sin.

Savanna, in the end, is left alone. However, this solitude is unlike her scene of meditation and personal strength at the beginning of the novel. Her husband Walter has died (although she does not yet know that), her only child Foster will soon be going away to college, her lover Roy has left town, and her sister Laura has married a man whom Savanna despises:

> When the telephone began to ring, she did not move: she would give herself the time it would take to get out of bed and come downstairs. Then as she touched the receiver she thought: It's something bad; I can feel it's something bad and I'm here all by myself. (279)

In her quest for the paradise of salvation and God's love and grace, she has lost any semblance of the pastoral peace she has doggedly sought. Rather, she is suffering anti-pastoral pain and loss. Savanna can be seen not only as a lost pilgrim but also as a tragic hero, her religiosity being her hubris.

Aside from Savanna and her church congregation, much of the atmosphere of Phillip's South is tolerant of and eager for, popular music. In addition to Kirby's blues and jazz, the music playing on the radio is hillbilly music. This is significant because, in American popular culture, the difference between rural and urban can often be seen in the divide in music. Jazz is historically considered Black music, and country music is associated with the rural and often with the poor. The boundaries in music between race, class, and region have softened in recent years, but in the 1950s, there was a strong, sometimes harsh division, especially in the elitism directed toward Southerners in general and country music in particular; country music is nearly always associated with the South and those who are perceived as backward Southerners.

Additionally, this hillbilly music is used, perhaps ironically, to illustrate socially suspect, possibly criminal, behaviour among the residents of Mississippi. In *Kangaroo Hollow*, the character Cleve's house is dark green with an empty porch and drawn shades. At night people "sometimes saw light behind the shades and heard hill-billy music low and clear." Also, when Dean first visits Cleve, "He smiled at the thought of Cleve listening to music, even hill-billy stuff" (190). However, Cleve is not listening to the music; rather, Jen, Cleve's girlfriend, is playing the music on the radio, just as she does in the working-class diner, the Moon Harvest Café, where she works. Hill-Billy music in the workplace indicates an urbanized rural in a sense. Only in a relatively urban setting, with reliable electricity and adequate broadcasting facilities, can rural working-class music play on the radio.

For most rural folks, including landowners, life is neither pastoral nor anti-pastoral but rather a locus of indifference to any notion of *pastoral*, with very little thought given to the beauty of the panorama or the tranquil ambience of the setting. Instead, rural farm life, like any other job, can be monotonous daily drudgery for the workers, including the sharecroppers and field hands of Phillips's often-paradisical countryside. This non-pastoral idea is a type of realism, a verisimilitude regarding real-world details. Harold E. Toliver in *Pastoral: Forms and Attitudes* explains this:

> The difficulty in finding an effective balance between idyllic dreams and the everyday functions of complex societies is increased when paradise becomes a distant Eden or future paradise, which are all the more unreachable and hostile to business as usual. (211)

Accordingly, Darrell Barclay, the protagonist of *The Bitterweed Path*, experiences moments of the non-pastoral in his work as he settles into his life with the Pitt family:

> Darrell marked his days by tracks across the new furrowed earth, sometimes with Roger, sometimes with Malcolm Pitt, but more often in his father's fields carrying water, following the harrow, or sprouting with the poleax, which was too heavy for him, the five acres of new-ground along Winter Creek. (44)

However, especially with Roger Pitt, Darrell experiences moments of pastoral bliss because he is in love with Roger. Darrell and Roger go watermelon picking one day in late summer:

> They went barefooted through the tall corn toward the creek and the watermelon patch; and there, after expert thumping, selected the right melon and took it across the dying vines to the gum tree at the end of the rows. They stripped naked, dropping their clothes on the gum tree roots, and buried the melon knee-deep in the cold blue creek. (48)

Most probably, the two young men would not be swimming in the nude in an urban pool, certainly not an outdoor public pool. Furthermore, their comfort with being naked outdoors is a sign of the pastoral, even the classical Greek and Roman idea of the human body being part of nature.

Early in *The Bitterweed Path*, Malcolm Pitt's attitude toward nudity sets the tone of the pastoral. Nudity is natural, and one need not feel ashamed of it:

> That's a big pond,' Darrell said. 'Sure,' Roger said. 'We'll go swimming when April comes. You can go with us.' 'You have to have clothes on?' 'No. We go naked. Father said all the trouble in the world started, anyhow, when folks put on the first fig leaves. (22)

This reference evokes the simplicity and freedom, and the guileless nudity, before the fall of the Garden of Eden. This is an example of Phillips's male characters' relaxed attitudes toward nudity and its place in the soothing, usually bucolic environment. Amid the turbulence and volatility of the environment and the other characters, Darrell and Roger have found the retreat so often associated with the ideal pastoral. Eventually, this physical retreat gives way to the urban for Roger. He returns to the city to work as an obstetrician leaving Darrell and the rural life behind.

Additionally, other characters leave and do not return to the farming villages. For example, in *Kangaroo Hollow*, Todda, pregnant with Rufus's child, loses herself in the anonymity and moral ambiguities of the big city. She changes her surname from Hurley to Temple, adding another layer of removal from her rural background. She raises Rufus's child Dean by herself, except for some help from her Black friend Lizzie. Memphis for Todda is an escape from the rural, an urban retreat, withdrawing from any moral censure, and forging her reality. Also, she works as a waitress, an urban occupation far from the home-cooked meals routinely associated with the rural. Although she has escaped the constraints and judgments of the small town, she cannot escape her past and her indelible ties to Kangaroo Hollow, if only because Rufus still lives there. When Rufus visits Todda in Memphis, he becomes aware of the differences between the rural of the past and the urban of the present:

> He thought she was telling him to forget the old world, set in its playhouse atmosphere, and wake up to the present where men scratched in garbage cans for worm-eaten apples and moulded bread. (144)

The imagery of the playhouse is of the tranquil rural environs and the garbage cans of the harsh urban setting which Todda has comfortably adapted. Another notable example of the exodus from the village is Maxwell Harper. Max is sentenced to death for murder. After he is pardoned, he hops onto a freight train to leave town. Indeed, for Max, prison has proven to be safer and less hostile than his village. Also, the open road, or a life on the rails, seems to be safer.

For most of Phillips's characters, life proves to be a spatial fluidity with lots of comings and goings between the rural villages and farm areas and the urban life of cities, riverboats, and trains. The showboats exist as sophisticated and worldly in the pristine nature of the Mississippi, a liminal space between the rural and the urban. The trains themselves are nearly characters, moving the people from rural to urban, moving them from the pastoral to the non-pastoral, frequently being background sights and sounds, going about their business within and beyond the village and the farmlands. The characters in the novels of Thomas Hal Phillips easily become urbanized, especially in the novels set in later years, during the age of telegrams, radios, and telephones.

The protagonists mostly are the sons of sharecroppers, and, in the socially fluid world of Phillips's Mississippi hill country, they often rise to positions of social and financial comfort. Usually, they are helped by powerful older men who, incidentally, wield considerable, although geographically limited, political power. These are rural self-made men, relying for their livelihoods, and their power, on the products of rural life, farming, sawmills, and cotton gins. They also control the lives of their employees, the community, the bankers and the merchants. Although they are self-sufficient, they are not self-sustaining. Rather, they rely on urbanized industry and the urban markets for their livelihood.

The twentieth-century move away from the Virgilian pastoral was most noticeable during the Great Depression when farmers were losing their land and slaughtering their livestock because they could not afford to feed them or ship them to market. Thus, poverty often mars the sense of the pastoral, especially in the rural South. While travelling by train, Howard Hurley, a sharecropper heading off to war, notes their fellow passengers; "His stares fastened on the sunken, toothless faces of old men; the malarial yellow skin of fattening women; the bright, journey-proud eyes of children" (63).

Howard's parents live in a "lumberjack room" with "the calendar hanging from a sixpenny nail, the unframed picture of a horse which came with the purchase of a box of Red Rooster salve, the year-old Christmas cards tacked in a triangular design, and the several Biblical scenes cut from Sunday school books. Ephriam Hurley sat before the log fire with the Bible closed on his thumb" (72). This can be read as the poor being too rigid and old-fashioned to be capable of attaining wealth, or, that the rich are neither religious nor righteous because financial success requires unscrupulous attitudes and behavior.

In *Kangaroo Hollow*, socioeconomic class divides the characters. It would seem, at least in the cases of Tom Phelps and Rufus Scott, that wealth brings with it corruption and a loss of the usual moral and ethical standards. Tom Phelps (who proves to be a crooked, unethical politician) "was the owner of two farms in the Hollow, of a mule stable in Cross City; and he was considered the shrewdest politician in Woodall County" (73). In addition to buying votes, he also attempts, and fails, to buy and bully his way to prevent his son Nile from serving in the army in World War II. The Woodall County Draft Board is beyond Tom Phelps's influence. This political reckoning proves to be an epiphany of sorts for his son, that his money and influence operate in a sphere limited to his rural environs, too weak to extend far beyond those bounds. "Nile Phelps sat at the huge table brooding, thinking of the time when his father's arm and devious brain could no longer protect him" (74) and "He seized his father's shoulder and broke into a stifled, funereal sob. "I'll be killed, Papa! I know I'll be killed" (75). Although Nile is from the rural area, he proves not to be a stalwart pastoral figure, but rather a young man who has been citified and pampered by wealth and power.

Likewise, in a pivotal scene, Malcolm Pitt compares Roger, his blood son, and Darrell, his emotional son. He is also making a statement, a definition of sort, about what he sees as pastoral. Malcolm "crossed the room to Darrell and put his arm around Darrell's neck. 'This is my real son. We're just farmers and we can't factor, but we by God can raise the best cotton in the county. Roger is a schoolboy, soft; well, let him be a doctor.' He pulled Darrell close. 'We're going to build a gin—half and half. You couldn't work like we do, Roger—us men. You're pale—like winter butter. But look at Darrell…' He began to feel Darrell's arm" (93). Here Malcolm is mixing the pastoral (cotton farming) with the masculine; real men are countrymen, not needing or wanting education like a soft schoolboy or a doctor. Real country men are sun-burnt, and dark, unlike pale butter. However, these real countrymen are as urbanized as Roger. They own and manage successful cotton gins, marketing themselves and their products to urban outsiders. Because they are financially comfortable, they can travel freely on steamboats and trains, making frequent visits to the cities: of Jackson, Vicksburg, and New Orleans. Malcolm, therefore, regardless of his speech about rural businessmen, is dependent upon urban industry, especially when he needs parts for his machinery or markets for his goods.

Sometimes, the urban setting, ironically, can provide an escape from the country into a safe and tolerant anonymity. Kindness and civility are seen in the city, especially in an older prostitute's mother-like concern toward the protagonist Darrell Barclay in *The Bitterweed Path*. When Darrell and Roger visit Nanette, a prostitute in New Orleans, she says, "Darrell, you have a beautiful body and you have a beautiful soul. I can see one. I can feel the other" (122). She even obliquely comments on the relationship of these two brother-friends, "Go home and love your friend. When ten years have gone, you can come to me" (123). Thus, she offers the boys companionship and wisdom, refusing to have sex with them until they are older. Nanette stands in sharp contrast to the stereotype of the callous and jaded prostitute, especially an older prostitute in a big city seen as decadent and profligate as New Orleans.

Another time, a few years later, Darrell and Roger are visiting Vicksburg, Mississippi, to pay off a loan. Finally, they are alone in a hotel room, similar to the one in New Orleans. Yet, this room allows them intimacy and silence. Their maturity, and the solitude found in the city, have finally freed them to admit and share their true feelings, here away from the confines of Leighton, their relatively isolated village home. Roger brings up the topic of Malcolm Pitt and Darrell's attraction to the man they both call father:

> Did you love Father? I mean really love him?' Darrell touched Roger's shoulder as if his hands might speak, for his lips had failed him for a space of time. 'Would you make something ugly out of that Roger?' 'No, I think I'd be the last person in the world to do that. (310)

In this same conversation, Darrell tells Roger about their father: "I never saw him in my life but that something moved inside me." And further, "Suddenly, he put his arm around Roger, and he said, "I love you, Roger. I always have. But not that much." Finally, in this conversation, Darrell tells Roger, in words and actions, about his love for his brother-friend: "His fingers moved along Roger's face and he knew that Roger was crying. He leaned over as he had done in that lost and younger time and touched Roger's face with his lips; 'You mean more to me now than anybody" (310-311). For Darrell Barclay, at least, the rural countryside holds the possibility of peace and personal fulfilment.

Furthermore, the pastoral retreat proves not to be escapism for Darrell but rather a place of gaining self-knowledge and experiencing reality. As he stands in the pouring rain outside town:

> …. until his clothes were soaked,
> Somewhere, he thought, beyond my reach lies what I am looking for; perhaps it lies in the smell of freshly plowed earth, of cool spring water, of early frost, of good clean strength, and with no more form than the shape of darkness, so that my fingers close always on emptiness. (298)

Here, he believes that the country life, the earth and water themselves will provide what he seeks. Conversely, at Vicksburg, he surveys the Showboat's gambling room: "filled with smoke and walking-canes and tall hats. At the bar, they drank bourbon and for a while watched the floor show. A heaviness seemed to settle on Darrell, he felt choked. He leaned against Roger and whispered, 'We won't find it here.' 'What?' Roger said. 'Whatever we're looking for'" (306-307). Darrell finds his peace, what he has been looking for, in the country, in nature, and in working the land. Roger finds his peace in practising medicine in the city.

Roger and Darrell have found their places in the world, emerging from callow rural youth to intelligent maturity, comfortable in both rural and urban settings. Each has his realm of peace. Likewise, most of Phillips's characters make their way in the world regardless of where they have been or what they have survived. Several, like Phillips himself, leave the rural setting, usually temporarily, by leaving to become part of larger pseudo-urban populations: military service, college, prison, or careers. Although some of these departures are voluntary, college and careers, others are forced departures, being drafted into military duty and being sentenced to prison. Even after experiencing life outside the South, Thomas Hal Phillips's characters mostly return to rural life, affected by their time out of the rural environment and bringing a sense of the urban back to their homes. Finally, considering the eccentricities of Phillips and his characters, the rigid notions of *pastoral* and *non-pastoral* tend to blur and fade away.

Works cited

Gifford, T. (2020) *Pastoral*. 2nd edn. London Routledge.

Lindheim, N. (2005) *The Virgilian Pastoral Tradition: from the Renaissance to the Modern Era*. Pittsburgh: Duquesne UP.

Phillips, T. H. (1996) *The Bitterweed Path*. Chapel Hill: U of North Carolina P.

— — — (1951) *The Golden Lie*. New York: Rinehart & Co., Inc.

— — —. (2000) *Kangaroo Hollow*. Jackson: UP of Mississippi.

— — —. (1998) *The Loved and the Unloved.* Jackson: UP of Mississippi.

— — —. (2002) *Red Midnight*. Jackson: UP of Mississippi.

— — —. (1952) *Search for a Hero*. New York: Rinehart & Co., Inc.

Ransom, J. C., et al., Twelve Southerners (1995) *I'll Take My Stand: The South and the Agrarian Tradition*. Baton Rouge; Louisiana State UP.

Toliver, H. E. (1971) *Pastoral: Forms and Attitudes*. U of California P, Berkeley.

Virgil (1999) *Eclogues, Georgics, Aeneid I-VI*. Translated from the Latin by H. Rushton Fairclough. Cambridge: Harvard UP.

Culture, Identity, Diaspora and Displacement in Monica Ali's *Brick Lane*

In 1982 Salman Rushdie claimed that the "Empire writes back to the Centre" (8). Rushdie's postulate has since been proved by many literary works—for example, V.S. Naipaul's *The Enigma of Arrival* (1987), Salman Rushdie's *Satanic Verses* (1988), Hanif Kureishi's *The Buddha of Suburbia* (1990), Meera Syal's *Anita and Me* (1996), Andrea Levy's *Small Island*, and Derek Walcott's *Omeros*—that have widened the anglophone literary canon, which has, since the 1980s, become very multicultural. Ritushree Sengupta claims that "the tradition of silencing women's voices in the name of gender as well as race has been supported by various agents and the situation only worsens when the issue of migration is involved. The trauma of displacement has timelessly affected women denying them of several things such as social position, cultural acceptance or even economic empowerment" (2021).

Among the diasporic writers, Monica Ali has been praised as well as heavily criticized for her debut novel *Brick Lane* (2003). Based on the constant comparison and contrast of the Bangladeshi village the main protagonist, Nazneen, comes from and the city of London, to which she has moved because of an arranged marriage, the author highlights the pitfalls of multiculturalism and assimilation of the 1980s and 1990s. As Asim Karim and Zakia Nasir have pointed out, the women protagonists in the novel "are generally semi-literate and unaccustomed and unfamiliar to the ways of the liberal, multicultural West and therefore remain deprived of the opportunity to progress and this constantly implicated in their men's fear of probable negative Western influence on them" (126). This goes hand in hand with the class the female protagonists of South Asian diasporic novels come from. They are not "the upper-class women . . . rather they depict the lives of the class which has migrated to the West for economic or political reasons" (216). As a consequence, they have almost no chance of social and economic mobility and, therefore, they remain outsiders in a society that is alien to them. Nazneen's husband Chanu is well aware of the constant pressure that results from the coexistence of different cultures and their values. The constant juggling of both cultures side by side results in the permanent tension the protagonists experience. A very striking example is given by Chanu in relation to alcohol: "it's part of the culture here. It's so ingrained in the fabric of society. Back home, if you drink you risk being an outcast. In London, if you don't drink you risk the same thing" (110) However, his view is strongly opposed by the very liberal view of the emancipated wife of Dr. Azad: "Listen, when I'm in Bangladesh I put on a sari and cover my head and all that. But here I go out to work. I work with white girls and I'm just one of them. If I want to come home and eat curry, that's my business" (114). That is why it can be claimed that she recommends distinguishing between assimilation abroad and acting like a local while visiting her native country. However, Nazneen is far from being able to understand this dualism and she is not capable of acting differently in the public and private spheres.

Village versus city

Nazneen is caught in a triple bind. First, she comes from a village in Eastern society and arrives in Western society in London. Whereas in her native village of Gouripur in Mymensingh District she was always surrounded by people, in London, she is metaphorically imprisoned in Tower Hamlets. She does not know the language, which makes her isolation even more perceptible. She is destined to live in isolation. She comments on it thus, "In all her eighteen years, she could scarcely remember a moment that she had spent alone. Until she married. And came to London to sit day after day in this large box with the furniture to dust, and the muffled sound of private lives sealed away above, below and around her" (24). Even the sounds are only second-hand. Nazneen knows that life around her is vibrant, but she is not to be an active participant in it. Her married life is characterized by the monotonous execution of menial domestic tasks. Her routine around the household, her blind devotion to her husband who she still has to learn, and the isolation and desolation are metaphorically signalled by the broken pavement or the dead grass within the estate. As an escape, Nazneen mentally returns all the time to her native country, where women feel strongly attached to their birthplace: "The pull of the land is stronger even than the pull of the blood... They don't leave home. Their bodies are here but their hearts are back there. And anyway, look how they live: just re-creating the villages here" (16). Nazneen, as a girl from a village, finds it difficult to fit in in Britain. Although she landed in the centre of the British metropolis, she remains at its periphery, in both the physical and metaphorical sense. As Cormack argues, she is "displaced from the village life whence it sprung and landed in urban London, the story that locates her source of fatalism becomes less able to maintain its organicism and project a coherent identity for her" (701-702). The third dimension of her oppression is the fact that she is a woman who is used to behaving by the rules, which strictly dictate the role and behaviour appropriate for women. Nazneen feels obliged to observe these cultural rules.

However, a different view on emancipation and the role of women in both Western and Eastern society is provided by Nazneen's sister Hasina. Similarly, to Nazneen, she leaves the village and goes to a town. However, she remains in Bangladesh. The reality of the town in London and Dhaka is mediated through letters that the sisters exchange. The epistolary part is an allusion to Jane Austen. Similarly, to Austen's female protagonists, Ali's characters resort to writing letters whenever they are in trouble. In such moments, they return in their thoughts to their native village and describe to each other some physical particularity of their native place, for example, "It is hot like anything leaves falling. Even coconut tree looks hot. I think of Gouripur never so hot in the village. Only a few trees here no shade roads melting. In London do roads ever melting?" (154) By a simple accident, Nazneen reveals that "was the point of being lost. She, like Hasina, could not simply go home. They were both lost in cities that would not pause even to shrug" (59) In the end, both women fail to assimilate and to live as Western women with no possibility of returning to Gouripur, as this would be a revelation of their failure to all.

English — Bangladeshi Domestic Novel

If *Brick Lane* is to be considered within the axis of centre vs. periphery or, in other words, city or village, the novel can be compared to the domestic novels by Jane Austen in which her female characters are also confined to a limited space. For example, in *Pride and Prejudice,* the reader learns hardly anything about the town settings beyond the village where the Bennet family lives and beyond the limits of the Bingley country estate. Whereas Elizabeth Bennet admits "confined homes", Nazneen at first enjoys her confinement in the flat and within the boundaries of the estate for reasons of uncertainty and security. Whereas Monica Ali indirectly alludes to Jane Austen, she makes a transition to the twentieth century when she admits that not many writers have written about the Bengali minority in Britain: "not many voices have emerged from that community. It is showing another side of Britain — a confined, tight-knit, ghettoesque place in Britain". (1) Returning to Nazneen's view of the world, upon her arrival in England, it is limited not only by Brick Lane or by the tightly knit and restricted area of Tower Hamlets, but most significantly by the field of vision from her curtained window. She experiences a double limitation — she can only see through her window and the view it provides again shows the very tightly limited community in Tower Hamlets. As Barker claims, "a quarter of Britain's 283,000 Bangladeshis live in Tower Hamlets: a unique concentration of a single ethnic minority in one local authority. The plus is a close network of family support. The minus is social inwardness and small conservatism."[15] Although Nazneen lives in the Brick Lane area, she does not know it at first. She does not have the slightest idea of the history and current situation of the suburb. Brick Lane's rich history begins with French Huguenots seeking religious refuge. When they left, the Jews who faced pogroms in continental Europe arrived. In the twentieth century, the area became an Asian ghetto which was dominated by the Indians who traded here in rags and opened bistros and by the Bangladeshi

---

15 Paul Barker, "The Taste of Banglatown: Britain's curry capital is a classic tale of migrant success. But the Bangladeshis of Brick Lane face new problems," *Guardian* 13 Apr 2004: 20.

community. Thus, in modern times, Brick Lane represents Bangladeshi success in gastronomy. As Sean Carey has documented:

> The story began when seamen from the Bangladesh up-country district of Sylhet gained a near-monopoly as cooks and galley-hands on imperial ships. They started to set up cafes ashore, which spread out from the docks. Today, the curry capital is Brick Lane, on the City of London's eastern fringe. (20)

In addition, based on a sociological survey conducted by Carey, he points out the gentrification still present in public places in the area under discussion; he states that:

> the ethnic and gender patterns are striking. Almost all the customers are white. Going out from the City for a curry is like white New Yorkers in the 1920s dining out at Harlem's Cotton Club... Almost all the staff are male... [b]ut Bengali women won't work in our restaurants for religious reasons. (20)

However, the social representation in the council houses is slowly changing at present because third-generation immigrant children do not wish to continue the tradition set by their parents. They aspire to smarter suburbs and better-paid jobs. They can dream about these as, unlike the protagonists of the novel Brick Lane, they are British citizens and are educated in the United Kingdom.

Nazneen can see the limited world outside her flat without being seen. This metaphorically signifies Nazneen's position as a silent observer who does not share her opinion with anyone. Another window into the external world is the TV. As a woman from a rural culture, she is appalled and at the same time fascinated by ice skating, the closeness of the partners on the ice, and their costumes. The narrator describes it thus: "Nazneen held a pile of the last dirty dishes to take to the kitchen, but the screen held her. A man in a very tight suit (so tight that it made his private parts stand out on display) and a woman in a skirt that did not even cover her bottom gripped each other as an invisible force hurtled them across an oval arena" (36). She does not comprehend the culture that permits showing bodily parts publicly, such as when she witnesses the neighbouring tattoo lady who shamelessly exposes herself in a curtainless window. On the one hand, Nazneen has never seen anything similar in her native village or country, but, on the other hand, she admires it and in secret, she later tries for a vain moment in privacy to imitate the ice-skaters, including their dress, when she unusually folds her sari. These private adventures remain hidden from the rest of the world and are little epiphanies for Nazneen in her daily routine.

When Nazneen desires to assimilate, she step by step tries to persuade her husband, who, however, always dismisses her goals and necessities. For example, he does not let her attend a language course with a fellow Bangladeshi woman from the Hamlets as this would not only mean a gateway to meeting and speaking to the British natives but it would also signify a substantial degree of emancipation that Chanu does not want to allow. He solves her request quickly by rejecting it with the following explanation: "Where's the need anyway?" (37) On another occasion, she wants to leave the flat but Chanu again does not see any purpose for it and therefore, he only rhetorically asks "Why should you go out?" (37). She becomes imprisoned within their flat, which she only slowly comes to realize, as she has been taught by her culture to abide mostly at home. After some time spent in Britain, she thinks for herself that she is "trapped inside the room, inside this flat, inside this concrete slab of entombed humanity" (76).

Fate

Another element that drives Nazneen's life and that relates closely to her upbringing in a traditional Bangladeshi village is fate. The novel *Brick Lane* is introduced by two quotes relating to fate. The first one, from Ivan Turgenev, talks about fate as being the leading phenomenon in human life: "Sternly, remorselessly, fate guides each of us; only at the beginning, when we're absorbed in details, in all sorts of nonsense, in ourselves, are we unaware of its harsh hand" (9). The second quote, from Heraclitus, "A man's character is his fate" (9) foreshadows Nazneen's way of life. Interestingly, it is Chanu, who is in love with English literature and even has a degree in it, who also indirectly often alludes to fate as well. However, he carefully avoids mentioning classic women writers in English and always provides examples of idols such as Thackeray or Hardy. These authors were very much preoccupied with fate. The style of the novel *Brick Lane* very much copies the smoothness of the style of Jane Austen. Both Ali and Austen do not surprise the reader by introducing innovations in style or by experimenting with form; rather, the twists are put across by small changes in the protagonists' lives and destinies. In addition, Ali chooses a third-person narrator. However, as Noemi Pereira-Ares points out:

> *Brick Lane* is mostly rendered from Nazneen's point of view. At first credulous and naïve, later on, sophisticated and mature, Nazneen's perspective dominates that of the narrator in a very palpable way at the beginning of the novel, merges with it almost imperceptibly towards the middle section and makes it almost unfelt towards the end. Consequently, as the novel progresses, the reader gets closer and closer to the protagonist, forgetting the presence of the narrator who mediates between them. In so doing, the novel creates a parallelism between the emancipation of Nazneen's voice at the formal level and her process of self-empowerment at the diegetic level where Nazneen goes from being a submissive wife to becoming an independent woman and the breadwinner for the family. (73)

The turning point is when Nazneen is given a sewing machine by Chanu. This act bears a multiple significance. On the one hand, Chanu wants to save their economic situation after his promotion prospects fail; on the other hand, it is the turning point and a chance for Nazneen to become independent emotionally and partly economically. At the same time, sewing is still a domestic and traditionally female activity and therefore, it is in line with Chanu's opinion that Nazneen should remain a "girl from the village".

Religion and upbringing as a girl from a village dictate that Nazneen does not revolt most of the time. If she rebels, she does so secretly and her rebellions are small and meaningless and do not influence anyone else as she is a full believer in fate. Chanu often talks about fate as well and it explains his deep interest in Thackeray and Hardy, who both focused on fate in their novels. Having been told that she was believed to be a stillborn child, Nazneen considers her life to be a gift and, therefore, she follows Fate almost blindly:

> As Nazneen grew she heard many times this story ... It was because of her mother's wise decision that Nazneen lived to become the wide-faced, watchful girl that she was. Fighting against one's Fate can weaken the blood. Sometimes, or perhaps most times, it can be fatal. Not once did Nazneen question the logic of the story ... What could not be changed must be borne. And since nothing could be changed, everything had to be borne. This principle ruled her life. (16)

She applies the same logic when her first son Ruku is dying in the hospital: "We must not stand in the way of Fate. Whatever happens, I accept it. And my child must not waste any energy fighting against Fate. That way, he will be stronger" (14). Although, of course, she is in deep sorrow, she overcomes it by believing that the death of her son will make her stronger for the future:

> So that when, at the age of thirty-four, after she had been given three children and had one taken away, when she had a futile husband and had been fated a young and demanding lover when for the first time, she could not wait for the future to be revealed but had to make it for herself, she was as startled by her agency as an infant who waves a clenched fist and strikes itself upon the eye. (16)

Nevertheless, at certain moments of uncertainty and at the point when she hesitates to make a decision, she is still lost.

Sexual awakening

Nazneen's growing economic independence secondarily brings about her sexual awakening. In addition, she loves just to observe male bodies—whereas Nazneen indirectly detests the fat body of Chanu and compares it to various elements of furniture, the body of her lover Karim is the object of admiration: "She thought of [Karim's] forearms and she rejoiced that they were not thin. She thought about the small flat mole on the left ridge of his jaw and how stunned she had been to discover it only this week" (264) Such sexual adventure would hardly be possible in a Bangladeshi village, unlike the English metropolis, where anonymity and at least the isolation of the individual flats within Tower Hamlets provide a shelter for the forbidden fruit. Still, she is very much aware of the conflict between her native culture and the culture of the multicultural city in which sexual practices are governed by different rules. Therefore, as Karim and Nasir postulate, "she can neither adopt the Western dating practice not have an adulterous relationship" (129). At the same time, for her Karim is a link between Bangladeshi and English culture. He initiates her into an implicit political awareness as she at first unwillingly attends the meetings of the radicalized Muslim group of Bengal Tigers. However, this political, social, and emotional awakening is only short-lived as she realizes that it has no future and therefore, she ends the love affair. However, in the novel her being mentally indecisive and unable to make decisions on her own are signified by her breakdown. Metaphorically, she is unconscious for a while and hesitates to come back to reality. Interestingly, at this point, Chanu, having no other option and not having around any other adult Bangladeshi women who would normally take care of her back home in Bangladesh, steps in and provides service to her. It might be partly his adaptation to Western standards but, more likely, it is because he is afraid of another loss and failure in his life.

Karim presents the ambiguity of assimilation. When Nazneen meets him for the first time, she admires him because he "made her feel as if she had said a weighty piece, as if she had stated a new truth" (216). She has the impression that she is being listened to, which is an experience she does not encounter with her husband. Unlike Chanu, who keeps repeating his mantra that sees Nazneen as "an unspoilt girl. From the village. All things considered, I am satisfied" (320), for Nazneen, Karim truly represents Western values. This is manifested by the way he thinks, by his attire and his style. However, after the 9/11 events in America, he slips back to a Bengali/Muslim way of behaviour and becomes radicalized. He explains to Nazneen his view on immigrant women:

> There's your westernized girl, wears what she likes, all the make-up going on, short skirts and that soon as she's out of her father's

> sight. She's into going out, getting good jobs, having a laugh. Then there's your religious girl, wears the scarf or even the burkha. You'd think, right, they'd be good wife material. But they ain't. Because all they want to do is argue. And they always think they know best because they've been off to all these summer camps for Muslim sisters. (321)

Based on this change of view, behaviour, and style, Nazneen finds the courage to refuse Karim because she finally understands that he saw in her "a Bengali wife. A Bengali mother. An ideal home. An idea of himself that he found in her" (380). Nazneen concludes that with Karim, even if she divorced, by which act she would trespass the laws of the ancestral culture, she would not become assimilated. Her situation and societal position in a relationship with Karim would just repeat her status, which would be very similar to what she has already experienced in her marriage to Chanu.

It is not only Nazneen who struggles. Sexual awakening, although in a different form, comes to her sister. In her letters, Hasina, having stayed in Bangladesh, compares her situation to that of Nazneen. Hasina similarly struggles in her marriage even though she eloped to avoid an arranged marriage. However, unlike Nazneen, she dares to leave the village, go to the city, and try her luck to support herself financially. She does not want to succumb to enduring mental as well as physical exploitation because she does not believe that "it is better to get beaten by your husband than beaten by a stranger" (58). This advice given to her by her landlady to endure domestic violence typifies the view of the older generations of Bangladeshi women. However, Hasina represents the revolt against the norms of the village; she is simply a young woman who opposes the stereotypes regarding gender roles in her native culture. In this respect, she is more progressive than Nazneen, who, in Western society, had a better opportunity to become assimilated and to adopt Western attitudes to gender and roles in marriage. Yet, as Elsa Gaztambide states, "Nazneen cannot help but feel trapped by the restrictions of her Muslim society in a land teeming with opportunity" (150) Although both women live in a metropolis, Nazneen does not use her chance. Hasina tries hard, but in the end, even Dhaka is hostile to her and she ends up as a prostitute. Having no other choice, "she'd have to propel herself into the future by whatever means possible or she'd be trapped forever in a place whose time had already passed". (54)

Another example of an emancipated woman who made it as regards assimilation and appropriation of Western values is Mrs. Azad. Based on her behaviour during the visit of Chanu's family to the house of the doctor, Chanu comments:

> I'm talking about the clash between Western values and our own. I'm talking about the struggle to assimilate and the need to preserve one's identity and heritage. I'm talking about children who don't know what their identity is. I'm talking about the feelings of alienation engendered by a society where racism is prevalent. I'm talking about the terrific struggle to preserve one's sanity while striving to achieve the best for one's family. (88)

This Whitmanesque litany highlights the struggle, identity, heritage, and family issues. Chanu does not provide answers; he just lists the problems. By not having any solutions ready, he shows that after all those years spent in England, he has not been able to assimilate. He has stayed on the periphery of the British culture and society that he admired so much at the beginning. On the contrary, Mrs Azad refuses to not integrate and adapt; she does not want to be like other immigrant women who "spend ten, twenty years here and they sit in the kitchen grinding spices all day and learn only two or three words of English". (93)

Muslim radicalization and 9/11

Nazneen was well aware of the pitfalls of Muslim radicalization. However, as a girl from a village, she does not understand the political agenda of the Westernized world and, in addition, as a woman, it does not feel proper for her to get actively engaged. But it is through the prohibited and secret love and admiration for Karim that she steps over her shadow and takes a passive part in the meeting of the Bengal Tigers. Ali, however, was careful about foregrounding the political ambitions of the Bengali inhabitants of Tower Hamlets. Although they plan various actions, even within their small communities, there are factions and disputes. On top of that, Ali indirectly reflects the post-9/11 worldwide atmosphere with the fear of radical Muslim actions. In an interview, Ali commented on her choice of depiction of the terrorist action in the USA and its aftermath in the novel, "in *Brick Lane*, the first reaction of some of the characters to 9/11, instead of shock and horror, is fear for themselves and Muslims around the world. That's not something they might want to read about in nonfiction form. A work of fiction is more open to a different human situation; the fiction is more deeply woven. You go to walk a mile in another man's shoes because it enables you to understand where the fundamental similarities are". (1)

Given the political turmoil that is expected as an aftermath of 9/11, Chanu realizes that his dream of becoming a high official has failed. Cormick agrees with this view, suggesting that Chanu "constructs a mythic Bangladesh to compensate for his failure to succeed in English culture" (702). The British certificates he once so admired and appreciated now gather dust at the bottom of a wardrobe. As a consequence, he changes his focus from Britain back to Bangladesh. However, the lessons he gives to his daughters about the country of their ancestors are not welcomed by the girls, for whom Bangladesh is not their native country. He explains to his children:

> In the sixteenth century, Bengal was called the Paradise of Nations. These are our roots. Do they teach these things in the school here? Does Shahana know about the Paradise of Nations? All she knows about is flood and famine. The whole bloody country is just a bloody basket case to her. (151)

Therefore, he highlights that children in Western schools are not taught a full picture of far-away countries that were once connected to the Empire, but they rather present a distorted picture that emphasizes the negative aspects of the native culture and history in contemporary Bangladesh. Chanu's lessons, which are intended to have a corrective character, are not very successful and are met with disdain by his daughters. For example, he forces Shahana and Bibi to memorize a poem, "Golden Bengal", by the Bengali national poet Rabindranath Tagore. Despite having no interest, they learn it by heart and they unwillingly have to recite it in the presence of a distinguished guest, Dr Azad. They do not understand the essence of it and therefore their performance is very static and emotionless.

Conclusion

Brick Lane by Monica Ali proves that the road to emancipation for a girl from a Bangladeshi village who is displaced in a British metropolis is hard to achieve. She has to overcome not only cultural and language barriers but also, she has to find the courage to make her own decisions and to act in favour of her children. Although she keeps hesitating about her independence and relies heavily on fate, in the end, she manages to free her thinking from the stereotypical roles when stays in England with her children while her husband moves to Bangladesh. Whereas Chanu leaves England as a loser, Nazneen is the victor who has succeeded in assimilating to a degree that enables her to retain some features of her native culture that she considers important.

Works Cited

Ali, M. *Brick Lane*. 2003. London: Black Swan.

Barker, P., 2004. "The Taste of Banglatown: Britain's curry Capital is a classic tale of migrant success. But the Bangladeshis of Brick Lane face new problems." *Guardian*, 13 Apr. p 20.

"Best of British: Booker Hopeful Monica Ali on Her Novel Brick Lane," 2003. *Publishers Weekly* 2, p.1.

Cormack, A., 2006. "Migration and the Politics of Narrative Form: Realism and the Postcolonial Subject in Brick Lane." *Contemporary Literature*, 47(4), pp.695-721.

Gaztambide, E., 2005. "Ali, Monica." *Booklist*, August (2003): 1950.

Karim, A., and Nasir, Z., 2014. "Multiculturalism and Feminist Concerns in South Asian Diaspora Novels." *Southeast Asian Journal of English Language Studies* 20 (3), pp.125-134.

Pereira-Ares, N., 2012. "The East Looks at the West, the Woman Looks at the Man: A Study of the Gaze in *Brick Lane* by Monica Ali," *Miscelánea* 46, pp.71-81.

Rushdie, S., 1982. "The Empire Writes Back with a Vengeance." *The Times*, 3 July, p.8.

Sengupta, R., 2021. "Women Writers of the South Asian Diaspora: Interpreting Gender, Texts and Contexts." *Journal of Comparative Literature and Aesthetics*, 44(1), p.99. Available at <https://go.gale.com/ps/i.do?id=GALE%7CA655104010&sid=googleScholar&v=2.1&it=r&linkaccess=abs&issn=02528169&p=LitRC&sw=w&userGroupName=anon%7E254b723a> [Accessed December 14, 2021].

This work was supported by the Erasmus+ Programme of the European Union, Key Action 2: Strategic Partnerships, under the Grant "Reflection of National and European Identity in the New Millennium" [2019-1-CZ01-KA203-061227].

The London Underground in Neil Gaiman's *Neverwhere*

A tale of London

Neil Gaiman is undisputedly one of the most acclaimed and popular British authors of our time across a variety of media and genres, as well as one of the most productive. Among his many stories, *Neverwhere* stands out as a narration that appears to have an extraordinarily abiding appeal, as it has been rewritten and readapted multiple times:

> Beginning life as a BBC TV series in 1996, Gaiman released a novelization of his script later that same year. In 2005, it was turned into a comic book by writer Mike Carey and artist Glenn Fabry and in 2013, a BBC radio adaptation with Dirk Maggs at the tiller was broadcast. The story has also been adapted for the stage several times (Barnett 2017).

One cannot help but wonder why a story as fantastical as *Neverwhere* is so high in demand. After all, at the time of its publication, fantasy was still a fringe phenomenon, only just on the verge of becoming "one of the great pillars of popular culture" (Grossman 2014).

To begin with, the story's protagonist, Richard, is an average young man in a committed relationship, with a secure job and everyday life problems, which makes him an easily relatable character. Secondly, it is a story of nostalgia for a simpler past, a better world. It criticizes contemporary values and imagines a (to some extent utopian) alternative society, which makes it appealing as well. I argue that, with these textual functions in mind, *Neverwhere* can be read as a work of the pastoral, despite its entirely urban setting. This leads us to the third and perhaps most substantial element to increase *Neverwhere*'s popularity: it's being set in London, a place that is exceedingly familiar to most British and many international readers. London is much more than just a backdrop setting; it is essential to the plot, even indispensable since there would not be much of a story left if the parts about the city were to be deleted. *Neverwhere* is a tale of London.

The London in the centre of the narration lies mostly under the city's surface — partly deliberately hidden away, such as sewers, buried ruins and abandoned buildings, and partly all-too-familiar and mundane, such as the Tube, London's Underground system. Around these constituents of the real-life city, Gaiman creates "an alternative magical world which coexists with ours" (Beaudry 2012, p. 73), seemingly in the same spaces, but strictly separated from one another. This becomes especially obvious in the scenes that are connected to the Tube. With its peculiar station names the London Underground "has always exercised a powerful influence on London's urban imaginary" (Gomel 2014, p. 185). Any person reading or hearing them for the first time would wonder about the origins of these names.

In this sense, "[t]he Underground is also a place of collective memory. The names of the stations prompt historical associations" (Ackroyd 2011, p. 160). There is more than one layer of knowledge available for each place in London. It is easily possible to be familiar with a place in modern-day London, to visit it every day and even connect deeply personal memories with it, while simultaneously being completely unaware of the place's history and most other stories connected to it. This notion of the city as a palimpsest, casting one layer of history and subjective experience over the next and thus rendering the ones at the bottom illegible, is a very prominent one in urban writing and forms a perfect foundation for fantasy literature. After all, if the original appearances, functions and meanings of places are continuously supplanted by new places, new purposes or associations, then how could anybody ever know with certainty how many layers there are? Fantasy authors "use the idea of the palimpsest — a surface of vellum or parchment used for writing on more than once — as a guiding principle because it shows that imaginative writing *can* contain many different versions of the city within the same space" (Groes 2011, p. 123; cf. Elber-Aviram 2013, p. 2). This technique of creating alternative worlds which the characters, as well as the readers, can enter, is one that fantasy literature shares with the pastoral. After all, the pastoral is essentially "a retreat from 'our manners', 'our climate', 'our age', into a literary construct"; it generates a "discourse, a way of using language that constructs a different kind of world from that of realism" (Gifford 1999, p. 45).

How this method is executed in the particular example of *Neverwhere* will be the central question of this chapter. To begin with, the London Underground Map will be briefly discussed, which is the medium to first convey an idea of the Tube to many people. Although its design is a highly abstract diagram and ignores any basic rules of geography (Hadlaw 2003, p. 32; Groes 2011, p. 134), the map is mostly understood and utilized as a truthful representation of London and therefore comprises an ambivalent rapport of fiction and reality in itself. After having examined this issue with Baudrillard's theory of Simulation and Simulacra, the chapter will move on to Neil Gaiman's alternative representation of the Underground system, which includes the map, but gradually alters all knowledge it ought to impart. His procedure of rewriting is examined more closely concerning distinct Underground Stations, namely Knightsbridge, Earl's Court, and Blackfriars, which will be placed in the context of their historical development and juxtaposed and complemented with Gaiman's presentation of them. Throughout the argumentation, it will be pointed out where Neverwhere exhibits characteristics of the urban pastoral by "find[ing] or creat[ing] within the city spaces or images conducive to pastoral moods" (McNamara and Gray 2014, p. 246).

"Handy Fiction" — The London Underground Map

> No visitor to London can avoid the ubiquitous London Underground Map […]; like many public transit maps, it is regularly posted on city streets outside stations, and strategically placed inside train cars and on platforms at regulated locations and angles for maximum exposure. But the map exceeds the confines of the transit system: the famous design is plastered all over the city on tourist trinkets such as T-shirts, mugs, umbrellas, lighters, and postcards, and an estimated 95% of Londoners are said to have a copy at home (Vertesi 2008, p. 9; cf. Hadlaw 2003, p. 25).

The omnipresence of the so-called Tube Map[16] is unparalleled and exerts substantial influence on the general public, even more so because the design is not only passively perceived and consumed, but put to active use in uncountable situations. Not only is it utilized for its original purpose — making sense of the different subway lines and finding one's way from one station to another — but in the eyes of many it becomes an image of London itself. As Janet Vertesi explains, "The map is not only an interface to the subway system but is also metonymically used as an interface to the city as a whole" (11). Of course, this approach to the Tube Map is rather problematic due to the high degree of abstraction used in the design. Showing no visible landmarks apart from a stylized, angular version of the river Thames (Hadlaw 2003, 32) and distorting the distances between stations,[17] it does not apply to the city above ground. Nonetheless, people imagine the city as a grid whose principal axes are the Underground lines on which any given place can then be located (Vertesi 2008, pp. 15-6) and which serve to measure the spatial and temporal distances between those places, for instance as 'five stops' or 'a twenty-minute ride' (18-9). Due to this manner of visualizing the city, "localities become 'stops' on the map; spaces to surface from the warp of the underground and encounter the above-ground locality" (16), taken out of their actual context in the cityscape and, consequently, hard to find on a city map of London. What the Tube Map does, accordingly, is to establish "a virtual space in which the analogue urban environment can be explored, constructed, narrated and understood" (11).

---

16 As the London Underground is the oldest subway system worldwide, having been in use since 1863 (Ackroyd 2011, p. 136), the Tube Map was also one of the earliest of its kind and has influenced many similar designs. Henry Beck constructed it in the early 1930s — however, the exact year of its creation and/or publication appears to be contested, e.g. Ackroyd names it as 1931 (2011, p. 150), Hadlaw as 1931 and 1933 respectively (2003, p. 25), Vertesi as 1932 (2008, p. 9), and Groes as 1935 (2011, p. 133).

17 The proportions are distorted insofar as "the cartographic projection is non-traditional, inflating the centre and conflating the periphery" (Vertesi 2008, pp. 9-10). Moreover, on the map "proximity of place was determined by *typographic* (as opposed to geographic) concerns: that is to say that the representation of the distance between stations had to do with the layout of text and graphics, rather than the actual geographic relationship between places" (Hadlaw 2003, p. 33).

Following this train of thought, the London Underground Map might be considered a simulacrum as defined by Jean Baudrillard in 1981. In earlier discussions of the term, simulation was understood as the act of copying real-life objects, people, situations or spaces and regarding these copies as equivalent to the original, for instance, a classical city map would duplicate the city and be read as if it were the city itself. However:

> [a]bstraction today is no longer that of the map, the double, the mirror or the concept. Simulation is no longer that of a territory, a referential being or a substance. It is the generation by models of a real without origin or reality: a hyperreal. The territory no longer precedes the map, nor survives it. Henceforth it is the map that precedes the territory — *precession of simulacra* — it is the map that engenders the territory (Baudrillard 2004, pp. 365-6).

The London Underground Map appears to be the perfect example of such a "model of a real without origin or reality" — it is, after all, taken as an authentic copy of the subway system, despite depicting it in an abstract manner in which that system does not exist. In the great majority of human minds, the Tube Map "engenders" the Underground territory.

Giving a further description of the simulacrum, Baudrillard states that:

> [i]t is no longer a question of imitation, nor of reduplication, nor even of parody. It is rather a question of substituting signs of the real for the real itself; that is, an operation to deter every real process by its operational double, a metastable, programmatic, perfect descriptive machine which provides all the signs of the real and short-circuits all its vicissitudes. Never again will the real have to be produced (2004, p. 366).

never again would anyone need precise knowledge of the real London Underground landscape when the Tube Map is so thoroughly applicable. There is simply no need for the common public to know any other "reality" than the one offered by the simulacrum. Henry Beck, the designer of the map, was fully aware of that: "If you're going underground, why do you need to bother about geography?", he asked. "It's not so important. *Connections ... are the thing*" (cited in Hadlaw 2003, p. 32).

As legitimate as this question may be, we ought to keep in mind that "an abstraction like Beck's Underground map represents only the desire for order, a trope of coherence, not its realization" (Phillips 2010, p. 180; cf. Ackroyd 2001, p. 112). It is undoubtedly beneficial for daily journey-planning purposes, but it leaves a disconcerting void behind. "[W]hat is unsettling is the deceptive gap between reality and representation with which it confronts us" (Groes 2011, p. 134). It is this gap precisely that Gaiman fills with his story. Tracy Bealer and Rachel Luria state that "Gaiman provides a new map for once familiar territory" (2012, p. viii), yet, especially about *Neverwhere*, it seems more accurate to say that he provides an utterly new, unexplored territory for an old, familiar map.

The relevance the Tube Map has for *Neverwhere* is emphasized early on in the novel: first, an excerpt of it is included in print on the pages preceding the text, and second, it takes centre stage in its prologue. Even though the first scene is set in a small Scottish town, the second sentence reports that Richard has received "warnings about the evils and dangers of London" along with a "white umbrella with the map of the London Underground on it" as a farewell gift from his friends (Gaiman 1996, p. 1). Thus introduced, the design is spotlighted even more when Richard passes the umbrella on to a friendly elderly lady:

> [A] click, and it blossomed into a huge white map of the London Underground network, each line drawn in a different colour, every station marked and named. The old woman took the umbrella, gratefully, and smiled her thanks. [...] Then she walked away into the rain and the night, a round white shape covered with the names of London Tube stations—Earl's Court, Marble Arch, Blackfriars, White City, Victoria, Angel, Oxford Circus ... Richard found himself pondering, drunkenly, whether there was a circus at Oxford Circus: a real circus with clowns, beautiful women, and dangerous beasts (pp. 3-4).

To this effect, the prologue uses the London Underground to foreshadow the ensuing story in two ways. On the one hand, it introduces Richard as a helpful young man and a stranger to London, a newcomer who is a bit naïve about the city and views it with childlike curiosity and imagination, as his musings about the station name Oxford Circus indicate. On the other hand, it introduces specific places in London that are to become important elements to the plot, such as Earl's Court, Blackfriars, or Angel, and conjures images of troubling doors, beautiful women, dangerous beasts, and drowning rats (p. 4), all of which are to feature extensively later on (Jódar 2006, p. 169).

Richard's friends make a great effort to prepare him for his new city life and its dangers by giving him good advice as well as the umbrella, a device to read the London Underground system and simultaneously ward off London weather. Nevertheless, the immediate outcome of the farewell party is a sense of confusion. Richard "remembered only the feeling that he was about to leave somewhere small and rational — a place that made sense — for somewhere huge and old that didn't" (Gaiman 1996, pp. 4-5). This disorientation seems to be dispersed at the beginning of the main plot line in chapter one, which starts after a considerable time gap:

> Three years in London [...] had changed the way he perceived the city. [...] When he had first arrived, he had found London huge, odd, fundamentally incomprehensible, with only the Tube map, that elegant multicolored topographical display of underground railway lines and stations, giving it any semblance of order. Gradually he realized that the Tube map was a handy fiction that made life easier but bore no resemblance to the reality of the shape of the city above (p. 8).

To a certain degree, Richard becomes aware of the hyperreality of the Tube Map. He acknowledges that the map is fiction about London Above, the cityscape on the surface of the earth, and can hardly ever be of practical use there. However, he seems to hold onto it as an absolute truth for the Underground system. Moreover, Richard is also conscious of London's colourful history, that is of the fact that today's city is a conglomerate of the different villages it has absorbed over centuries, together with their histories, "leaving only their names behind" (p. 10). In this respect, he realizes that there are numerous levels of history and reality in the city. Nonetheless, the entire scope of the city's palimpsestuous character and its functioning as a simulacrum has not yet entered Richard's mind at that point.

In the early scenes, no connection is made between Richard's regular London life—of which the quotidian use of the Tube is an essential part—and Door's adventures in an unspecified Underworld, even though the two storylines are taken up alternately and are thus physically interwoven on the page. The fantastic elements that are visible in Door's story do not affect Richard or his surroundings up to their first encounter during which Richard is confronted with various forms of magic and forced to accept that something is happening that he does not understand; however, he does not feel the impact of recent events until the next morning.

Interestingly, it is in the London Underground that Richard begins to realize that his status has been crucially altered. Having been ignored by a taxi driver, which had not seemed too unusual to him, he attempts to buy a Tube ticket but fails, since three different ticket machines as well as the ticket seller ignore him and his coins. "'Fuck it,' announced Richard and he vaulted the barrier. No one stopped him; no one seemed to care. [...] As a child, Richard had had nightmares in which he simply wasn't there, in which no matter how much noise he made, no matter what he did, nobody ever noticed him at all. He began to feel like that now" (p. 57). His everyday routine of getting to work thus becomes gradually uncanny. It turns from being an unspectacular nuisance into a reassuring ritual of normality that is deeply missed as soon as it is gone. The Tube as the embodiment of "rationalized space and time, as [a place] where the unexpected is not meant to happen" (Mengham and Atkins 2012, p. 169), is astoundingly the first indicator of Richard's nightmarish expulsion from his world. Like many others before him, Richard has fallen "through the cracks in the world" (Gaiman 1996, p. 127) and landed in London Below. His change of location, albeit involuntary, can be read as the first instance of the motif of retreat, which is a central component of the pastoral form (Gifford 1999, pp. 1-5, pp. 45-80). The Tube is the indicator and site of Richard's transformation and as such represents the borderline between both worlds, Above and Below. It becomes a "liminal zone where the past and the present, the poor and the rich, the metaphorical and the literal meet and mingle" (Gomel 2014, p. 187; cf. Rață 2017, p. 98). How London Above and London Below are continuously juxtaposed, compared and contrasted, supports the reading of London Below as a pastoral landscape, an alternative space to the city as we know it (Gifford 1999, p. 2).

Re-imagining Underground stations

The first Underground Station to be mentioned by name is Knightsbridge, a place which originally referenced a medieval bridge over the Westbourne stream and later came to denote the entire surrounding neighbourhood as well as its Tube station (Hilliam 2016, p. 74). Being the first stop on Richard's underground travels and accessible from both London Above and Below, it illustrates particularly well how certain spaces may be perceived completely contrariwise in the two worlds. Whereas Anaesthesia, an inhabitant of Below and Richard's new escort, describes Knightsbridge as "a really nasty neighborhood" (Gaiman 1996, p. 92), Richard associates the name with a middle to upper-class housing area which is not scary at all, in fact, according to Gaiman "this is the nicest area of London" (White 1999). Although the place could not be characterized in a more contrary manner, both descriptions are accurate as the events taking place at Knightsbridge show.

When Richard and Anaesthesia arrive at their destination, it is the original eponymous bridge, long gone in London Above but still existent in Below, that they see. "[T]here was no sky above it, no water below. It rose into darkness. Richard wondered who had built it and when. He wondered how something like this could exist, beneath the city of London, without everyone knowing. He felt a sinking feeling in the pit of his stomach. He was, he realized, deeply, pathetically scared of the bridge itself" (Gaiman 1996, p. 100). Hunter, whom Richard and Anaesthesia meet at the foot of the bridge, augments Richard's confusion and anxiety by warning him that the name is Night's Bridge rather than Knightsbridge and that the night, i.e., the darkness on it, must indeed be feared (p. 102).

Her remark indicates for the first time that well-known names, especially those of the Tube system, need to be reconsidered in this alternative city because they might acquire different, very literal meanings. London Below presents "a world where language achieves absolute referentiality, even in place names" (Błaszkiewicz 2014, p. 130; cf. Michaeli 2017, p. 25).

Hunter's sinister warning about the Night's dangers comes to fruition when the group crosses the bridge. Richard feels physically suffocated by the darkness, which resembles a living organism more than anything, and "[i]t was then that the hallucinations started" (Gaiman 1996, p. 104). He is confronted with a string of visions, memories from his past as well as premonitions of potential futures, which are all horrifying to Richard. Despite this attack, he reaches the other end of the bridge, only to realize that his companion is not so lucky. Anaesthesia has been taken by the darkness as a toll, and there is nothing left of her except for a small bead from her necklace which Richard takes with him to remember her and the passage (p. 105).

Thus, the first experience Richard has with the London Underground in its 'Below' variant establishes right away that he has stepped into a life-threatening atmosphere. It is quite typical for urban fantasy literature that "the counter-world is a place where our fears and anxieties are re-negotiated, where our instinctive responses of terror and disgust are simultaneously tested and challenged, and where the repugnant and repulsive are revealed as integral parts of our world" (Vanderbeke 2014, p. 153). Patterns of this kind are also typical of what Leo Marx has famously termed the 'complex pastoral'. Works of this kind stand in opposition to the rather simple 'sentimental pastoral', which fully and unquestioningly idealizes nature. The complex pastoral, however, explores nature more critically, and it always bears a *counterforce* which establishes the natural world as "a larger, more complicated order of experience" and "brings a world which is more 'real' into juxtaposition with an idyllic vision" (1964, p. 25). If we disregard the fact that Marx's definition of the pastoral was restricted to a natural arcadia and consider London Below as a pastoral landscape in its own right, as argued above, we can identify his counterforce for the first time in this passage and the complexity of this world's design is revealed. Richard is forced to recognize the reality of London-Below, which, so far, had been dream-like, if slightly scary for him, in two stages: First, through the series of images he is faced with which include rather intimate, enclosed traumas and anxieties as well as frightening events that may take place in the future. By producing or recalling these visions realistically in his mind and memory, Knightsbridge exerts an effective form of psychological terror over Richard. As soon as he has successfully crossed the bridge and his horror starts to dissolve, he is hit by a second wave of fear, guilt and mourning when he slowly apprehends Anaesthesia's death and realizes how immediate the danger to his own life is (Gaiman 1996, pp. 105-6).

As the name Knightsbridge or Night's Bridge has been mentioned a couple of times, the reader will have made a connection between this eerie place in London Below and the real-life Tube station already, but only at the very end of the scene does the novel address it. When Richard and Hunter have passed the bridge successfully, they emerge at a familiar spot: "They were in an Underground station" and "[t]he sign of the station said KNIGHTSBRIDGE" (pp. 107-8). The familiar image that Richard has been expecting is finally evoked, but now that he has seen its uncanny counterpart, his personality is significantly altered and his former view of the world cannot be restored. He has started to gradually comprehend that spaces like Knightsbridge are hyperreal, with more than one original reality lurking behind them.

In summary, Knightsbridge has three relevant functions: firstly, it introduces Richard to Below and clarifies some of its rules — for instance, that, down there, inexplicable places can exist despite any London Above logic, that names are to be taken seriously, that dangers might wait in every corner and death is a definite possibility, and that the past and history are relative notions. Secondly, it foreshadows some of the upcoming events through the visions imposed on Richard. Thirdly, it provides him with some of the tools he needs to survive in Below, in the form of knowledge, memories and self-awareness, but also materially speaking, as Anaesthesia's pearl will become the key to his survival in the ordeal later on. The crossing of the bridge represents Richard's transfer from one world into the next.

When the next Tube Station comes into play, Richard is better prepared. Having found Door, the Marquis and Hunter once more, the declared new aim of his travel companions is to find Earl's Court. "Richard was beginning to catch on. He assumed that the Earl's Court he referred to wasn't the familiar Tube station he had waited in innumerable times, reading a paper, or just daydreaming" (p. 139). Although Richard says he is not expecting the familiar station any more, his further actions and reactions prove him wrong. He cannot help holding on to the knowledge he has collected with care over three years of living in London and therefore keeps voicing his fundamental truths. When, for instance, the Marquis leads the others to a Central Line platform after consulting a special train schedule, and pronounces "'We're in luck,' [...] 'The Earl's Court train should be coming through here in about half an hour', Richard replies doubtfully "'Earl's Court Station isn't on the Central Line,' [...]. The marquis stared at Richard, openly amused. 'What a refreshing mind you have, young man,' he said. 'There is nothing quite like total ignorance, is there?'" (p. 143). Despite having warmed to the idea that there might be alternate versions of the Tube stations themselves, Richard has never doubted the fixity of their locations until then. He is proved wrong when the Earl's train arrives:

> The car that had pulled up in front of Richard was quite empty: its lights were turned off; it was bleak and empty and dark. From time-to-time Richard had noticed cars like this one, locked and shadowy, on Tube trains, and he had wondered what purpose they served. The other doors on the train hissed open, and passengers got on and got off. The doors of the darkened car remained closed. The marquis drummed on the door with his fist, an intricate rhythmic rap. Nothing happened. Richard was just wondering if the train would now pull out without them on it, when the door of the dark car was pushed open from the inside (p. 148).

The fact that he remembers having seen cars like this before shows one more point of contact between London Above and Below.

However, contrary to his belief up to then, the car in question is not empty and useless but contains the most improbable scene. Upon entering it Richard finds an open log fire, chicken on a straw-covered floor, men-at-arms, a wolfhound, a lute player, a falconer alongside his falcon, some damsels, a herald with a bugle, a jester, and, finally the ruler over all this entourage — the Earl. "It was, Richard realized, as if someone had taken a small medieval court and put it, as best they could, in one car of an Underground train" (p. 151), an image that seems in line with the associations produced by both the literal meaning of the station's name, as well as the place's history as a small hamlet surrounding the manor house or 'court' of the Earls of Oxford (Hilliam 2016, p. 44).

However, after a brief moment of astonishment, Richard has to realize that this prospect is not completely truthful either. Following the common laws of hospitality, the visitors are offered food and drinks. In a readjustment of the medieval tradition, these provisions are sweets and Coca-Cola taken from the vending machines in the stations (Gaiman 1996, p. 157), to be then served in silver goblets (p. 160). The preparation and display of the food thus demonstrates perfectly the palimpsestuous mixture of history and modernity that prevails in *Neverwhere*. The court members hardly react at all, since these are daily commodities of their lives, just a tinge of nostalgia is visible in one of the guard's wistful memories of the days when wine was the standard drink (p. 160).

Another reason for nostalgia becomes apparent while inspecting the Earl himself more closely. He is described as:

> an immense, elderly man, in a huge fur-lined dressing gown and carpet slippers, […] his arm resting on the shoulder of a jester in shabby motley. The old man was larger than life in every way: he wore an eye-patch over his left eye, which had the effect of making him look slightly helpless, and unbalanced, like a one-eyed hawk. There were fragments of food in his red-gray beard, and what appeared to be pajama pants were visible at the bottom of his shabby fur gown (p. 151).

Although he is addressed respectfully as "His Grace the Earl" (p. 152) and still considered Lord of most Underground lines (p. 161), he is by far not an elegant, sophisticated figure. On the contrary, he has a shabby, neglected exterior, and his mental capabilities seem to be impaired by either dementia or insanity. Hence, he does not conform to Richard's image of the powerful, strong, noble aristocracy of the Middle Ages (p. 163). This scene, alongside several others, illustrates again that London Below is pastoralized, with its nostalgia for past centuries, simpler hierarchies, and even the feudal system. After all, what contributes significantly to the appeal of 'subterranean pastorals', according to David Pike, is their timelessness and their connection to history (2005, pp. 170-172). However, the Earl's Court episode also proves the complexity of *Neverwhere*'s pastoral design once more, with its critical point of view and references to 'real life'.

Finally, in addition to his representative and governmental responsibilities, the Earl is in charge of any object that shares his fate of being outdated and obsolete. The Earl's "real domain" is his library which is "a tiny empire of lost property" holding a massive amount of "[t]hings lost, things forgotten" (Gaiman 1996, p. 162), and therefore gives access to all kinds of knowledge and cultures. Thus, Earl's Court is not only a perfect example of an urban space that is co-inhabited by history and modernity and belongs to both London Below and Above but also represents an archive of things that have gone from one state and place to the other. It is proof and witness of the dynamic relation between the worlds and keeps impeding Richard's unconscious quest for a simplification of this dynamic and the restoration of the old London Above logic.

A later interim goal of the group's journey is Blackfriars, where they ought to find a key. On the way there, the narrative pattern used before is repeated. Richard states that "[h]e had crossed Blackfriars Bridge, in the City of London, many times, and he had often passed through Blackfriars station, but he had learned by now not to assume anything" (p. 203). Nonetheless, he does undoubtedly bear certain expectations in mind, namely that the Black Friars will be "a bunch of monks" (p. 204), the concomitant image being one of elderly, peaceful, Christian men who live in an abbey. What awaits him at the destination is therefore surprising.

The first sight upon the group's arrival at Blackfriars might be considered a mirror image of Knightsbridge, as "[t]here was a bridge ahead of them [...]. A figure, dressed in black, waited at the foot of the bridge. He wore the black robes of a Dominican monk. His skin was the dark brown of old mahogany. He was a tall man, and he held a wooden staff as tall as he was" (p. 230). His name is Brother Sable (p. 231) and the bridge can only be passed when Hunter has successfully defeated him in battle. Then:

> [a]t the apex of the bridge, another monk was waiting for them: Brother Fuliginous. He was younger and smaller than the first monk they had met, but he was dressed the same way. His skin was a deep, rich brown. There were other black-clad figures, just barely visible, further into the yellow fog. These were the Black Friars, then, Richard realized (p. 231).

Even though the Black Friars partly fulfil Richard's imagination, insofar as they wear Dominican monks' robes and call each other 'Brother', he does not, at first, recognize them as the friars they are looking for. This is most probably the case because they deviate from the stereotypical image of a friar in many ways: they are not elderly and plump, but young, tall and athletic. They are not pacifistic, but initiate a physical fight with them for no obvious reason. They are all black and have strange-sounding telling names, which are all synonyms of the word 'black'. These deviations from the picture in Richard's mind create a rather uncanny effect.

In contrast, the blind, wise abbot is a stock character of many stories set in monasteries who unfailingly rule over Blackfriars in London Below as well. Maybe it is because of this familiarity that "Richard liked him on sight" (p. 232), although he is the one to explain the ordeal Richard has to undergo to obtain the key they are searching for. While making it clear that the undertaking is rather hopeless since every person who has attempted it so far has failed, he at least tries to be nice about it:

> [...] do not fret, perhaps you will be the one to win the key, eh?' There was a ghastly attempt at reassurance in his voice, more terrifying than any attempt to scare him could have been. 'You would kill me?' The abbot stared ahead with blue-milk eyes. There was a

touch of reproof in his voice. 'We are holy men,' he said. 'No, it is the ordeal that kills you (pp. 234-5).

He willfully plays with Richard's uncertainty about the monks' true nature by assuring him that he and his brethren would never harm him, only to add that the ordeal, to which he leads Richard at that moment, will kill him nonetheless.

Accordingly, this ordeal is feared most intensely by Richard, but to his surprise, he finds a familiar image when he enters the room in which it is to take place: "It was a District Line station: the sign said BLACKFRIARS" (p. 241). Again, his experience in Knightsbridge is paralleled: after having been confronted with a fantastic, new and scary version of the place Blackfriars, he unexpectedly walks into its familiar London Above counterpart. The attack he fears seems to hold off at first, but after a while, it becomes clear that it just takes a different form from what he anticipated. Instead of being affected physically, there is a mental assault taking place, to be executed in several stages. Firstly:

> [t]here were footsteps on the platform, near him, and he looked up to see a prim little girl walking past him, hand in hand with a woman who looked like a larger, older version of the girl. They glanced at him and then, rather obviously, looked away. 'Don't get too near to him, Melanie,' advised the woman, in a very audible whisper. Melanie looked at Richard, staring in the way children stare, without embarrassment or self-consciousness. Then she looked back at her mother. 'Why do people like that stay alive?' she asked, curiously. 'Not enough guts to end it all,' explained her mother. Melanie risked another glance at Richard. 'Pathetic,' she said (pp. 241-2).

The bluntness of the exchange and the harsh judgment from a child, clearly advising him to kill himself, baffle Richard and leave him insecure. In this vulnerable state, he starts to reflect on his mental state. "He tried to remember why he was standing on this platform. Was he waiting for a Tube train? Where was he going? [...] Was he dreaming? [...] No. This was no dream. Wherever he was, was real. He felt odd: detached, and depressed, and horribly, strangely saddened" (p. 242).

Having started to doubt his purpose and state of existence, Richard is led deeper and deeper into confusion from then on. His former colleague Gary appears and starts talking to him. Friendly at first, he soon changes his appearance to look exactly like his vis-à-vis, thus creating the impression that Richard is talking to himself, and dares him to try and see the truth. Richard initially refuses, but then cannot help looking into the direction his double points out: "There was an Underground train waiting at the platform, and, reflected in its window, Richard could see himself. […] He was a crazy homeless person, standing on a platform of a busy Underground station, in the heart of the rush hour" (p. 244). After this first realization of his supposedly true state of insanity, Richard's doppelgänger is joined by his ex-fiancée Jessica, who reinforces the diagnosis. Although Richard tries to fight them off by explaining unconvincingly his quest and the ordeal, both Jessica and Gary eventually summon him to put his pitiful existence to an end, as Melanie and her mother did implicitly. Even the posters on the walls command Richard to kill himself (p. 249) and the announcements via speakers predict his suicide by referring to him as "an incident at Blackfriars Station" (p. 247). Richard is rescued only because he coincidentally finds the material evidence of his experiences in Below in his pockets — the bead from Anaesthesia's necklace. Due to his memory of his intense initiation to the world of London Below, the passage over Knightsbridge, he can resist the urge to jump to his death. Instead, "he stood on the platform and waited for the train to come in" (p. 250).

The Ordeal reveals to Richard once and for all the enormous extent of hyperreality that is present in the London Underground. It puts into question every firm knowledge or belief Richard ever had. He is almost led to believe that he is a madman with no chance for recovery, an image that seems plausible and familiar following the discourse that he has internalized as truth-telling for years. For regular Londoners, the Underground is a place that "generates greater fear and anxiety — of strangers, of thieves and of the mad who haunt its endlessly running trains" (Ackroyd 2001, p. 569). Richard comes to see himself as one of these mad, ghostlike figures and briefly accepts this image of himself as a fact until

Anaesthesia's bead in his pocket leads him to question the universal validity of this story. In conclusion, it is the realization that there is no one reality that saves Richard from death.[18]

The Ordeal can be overcome because "the experience [is] a test that finally enables Richard to come to terms with the duality of the world and his ability to perceive it" (Błaszkiewicz 2014, p. 136). The end of the ordeal is therefore quite fitting: "Richard had no idea who he was, anymore; no idea what was or what was not true; nor whether he was brave or cowardly, mad or sane, but he knew the next thing he had to do. He stepped onto the train, and all the lights went out" (Gaiman 1996, pp. 250-1). There is no further explanation, epiphany or closure because there cannot be if no singular truth exists. As soon as Richard becomes fully aware of the place's hyperreality, everything goes dark and the next thing told is how he is picked up by the Black Friars and brought back to his friends (p. 251).

The key he wins by passing the Ordeal adds to this interpretation towards the end of the story, when it is revealed that the key does not only lead to heaven, as Richard thought but really can lead its keeper anywhere. The abbot explains that "[t]he key is the key to all reality" (p. 341), and therefore Richard can go back to the reality he pursued all through the novel: London Above. The established pattern of retreat and return that is a key element of pastoral fiction seems to be fulfilled when Richard returns there, "changed and charged […] for more informed action in the present" (Gifford 1999, p. 80). Being back, he finds it exactly as it was before he left it, in some ways even better, as he gets a better job and a better flat and his ex-fiancée Jessica wants him back as well (Gaiman 1996, pp. 354-9). But with his newly gained knowledge that this world is not the whole truth but just one version of it, Richard feels too limited there. He cannot come to terms with the fact that in London Above, work, home, the pub, meeting girls and living in the city are all there is (p. 364), and, even though he is not sure that London Below

---

18   One could read the ordeal as another instance of the retreat and return motif, a retreat within the retreat so to speak, one from which Richard returns armed with insights that will be of great use to him.

is real either, he realizes that he would prefer to live in this uncertainty and discover more aspects of the simulacrum that is London. And luckily, he finds a way to return there (p. 370), presenting us with a return from the return. Following the rules of the pastoral design, Richard has returned "from that location [of retreat, i.e. London Below] to a context in which the results of the journey are to be understood [i.e. London Above]" (Gifford 1999, p. 81). Untypically, however, his understanding moves him to leave London Above once more, to return to his retreat. Thus, the narration exceeds a merely escapist function in which a return and reflection on the experiences made during the retreat never happens, and is lifted onto another level of complexity.

A third space?

Towards the end of this analysis, it becomes clearer than ever that the issue of the London Underground in Neil Gaiman's work is by far not exhausted yet. On the contrary, there are many more re-literalized Underground stations in *Neverwhere* than discussed here. Nonetheless, the three examples discussed sufficiently illustrate the central notion of Gaiman's world — that any representation of the city of London is a simulacrum. The City of London is a palimpsest consisting of uncountable layers and no representation can capture them all, therefore any attempt is bound to be untruthful. No matter what image any person living in London might have of the city, it is only one version of a place that does not exist as one entity at all. Richard has absorbed this philosophy step by step and the acceptance of London's hyperreality is essential for Richard's decision to return to London Below in the end. He appears to take pleasure in the endless possibilities this philosophy brings him. According to Andrés Romero Jódar, Neil Gaiman has provided *Neverwhere* "with a utopic feeling of belief in a better world, in a third space of integration, where the Imagination is the most important element in the construction of a reality that is seen as complex and many-sided" (2006, p. 193). Reading London as a simulacrum, however, means adding a fourth and a fifth and multitudinous other spaces to that, as many as ever could be imagined.

Works cited

Ackroyd, Peter. (2001) *London: The Biography*. London: Vintage.

---. (2011) *London Under: The Secret History Beneath the Streets*. New York: Doubleday.

Barnett, David. (2017) "Neil Gaiman announces *Neverwhere* sequel, *The Seven Sisters*", *The Guardian*, 17 February. Available at: www.theguardian.com/books/2017/feb/17/neil-gaiman-announces-neverwhere-sequel-the-seven-sisters. Accessed: 15 July 2021.

Baudrillard, Jean. (2004) "Simulacra and Simulations", in Rivkin, Julie and Ryan, Michael (eds.) *Literary Theory: An Anthology*. 2nd ed. Malden, Oxford, and Carlton: Blackwell Publishing, pp. 365-377.

Bealer, Tracy L. and Luria, Rachel. (2012) "Traveling with the Gods", in Bealer, Tracy L., Luria, Rachel, and Yuen, Wayne (eds.) *Neil Gaiman and Philosophy: Gods Gone Wild!* Chicago and LaSalle: Open Court, pp. vii-ix.

Beaudry, Jonas-Sébastien. (2012) "Apologizing to a Rat", in Bealer, Tracy L., Luria, Rachel, and Yuen, Wayne (eds.) *Neil Gaiman and Philosophy: Gods Gone Wild!* Chicago and LaSalle: Open Court, pp. 71-84.

Błaszkiewicz, Maria. (2014) "Allegorizing the Fantastic: A Spenserian Reading of Neil Gaiman's *Neverwhere*", in Wicher, Andrzej, Spyra, Piotr, and Matyaszczyk, Joanna (eds.) *Basic Categories of Fantastic Literature Revisited*. Newcastle upon Tyne: Cambridge Scholars Publishing, pp. 127-143.

Carey, Mike and Fabry, Glenn. (2007) *Neil Gaiman's Neverwhere*. New York: DC Comics.

Elber-Aviram, Hadas. (2013) "'The Past Is Below Us': Urban Fantasy, Urban Archaeology, and the Recovery of Suppressed History", *Papers from the Institute of Archaeology*, 23(1), pp. 1-10. Available at: dx.doi.org/10.5334/pia.426. Accessed: 23 January 2017.

Gaiman, Neil. (1996) *Neverwhere*. Reprint, New York: Harper, 2014.

Gifford, Terry. (1999) *Pastoral*. London and New York: Routledge.

Gomel, Elana. (2014) *Narrative Space and Time: Representing Impossible Topologies in Literature*. London and New York: Routledge.

Groes, Sebastian. (2011) *The Making of London: London in Contemporary Literature*. Basingstoke: Palgrave Macmillan.

Grossman, Lev. (2014) "How Magic Conquered Popular Culture", *TIME*, 19 August. Available at: time.com/lev-grossman-magicians-land-magic-pop-culture/. Accessed: 15 July 2021.

Hadlaw, Janin. (2003) "The London Underground Map: Imagining Modern Time and Space", *Design Issues*, 19(1), pp. 25-35. Available at: www.jstor.org/stable/1512052. Accessed: 15 July 2021.

Hilliam, David. (2016) *Why Do Shepherds Need a Bush? London's Underground History of Tube Station Names*. 2010. Stroud: The History Press.

Jódar, Andrés Romero. (2006) "Paradisiacal Hells: Subversions of the Mythical Canon in Neil Gaiman's Neverwhere", *Cuadernos de Investigación Filológica*, 31-32, pp. 163-195. Available at: dialnet.unirioja.es/servlet/articulo?codigo=3096523. Accessed: 15 July 2021.

Marx, Leo. (1964) *The Machine in the Garden: Technology and the Pastoral Ideal in America*. Reprint, Oxford: Oxford University Press, 2000.

McNamara, Kevin R. and Gray, Timothy. (2014) "Some Versions of Urban Pastoral", in McNamara, Kevin R. (ed.) *The Cambridge Companion to the City in Literature*. Cambridge: Cambridge University Press, pp. 245-260.

Mengham, Rod and Atkins, Marc. (2012) "End of the Line", in Kerr, Joe and Gibson, Andrew (eds.) *London: From Punk to Blair*. London: Reaktion Books, pp. 169-183.

Michaeli, Chen F. (2017) "'Back to the Real London'; or Mapping the City of the Past in Gaiman's *Neverwhere*", *Fafnir*, 4(1), pp. 20–30.

Neverwhere. (1996) Television series, Crucial Films Production and BBC. Created by Gaiman, Neil and Henry, Lenny.

Neverwhere. (2013) Full Cast Radio Dramatisation, BBC Worldwide Limited. Dramatised by Maggs, Dirk.

Phillips, Lawrence. (2010) "What Lies Beneath: The London Underground and Contemporary Gothic Film Horror", in Phillips, Lawrence and Witchard, Anne (eds.) *London Gothic: Place, Space and the Gothic Imagination*. London: Continuum, pp. 172-182.

Pike, David L. (2005) *Subterranean Cities: The World Beneath Paris and London, 1800-1945*. Ithaca: Cornell University Press.

Rață, Irina. (2017) "Trials and Tribulations in London Below", *Brumal: Revista de Investigación sobre lo Fantástico*, V (2), pp. 85-105.

Vanderbeke, Dirk. (2014) "The Sub-Creation of Sub-London: Neil Gaiman's and China Miéville's Urban Fantasy", in Honegger, Thomas and Vanderbeke, Dirk (eds.) *From Petersborough to Faëry: The Poetics and Mechanics of Secondary Worlds*. Zurich and Jena: Walking Tree Publishers, pp. 141-162.

Vertesi, Janet. (2008) "Mind the Gap: The London Underground Map and Users' Representations of Urban Space", *Social Studies of Science*, 38(1), pp. 7-33. Available at: www.jstor.org/stable/25474563. Accessed: 15 July 2021.

White, Claire E. (1999) "A Conversation with Neil Gaiman", *The Internet Writing Journal*, 3(3). Available at: www.writerswrite.com/journal/mar99/a-conversation-with-neil-gaiman-3991. Accessed: 15 July 2021.

Casteism and Countryside: A Literary Scrutiny

Media and popular culture have often portrayed a picturesque version of the countryside. It consistently presents the postcard image of a village, creating a myth of pastoral and bucolic life. This popular narrative associates the idea of pastoral with ideals of beauty and peace. However, beneath the layers of this simulated pastoral lies the harsh reality of antipastoralism. As explained, "If pastoral suggests that rural life offers freedom, antipastoral may declare it to be a prison-house, with the farmers as slaves" (Allison, 2003, 42). This chapter aims to modestly deconstruct the popular and grand narrative of pastoral, with a particular focus on casteism.

Background

Casteism is the antithesis of pastoral and peaceful countryside in India. It is a perennial social evil prevailing in India since time immemorial. Untouchability, caste-based violence, and the dehumanization of one community have been the repercussions of this caste system. However, with the advent of Western education, attitudinal modernity, and the intervention of democracy, there has been a considerable positive change. Eventually, the structural oppression in society was recognized, and 'Dalit studies' sprouted as an epistemological reform. "The word 'Dalit' means 'oppressed'" (Prakash, 2015, XX). Dalit writing has also played a vital role in transformative politics in India by rendering a voice of resistance, literary representation, and social awareness at large. There have been several leaders and writers from South India, particularly Tamil Nadu, who have voiced out the trials and tribulations of casteism and it's like.

To comprehend the antipastoral nature of caste-ridden villages and for the benefit of readers outside India who may be unfamiliar with casteism, it is important to explain that caste is a hierarchical classification of individuals based on their inherent vocation. This caste structure is ancient and has been practised for many centuries, dividing society into four castes that determine one's social, economic, and religious status. However, over time, these four divisions have further subdivided into several sub-castes. Caste is a contemporary problem, although its roots are deeply entrenched in history. As stated, "The Dalit perspective redefines caste as a contemporary form of social and cultural inequality and power relations that affects the whole of Indian society" (Satyanarayana et al., 2020, 3). This caste hierarchy establishes social hierarchy and distributes power. In the preface to his book, *Dalits: Past, Present and Future*, Teltumbde explains:" This book may serve as an introduction to a mass of people in India who until a century before lived at a subhuman level as untouchables, unapproachable and even unseeable. They were victims of the caste system, which has the veritable distinction of being the longest-surviving man-made system in the world. Although one finds remnants of caste-like stratifications in some parts of the world, they are not quite the same. The very fact that they died leaving just some reminders of their existence, pales before the caste system in India, which not only survives but also threatens the present. Indeed, it remains unique to India." (Teltumbde, 2017, XII)

Research Questions

The effect of casteism or caste discrimination is more intense in rural areas than in urbanized places, deconstructing the popular pastoral narrative. The village is a space characterized by all-pervading casteism and caste-based bigotry. This chapter addresses the intersection between the countryside and the degree of casteism through literary case studies, focusing on Bama's *Karukku* and Imayam's *Beasts of Burden*. The chapter aims to explore questions such as: How is casteism deeply rooted in the countryside compared to urban spaces? How do factors such as unemployment, power relations, poverty, and illiteracy contribute to casteism in rural areas? And how does the prevalence of caste oppression in rural areas dismantle the deeply ingrained notion of a rustic utopia?

Bama's *Karukku*

In her autobiographical novel *Karukku*, Bama justifies the title and its significance in her own life, stating, "There are many congruities between the saw-edged palmyra karukku and my own life" (Bama, 2000, 12). The setting of the book also reflects this dual nature, encompassing both the countryside and extreme casteism. The narrative takes place in a small village in the Western Ghats, representing numerous other villages that serve as hotspots of casteism. Bama initiates the story by describing the village, stating, "Our village is very beautiful. Even though you don't see much progress or anything like that here, I love this place for its beauty. Although it's only a small village, many different communities live here. But before I delve into the topic of castes and communities, I have much to say about the village itself" (Bama, 2000, 12). Bama's village is characterized by the presence of various castes and communities, with clear demarcations of caste boundaries.

The means of livelihood play a crucial role in the Indian caste system, determining the division of individuals into castes based on their adopted professions since time immemorial. Bama introduces readers to her community, stating, "Most of our people are agricultural labourers. When there is no work in the fields, they venture into the mountains to gather firewood and sell it. However, those belonging to the more privileged castes never face such difficulties. They own fields with clear boundaries, have dug wells and established pump-sets, can work their land all year round, and enjoy a comfortable lifestyle in their homes" (Bama, 2000, 13). As Bama catalogues the various communities and castes in her village, she makes sure to mention their vocations as well. The caste labels align with the occupations of the people, showcasing the intricate interplay between profession, social position, and geographic location. Bama presents an example, stating, "To the left, there is a small settlement of about twenty houses known as Odapatti. It is predominantly inhabited by Nadars who make a living by climbing Palmyra palms. To the right, there are the Koravar who work as street sweepers, followed by the leather-working Chakkiliyar. Some distance away, there are the Kusavar who specialize in making earthenware pots. Next to them is the Palla settlement." This division based on caste and hierarchical structure related to professions reflects bigotry. Furthermore, Bama describes her neighbourhood, saying, "Immediately adjacent to that is where we live, the Paraya settlement. To the east of the village lies the cemetery, and our settlement is located right next to it" (Bama, 2000, 15).

Accordingly, Bama presents an antipastoral map of her village, meticulously describing its topography, which is both caste-based and geographically defined. She explains the presence of visible and invisible walls and boundaries between different caste communities, with each community residing in its exclusive colony or ghetto. This vividly portrays the profound social segregation prevailing in Bama's village. She proceeds to map out the entire village, stating, "Apart from us, one after the other, there were houses of the Thevar, Chettiyaar, Aasaari, and Nadar. Beyond them were the Naicker streets. The Udaiyaar community also had a small settlement of their own... However, they kept to their part of the village, and we stayed in ours" (Bama, 2000, 16). In addition to this stark segregation, the upper-class inhabitants enjoy all the civic amenities. As Bama observes, "We only went to their side if we had work to do there. But they never came to our area. The post office, the panchayat board, the milk depot, the big shops, the church, the schools—all of these were located in their streets. So why would they need to come to our area? Besides, there was a large school in the Naicker Street exclusively meant for upper-caste children" (Bama, 2000, 16). This confirms the social inaccessibility and denial experienced by the marginalized castes.

The social alienation and inaccessibility become even more pronounced in the unequal distribution of natural resources. Even natural water bodies like ponds are caste-specific, such as the "aiyar kulam" (pond of the Aiyars). The availability of natural food sources like fish, which is abundant, becomes scarce and inaccessible for the lower caste. Bama explains, "We mostly bought and cooked curries with silebi kendai and paambu kendai because that was the cheapest option available to us. The upper castes bought and ate ayirai, keluti, and viraal. But we couldn't afford to pay that much for the food we consumed" (Bama, 2000, 13).

Caste discrimination deeply permeates village society, influencing aspects such as class, power, dignity, wealth, life, and health. The upper caste individuals always demand respect and deference from those belonging to lower castes, regardless of their age. Dignity is seen as an inherent property of the upper caste community. The author recalls, "Both my grandmothers worked as servants for Naicker families. In one instance, even tiny children, just born the other day, would call my grandmother by her name and order her around simply because they belonged to the Naicker caste. And my grandmother, like all the other labourers, would address the little boy as Ayya, Master, and rush to fulfil his requests" (Bama, 2000, 22). The master-slave relationship becomes even more entrenched due to the caste dimension. Another degrading custom of the upper caste masters towards their lower caste servants is described as follows: "Even the way they were given drinking water was distressing to witness. The Naicker women would pour the water from a height of four feet, while my grandmother and others had to receive and drink it with cupped hands held to their mouths" (Bama, 2000, 22). This image of humiliation and servitude casts a shadow over the lives of those belonging to lower castes.

The culture of untouchability is integral to understanding the dark nature of village life. Untouchability is practised both in private and public spaces. Bama provides numerous examples in the text where her elder brother experiences discrimination even at the village library. She recounts, "Apparently, it was the same at the library. The Paraya lads from the Cheri Street would be looked at in a certain way, with a certain contempt. Once, when Annan was checking out his books, he impulsively added his title, MA. Immediately, the attendant brought him a stool to sit on and started addressing him as 'Sir'" (Bama, 2000, 23). This sentence, although amusing, demonstrates that education makes a subtle difference in the treatment of lower caste individuals. Bama further explains in her brother's words, "'Because we are born into the Paraya jati, we are never given any honour or dignity or respect. We are stripped of all that. But if we study and progress, we can shed these indignities. So, study diligently, and learn all you can. If you are always ahead in your studies, people will come to you on their own and attach themselves to you. Work hard and learn'" (Bama, 2000, 23). This dialogue highlights the collective and individual efforts of Dalits to rise above their circumstances and attain self-worth.

The author recalls another instance of untouchability, where she witnesses a person of lower caste carrying a food package for an upper caste individual using a string, avoiding direct contact with the package out of fear of scorn and resentment. Bama recollects, "The elder went straight up to the Naicker, bowed low, and extended the packet towards him, cupping the hand that held the string with his other hand. The Naicker opened the parcel and began to eat the vadais" (Bama, 2000, 21). Upon realizing the reality of this scene, Bama becomes angry and reflects, "Why do we have to fetch and carry for these people, I wondered. Our respected elder goes meekly to the shops to fetch snacks and hands them over reverently, bowing and shrinking, to this person who just sits there and stuffs them into his mouth. The thought of it infuriated me" (Bama, 2000, 22). Bama also recalls the caste discrimination she experienced on public transport in her village, saying, "When I went home for holidays if a Naicker woman was sitting next to me on the bus, she would immediately ask me which place I was going to, what street. As soon as I mentioned 'Cheri,' she would get up and move to another seat. Or she would tell me to move elsewhere" (Bama, 2000, 25).

Casteism infiltrates even schools, where education and progressive thinking should prevail. However, deep-seated caste prejudice overrides any progressive outlook in the village. Bama notes, "But it was the same story at school. They always spoke ill of people from our caste. If anything, bad happened, they would immediately and without hesitation say, 'It must be one of the Cheri-children who did it'" (Bama, 2000, 23). This demonstrates that casteism exists at institutional levels as well. Untouchability is also observed in the village convent, where people visit to see Mother Superior. Bama recalls Mother Superior's words, "Very well, now you may all go home quickly without leaning on the walls or touching anything" (Bama, 2000, 57).

The text effectively highlights the institutional casteism in Bama's village, which starkly contrasts with the treatment and approach towards the caste system in urban areas. In the village, teachers exploit students from lower castes for their gain. These students are both scorned and used simultaneously. Bama observes, "Everyone seemed to think Harijan children were contemptible. But they didn't hesitate to use us for cheap labour. So, we carried water to the teacher's house; we watered the plants" (Bama, 2000, 24). This sheer exploitation and oppression weigh heavily on the lives of lower caste individuals in the village community.

The politics of blame, crime, and punishment also operate along caste lines in the village. The author recalls a painful school memory when she was falsely accused of stealing a coconut solely because of her caste. Although other children who were playing with her witnessed the coconut falling naturally, they were not even questioned. Ironically, even God's house and the clergy practice casteism. When she goes to the priest to seek absolution to return to school, he humiliates her based on her caste, saying, "After all, you are from the Cheri. You might have done it. You must have done it" (Bama, 2000, 24). This experience disillusioned Bama with God and the church. However, she encounters similar situations later in her life. It is worth noting that "religious celebrations in India are not completely separate from the domain of politics, especially in rural areas. Therefore, the actual impact of such religious celebrations on various social groups is undoubtedly more diverse in terms of nature and scale of effect at any given point in time" (Mocherla, 2021, 81).

Caste-based violence shatters the notion of a village as a space of simplicity and peaceful coexistence. Bama also recalls the prevalence of community violence in the village. The village, divided along caste community lines, witnesses the transformation of caste politics into a politics of violence that even involves the institution of law. Bama states, "It seems that the Chaaliyar folk invited some people known as the 'Reserve Police' all the way from Sivakasi, butchered a sheep for them, and arranged a feast. They've taken an oath to destroy our boys, they say, so without counting the cost they are slaughtering sheep at the rate of two a day and feasting with the police. Do we have such means?" (Bama, 2000, 36). As wealth translates into power, Bama's community is left painfully powerless due to their extreme poverty.

Karukku also depicts the politics of caste at the institutional level and the consequences of custodial violence. The Dalits are not only powerless due to their untouchable caste status, but their economic deprivation and lack of social influence further exacerbate their situation. Bama states, "What food? Nonsense. They'll give them a tiny bit of ragi or cholam gruel in the name of food, they say. Now if they were rich or upper caste, or if the police were indebted to them in some way, they would have just given them a couple of light taps. They would have taken good care of them" (Bama, 2000, 36). This illustrates the grim reality of discriminatory treatment in custodial settings based on caste.

Hard labour and poverty define the lives of Dalits in the countryside. The author shares her experience of every family member toiling to survive and make ends meet. She says, "On one occasion, she brought home a bundle of firewood, leaned it against the wall, and then began vomiting vast gobs of blood. But it was only through such relentless toil, without regard for their bodies as human flesh and blood, that people of my community could survive" (Bama, 2000, 46). In the villages, Dalits live an enslaved life, where they are bound to work for one wealthy upper-caste family. Bama explains, "People from our community work for them, with each Paraya family being attached to a Naicker family as pannaiyaal, bonded labourers. As far as I have observed, it is only the Palla and Paraya communities who have to work so hard, while other communities don't face the same level of hardship" (Bama, 2000, 44).

The Dalits endure various forms of exploitation—physical, economic, and emotional. They are paid less, and even in trading, they are given less value in exchange. Bama reveals, "And at that time, we never realized how badly we were cheated during these bartering sessions" (Bama, 2000, 47). Poverty exacerbates the suffering and hardships of Dalits in the countryside. Bama takes readers through her economic struggles and how they deepen the divide. She observes, "But our people, no matter how hard they toil, never seem to have that cash in hand. They work so tirelessly that they wear themselves out like fragments of pottery. They survive on meagre gruel every day, wearing nothing more than a couple of rags. They don't own any property, land, or even a decent house to live in. In such conditions, they work, solely for the benefit of the wealthy" (Bama, 2000, 63). This stark reality not only reveals the layers of injustice and inequality but also reinforces the anti-pastoral nature of village life.

Bama's metaphor of 'beast,' used to imply the inhumane treatment of the lower caste and Dalits, is also reflected in the writings of other Dalit writers. She observes, "They seem to conspire to keep us in our place: to think that we have worked throughout history like beasts, should live and die like that; we should never move on or forward" (Bama, 2000, 30). Bama succinctly captures the harsh reality of casteism and poverty that prevails not only in her village but also in rural India as a whole. She affirms, "Those who labour are the poorest of the poor Dalits. But those who reap the rewards are the wealthy, the upper castes. This continues to happen in my village, to this day" (Bama, 2000, 65). This underscores the plight of lower caste individuals in most villages in India.

Imayam's Beasts of Burden

Imayam is another Dalit writer who originally wrote in the Tamil language, giving voice to the oppressed Dalits from the Tamil countryside. *Beasts of Burden* is a widely read and highly acclaimed novel by Imayam, which depicts the everyday struggles of the lower caste washer community against a rich cultural backdrop. In this novel, the lower caste community portrayed are washer people, known as 'vannan', who wash the clothes of other lower caste individuals. This implies that there is a power hierarchy even within the lower caste community itself, and Imayam aims to provide an honest portrayal of this social stratum.

The novel also highlights the migration of oppressed community members to small towns and cities, where the level of subjugation and discrimination is relatively lower. However, rural spaces continue to be dominated by caste hegemony. The characters in the novel convey a sense of despair, encapsulating the situation with the following words, "'But wherever we go, we'll still be beneath someone else. They'll always treat us like that because we do the lowest duties to the lowest communities'" (Imayam, 2001, 6).

Savuri and Arokkyam, along with their family, belong to the vannan community, which is part of the lower caste society. The intersection of poverty and the lower caste community becomes apparent in the struggles faced by Savuri's family, including their hunger and labour. When Savuri's family expresses their desire to undertake a short pilgrimage to the church, Savuri, filled with bitterness, exclaims, "'There's a church and a God only for those who have rice to eat and a place to rest. Or even kith and kin. Where's all that for those of us who can't even cover their crotch?'" (Imayam, 2001, 2). This resentful tone reflects the sentiment of the deeply oppressed segment of humanity.

Further, Arokkyam and Savuri are bound to serve the upper members of their community and village, which obligates them to seek permission for their actions. They are anxious about displeasing their masters by taking a day off from work to go to church. Arokkyam, in particular, is filled with distress, as seen when she seeks permission from the elders: "Throughout the next week, Arokkyam flew about in distress. She went and asked the elders to give her permission to go" (Imayam, 2001, 2). They don't even have the freedom to lead their lives according to their own will and needs.

As Arokkyam and Savuri fear, they face verbal assaults from their masters who resent their decision to go to church for a day. The community members reprimand them, saying, "'What need is there for you to go to the church at an ordinary time like this?' 'And who's to wash our clothes meanwhile?'" (Imayam, 2001, 3). The entire village assumes authority in regulating and manipulating the lives of this poor family.

Charity and humility have become integral parts of the lives of the vannan community. Despite being physically strong and skilled, they are deprived of regular wages and instead receive leftover food as alms. However, this is not the case in city life, as Joseph and his family can conduct their trade and lead a dignified life.

Every evening, the vannan family visits the households they serve, asking for unwanted and leftover food. The young boy,

Peter, feels sorry for his family's situation when he is taunted by other street urchins. He expresses his regret, saying, "'Amma, why do we have to call at houses for our evening meal? Why can't we cook at home every day?'" (Imayam, 2001, 10). The act of relying on "leftovers from others" symbolizes the marginalized position of the vannan family. Arokkyam, in her desperation, pleads for a little charity for her daughter's marriage from those who own her. She supplicates, "'Think of this child as your sister and be generous, saami,' 'Where will she go when she leaves you?' 'It is at your feet that she must spend her lifetime'" (Imayam, 2001, 155).

Self-effacement and amnesia become survival mechanisms for the vannar community. In the face of the caste hierarchy system and abject poverty, Arokkyam's family chooses to endure the abuses thrown at them. Arokkyam reflects, "We are a humble community. What's the use of getting angry? She would forget about the incident immediately. It was important for her to put it right out of her mind. Otherwise, she would have gone mad. It was only by forgetting that she survived" (Imayam, 2001, 11). Arokkyam, at least, musters the courage to ask for something a second time, but Savuri remains voiceless in the presence of his masters and community members. The vannan community is not only economically subjugated but also emotionally oppressed. They endure inhumane treatment from others in the village, regardless of their age. Arokkyam sighs, "'The people here don't even call me by name. It's always 'vannaati woman, vannaati woman'" (Imayam, 2001, 11).

Hard labour becomes the sole means of survival for the vannan family in the village. Imayam informs the readers, "There were not less than two hundred families living in the colony. And there were only Savuri and Arokkyam to serve all of them" (Imayam, 2001, 53). The rest of the community manipulates and asserts authority over the vannan family. When Ramasaami requires Savuri's assistance at a funeral, he expects Savuri to abandon all his other duties. He barks his orders, "' If the washing is left for this one day, nobody is going to be ruined forever. Drag him along with you and run! You must be back before I draw a single breath" (Imayam, 2001, 27). Ramasaami and others like him exploit Savuri's family for their self-interest and treat them as mere puppets to be controlled.

The vannan community individuals are also treated as beasts of burden. They are forced to carry the loads of others, whether it be their laundry or acting as a funeral hearse. Arokkyam struggles as she carries several pots filled with grains stacked on top of each other. Imayam describes, "As for her, her neck was cutting deep into her shoulders. The top of her head had lost all sensation. Her feet could barely tread on the earth. They felt as if they were touching fire" (Imayam, 2001, 33). The vannan community is required to assist in various tasks such as childbirth, funerals, and other miscellaneous chores. The level of poverty and despair is evident in the custom of gathering rice grains that are sprinkled on a corpse. Savuri and Arokkyam eagerly pick and gather the grains from the corpse to cook a meal. Imayam writes, "He took off his waist cloth and spread it over the corpse to receive the vaaykkarisi... Tying together the rice that had fallen on his vetti into a single hasty knot, without even binding it properly, Savuri hoisted the bundle onto his head; at the same time, he covered the corpse and tied it onto the bier" (Imayam, 2001, 41-42). This spectacle of Savuri excitedly collecting funeral rice grains from the top of the corpse highlights the socio-economic condition of the vannan individuals.

The individuals from the upper strata of the community detest the vannans, calling them names and even referring to them as donkeys. When Arokkyam requests her fair share of what is due to her, Mottayyan admonishes her, saying, "'Have you gone that far? Shut your trap, you donkey'" (Imayam, 2001, 47). Arokkyam, as a vannan woman, has to work hard and for long hours to bring food to her family. Her list of duties at a particular time, when she also has her daughter to marry off, is extensive. Imayam writes, "Arokkyam was in a grand confusion about the jobs that needed to be done... There were the Pongal chores; more clothes to be washed than usual; and weddings as well. By chance, it happened that this was the time when there also were an unusual number of births. Next, there was the local festival" (Imayam, 2001, 152). The vannan family complies and endures everything without receiving the due reward or respect they deserve:

The women from the lowest caste suffer sexual exploitation and mistreatment as well, and this is the most heinous antipastoral characteristic. The vannan's daughter Mary is sexually attacked by a man who ranks higher than her family, and she is unable even to resist. She is aware of the threat which all men hold against her but she is at their mercy. One of her work rounds when she goes to collect the dirty clothes, she is trapped. She is unable to raise the alarm for help because she knows she is insignificant and because of her social position she will not be heard, "Chadayan could do whatever he wished. He could put it about that this vannaan was no good. He could say they needed a different vannaan in this town, and drive them away. He could install a new vannaan in their place. He could do anything. And he would. Savuri's family was a very lowly one" (Imayam, 2001, 100). She manages to return home hiding what happened to her. However, she is unable to contain it any further. She is in a state where she cannot express her sorrow or share her suffering. Mary is traumatised, but powerless. "Still no reply. Ceaseless weeping. A terrible weeping which grew out of helplessness, humiliation and extreme loss shook the hut" (Imayam, 2001, 102).

Historically, one of how upper-caste domination has been expressed, maintained and perpetuated is through the sexual exploitation of Dalit women. (Still, 2017, 14).

The raped Mary is racked with grief and shame. Mary and Mary's mother are unable even to share their grief with anyone, "Nobody should know what had happened; they must not even tell Savuri" (Imayam, 2001, 103). The two women suffer in silence and endure the torment in secret.

The vannans also segregate themselves based on the caste they belong to, "The upper-caste vannaan and vannaati departed to their washing place, having said their goodbyes. Arokkyam went to her thorapaadu" (Imayam, 2001, 161). Ironically, though they are both vannans, and washer folks, they do not mingle because they belong to different castes. Mary and Rani are friends, but due to their caste and class differences, where Mary belongs to the lowest caste, she is afraid to be seen visiting Rani at her home, "Although Rani's mother was a good sort, she would never allow Mary inside. She was fearful of the townsfolk. If anybody were to see Mary going in, a big fight might follow. Mary's family could be in grave danger"

(Imayam, 2001, 162). This absurd casteism is also a distinct trait of the countryside.

Caste violence is experienced by the lowest caste in various aspects of their lives, from work to festive gatherings. The villagers, in addition to being cruel to the vannans, also incite others to engage in mob violence. "Flog her! Scavenging bitch, I'll pull your teeth out! Several others in the crowd began to shout along with Ramasaami. They leapt about. Mottayyan shouted continually, without even seeming to draw breath" (Imayam, 2001, 181).

Arokkyam, when attending home births, patiently endures physical abuse and becomes a punching bag for the delivering women who kick and slap her in pain. However, she remains calm and continues to help them. "As soon as she regained consciousness, Chitra clamoured for water. Arokkyam gave her pungent rasam to drink. Chitra flung the hot rasam at Arokkyam's face, then bent down and wept. Arokkyam was stunned for a moment but recovered herself, laughed and comforted Chitra, 'A woman who has just given birth should never cry.' She poured out a couple of glasses of rasam" (Imayam, 2001, 262).

Imayam's craftsmanship is evident in his depiction of the places, people, and ethos. In the village, spaces of amusement include community cinemas and village festivals. Spaces of labour are fields owned by the upper and richer community members, thorappadu, and so on. The vannans live on the outskirts of the village, and even their geographical location is marginalized, to the extent that it is overlooked by the census counting party. "Later, Sahayam said they should make sure their names were on the electoral lists' hereafter. The people who made up the census lists had so far left out the household of the chakkili community leader, Periyaan, and Arokkyam's household. Nobody had told them about these two houses, at a distance from the main and colony streets. The enumerators had come to the very edge of the colony, and then gone away" (Imayam, 2001, 269).

> Dalit settlements are not only apart from the upper-caste Hindu settlements; they are actually outside the boundary of the village (Limbale, 2004, 9).

Even the ground level is determined by the caste hierarchy, with the upper caste individuals living on higher ground and the lower caste individuals living on lower-level ground. "Arokkyam's house was at an even lower level... The upper caste street was not on high ground as such, but certainly, it was higher than the rest of the town. The water flowed down from the upper caste street to a distance of three or four furlongs before it reached the colony." The dirty and filthy water reaches the Vannan settlement, symbolizing their forced state of inferiority and impurity. This murky water also represents the attitudes prevalent in the countryside. "The mingled water flowed past Arokkyam's house, coloured yellow and green, and finally reached the stream" (Imayam, 2001, 287).

Even politicians exploit hunger to gain votes, "'I only belong to the stomach-party,' Arokkyam would say ... Each person has their party, but each person has their stomach too; don't forget that, da, Joseppu,' Arokkyam would say" (Imayam, 2001, 267). Arokkyam laments her existence in heart-wrenching words, "What if the vannaan disappears in the shit pond? Who cares if he is washed away by the river? ... Why did you create me as the downtrodden of the Downtrodden, Saint Anthony?" (Imayam, 2001, 283).

The vannan family represented in the novel also suffers from the changing times. They are so enslaved that they are unable to accept change and find independence. Arokkyam observes, "How could they have the heart to betray the low-caste vannaan who lived by trusting them, who served them to the very end? Truly, people had changed. Not just Arokkyam, but those whom she knew, and her forefathers and mothers, had all worked here and served these people in an unbroken tradition" (Imayam, 2001, 133). The novel also narrates the experiences of characters like Sahayam and Joseph, who have moved on, both geographically and metaphorically. They have relocated to developed cities where they have better economic opportunities and encounter less casteism. Savuri's visit to his son's home in the city is highly symbolic of the much-needed transition and transformation.

Conclusion

Both Bama and Imayam, as Dalit writers, have presented a realistic and experiential account of casteism existing in the countryside, debunking the popular myth of pastoralism. Casteism is deeply entrenched in rural areas due to factors such as poverty, illiteracy, regressive attitudes, and various other subtle reasons. Consequently, villages become hostile spaces that foster caste segregation and oppression. This pervasive casteism renders the countryside antipastoral. However, cities exhibit comparatively less casteism and strive for inclusivity. According to the article "The Word and the World: Dalit Aesthetics as a critique of everyday life," which cites a newspaper to support this notion:

In 1907, the newspaper *Dinbandhu* (Friend of the Impoverished), an organ of the working-class and lower-caste movement in western India, carried an important essay on the city as a space of transformed (caste) sociality.4 The essay's anonymous author noted: "[In Bombay] we all drink water from the same tap, in hotels and Irani stores we sit at the same table and drink tea and eat bread and biscuits. On trains and steamboats, we sit with our thighs and shoulders touching". Urban migration and urban infrastructure—especially everyday technologies of travel and communication that appeared to shrink, even obviate, social distance—provoked key transformations of lower caste and Dalit selfhood. (Rao, 2017, 152)

In summary, the examination of casteism in rural and urban settings, as depicted in Bama's *Karukku* and Imayam's *Beasts of Burden*, reveals a stark contrast in the intensity and manifestation of caste-based discrimination. Rural areas serve as breeding grounds for casteism, where its effects are deeply ingrained and pervasive, debunking the romanticized notion of a pastoral idyll. This chapter has delved into the intricate relationship between the countryside and the degree of casteism, highlighting the pressing research questions that arise. By investigating the roots of casteism in rural areas compared to urban spaces and analyzing the contributing factors such as unemployment, power dynamics, poverty, and illiteracy, this study aims to dismantle the illusion of a rustic utopia and shed light on the urgent need for social change and inclusivity.

Works Cited

Allison, J. (2003) 'Patrick Kavanagh and antipastoral,' *In The Cambridge Companion to Contemporary Irish Poetry*, Vol. 10.

Bama. (2000) *Karukku*, (L. Holmstrom, Trans. & M. Krishnan, Ed.) MacMillan, New Delhi.

Imayam. (2001) *Beast of Burden*, (L. Holmstrom, Trans.), Manas, New Delhi.

Limbale, S. (2004) *Towards an Aesthetic of Dalit Literature: History Controversies Considerations*, (A. K. Mukherjee, Trans.), Orient Black Swan, New Delhi.

Mocherla, A. K. (2021) 'Dalit Christians: rituals, religious celebrations, and community politics,' *In Dalit Christians in South India*, (pp. 64-90). Routledge, New Delhi.

Prakash, A. (2015) 'Foreword,' *In Dalit Capital: State, Markets and Civil Society in Urban India*, Routledge, New Delhi.

Rao, A. (2017) 'The word and the world: Dalit aesthetics as a critique of everyday life,' *Journal of Postcolonial Writing*, Vol. 53No. 1-2, 147-161. DOI: ttps://doLorg/10.1080/17449855.2017.1288314

Satyanarayana, K., et al. (2020) *Dalit Text: Aesthetics and Politics Re-Imagined*, Routledge, New Delhi.

Still, C. (2017) *Dalit Women: Honour and Patriarchy in South India*, Routledge, New Delhi.

Teltumbde, A. (2020) *Dalits: Past, Present and Future* (2nd ed.), Routledge, New Delhi.

'Romantic Ireland's 'Dead and Gone': Reading the Anti-pastoral in Donal Ryan's *The Spinning Heart*

Ireland has long been associated with the pastoral and Irish literature has consistently engaged with nature, place, and landscape. The Irish pastoral genre historically displays a heightened sense of nostalgia and contemporary Irish versions of the pastoral engage in a dialogue with this tradition, often accompanied by melancholic tension and trauma. Donal Ryan's polyphonic novel *The Spinning Heart* offers an anti-pastoral portrait of rural Ireland in a panoply of voices that inhabit the vocabulary of conflict and violence, and a landscape where domestic life is represented as sacrifice rather than bliss. In Ryan's novel, the myth of an unspoiled rural land has crumbled, thereby challenging the Irish ethnoscape and questioning the relevance of Irishness. As Gifford (1999) observes, the critical observation and stark realism of the anti-pastoral replaces the idealisation of the pastoral as the schism between an idyllic pastoral existence and a recession-struck rural landscape reveals itself in a fractured portrait of modern rural Ireland. Alpers (1976) argues that pastoral is based upon a fundamental fiction and this chapter seeks to explore Ryan's fictional engagement with contemporary Ireland through the complex relationship between collective memory and places, between nostalgia and reality, and the unfolding of anti-pastoral literature as a response to embedded pastoral ideals in Irish literature.

A key feature of Irish pastoral writing is the celebration of rural life in the form of an idyll and Jordan (2013, p.13) remarks upon the way in *The Spinning Heart* 'Ryan reaches back to the archetypes of Irish literature—the terrible father, the wanton country girl; the peat-black comedy of Flann O'Brien and dramatic rhythms of Yeats and Synge'. Ryan excels in writing the Irish rural man, however, the abstraction of pastoral appropriations of Irish rural life based on sentiment and nostalgia are tempered in the novel by a broader context of ecological and socio-economic change. The novel is an amalgamation of twenty-one monologues delivered by the inhabitants of an unnamed small town in Ireland who are some of the many victims of the country's financial collapse. In Ryan's novel, each perspective bears a certain amount of weight and validity echoing Bakhtin's assertion that each person's experience is 'unique and irreplaceable'. Bakhtin (1982) defines polyphony as 'the plurality of independent and unmerged voices' and the portrayal of an 'objective world' in which characters share 'equal consciousness' (p.12). A key element of the polyphonic novel is enabling characters and types to develop into personalities by granting them freedom from others' perspectives and their environment. Ryan creates such a world in *The Spinning Heart* while gathering those independent and unmerged voices and subjective perspectives under the umbrella of the collective trauma of a recession. Different perspectives are not 'partial, complementary truth, rather the dynamic interplay and interruption of perspectives is taken to produce new realities and new ways of seeing' (Robinson 2011, p.11) that counter the foundational myth of Motherland. The narratives are melancholic and anti-pastoral in mode and thus disrupt prevailing pastoral conventions and idealized portrayals of rural life.

The interaction of Irish literature with place, nature and landscape extends back as far as the seventh century (Murphy 1932). Deep within the core of the Irish psyche lies an archaic memory of an idyllic land, presenting a symbiosis of nature and nation that reflects what Synge called the psychic memory that haunts Ireland's landscape, and creates a culture that relies on the natural world for continuity. The disruption of this natural world by rapid economic growth and structural transformation thus marks a break not only with the Theocritean pastoral that helped establish the defining elements of the mode but also a psychic break evident in the ruined relationships, shattered dreams and disembodied characters that haunt *The Spinning Heart*. Landscape is the work of the mind observes Schama (1996) and its scenery is 'built up as much from strata of memory as from layers of rock' (p.7). Landscape, therefore, is as much a human construct as our tools and the material things they produce. He further argues that:

> Landscapes are culture before they are nature; constructs of the imagination projected onto wood and water and rock...once a certain idea of landscape, a myth, a vision, establishes itself in an actual place, it has a peculiar way of muddling categories, of making metaphors more real than their referents; of becoming, in fact, part of the scenery.
> (Schama 1996, p.61)

Poetic representations of the Irish landscape since medieval times have emphasized people's sense of belonging and contributed to the elaboration of an ethnoscape etched in collective memory. The land is shaped by a long and complex history of interrelationships that are present in its contemporary composition and this sense of rootedness, of linking a people to the soil, is integral to national identity, as Lloyd (2003) observes; 'the concept of the Irish race is thus to be grafted to its roots in sensuous contact with the land, through which it imbibes the particular taste of its spirit' (p.65). This relationship with the homeland and the landscape was displaced by the economic crash and Ryan's novel accurately captures the loss of identity and grief experienced by the uprooted population of a small town in rural Ireland with an expansive array of topographies, interiors, and sharp human portraits. Emigration and exile form a part of every Irish family's history, a trauma formed by economic wounds inflicted decades ago that still run deep in the collective memory and were reopened in the aftermath of the Celtic Tiger. Indeed, Lentin (2001) underscores the traumatic experience of famine emigration and argues that 'when interrogating the Irish, we cannot evade interrogating the painful past of emigration, a wound still festering because it was never tended' (p.4). For this reason, migration may not be a new phenomenon. the experience of it is very much grounded in terms of specific landscapes, narratives, and myths.

The 'Celtic Tiger' refers to a period of time in Irish society from the mid-1990s until early 2008, when Ireland's economy boomed due to foreign investment and other neoliberal economic measures. The Celtic Tiger singularly transformed the Irish landscape with rapid property-led development followed by an economic meltdown that crippled the construction industry and left lasting scars on the Irish landscape. By focusing on rampant urbanization, forced emigration and ghost estates, writers like Donal Ryan deconstruct the deep-rooted connection between national identity and the land (Appadurai 1996, p. 9). The focal character of Bobby Mahon, the first character to speak in the novel, traces the collapse back to the shooting dead of the young Cunliffe boy by the armed response unit who 'never threw a shape nor said a cross word' (Ryan 2012, p.13). His aunt subsequently sold the land, a decision that led to ruin and decay as Pokey Burke's father, Josie, admits in hindsight:

> We should have known it would all end in tears. Around here, it all started with tears: that boy of the Cunliffes getting shot in his yard by the guards, and his land going to his auntie, who shared it out among us like the Roman soldiers with Our Lord's purple robe. That was no way for good times to start.
> (Ryan 2012, p. 26)

The division of the land and the removal of the Cunliffe 'family name,' serve as a curse on the village, sending many people's hearts 'spinning' as their worlds collapse. The disruption of the natural order represents a tear in the social fabric as the sacred relationship between people and the land is sacrificed for corporate gain, generating 'collective histories of displacement and violent loss' (Clifford 1994, p.8) and precipitating a new world order that cannot be accommodated in the realm of the pastoral 'and all that environmental shite that everyone says is going to be the saving of us all' (Ryan 2012, p.108). For instance, the idealized depiction of Irish country life offered by Goldsmith's 'The Deserted Village' blends recollections of the Irish village of his boyhood with the human desolation of the present, after land clearance and depopulation. Ryan's rural Ireland offers no such ideal or comfortable return to an untroubled past, presenting instead a place where 'it all started with tears', a world where nostalgia has been violently replaced by a social and material reality aligned with the emergence of anti-pastoral literature.

The features of anti-pastoral literature challenge the distortions of idealised literary genres and represent the harsh realism of contemporary rural life (Gifford 1999). In relation to the pastoral 'there are some things of an established nature in pastoral, which are essential to it, such as a country scene, innocence, simplicity' (Loughrey 1984, p.54), however, the acknowledgement of the limitations of the genre has paved the way for the development of the anti-pastoral which displaces this simple idealisation of pastoral life. In anti-pastoral literature, a conscious attempt is made to present rural life as irreconcilable with the simple and serene existence proposed by the pastoral genre. In *The Spinning Heart*, the very first page of the novel establishes the absence of the sympathetic or reassuring natural elements of pastoral conventions with a scene of decay and disillusionment:

> There's a red metal heart in the centre of the low front gate, skewered on a rotating hinge. It's flaking now, the red is nearly gone. It needs to be scraped and sanded and painted and oiled. It still spins in the wind though. I can hear it creak, creak, creak as I walk away. A flaking, creaking, spinning heart. (Ryan 2012, p.9)

Gifford refers to the ebbs and flows of growth and decay in anti-pastoral literature and Ryan's novel employs anti-pastoral imagery of rural poverty and decline to highlight the dialectical tension between the pastoral ideal and anti-pastoral reality engendered by the rapid transformation of contemporary rural Ireland 'a rustic and in large part wild landscape…transformed' beyond recognition (Marx 1969, p. 343). Innocence is also a feature of pastoral literature and the prelapsarian innocence of the central character, Bobby Mahon, is poignantly conveyed in his monologue: 'What reason would I have ever had not to trust Pokey Burke?' accompanied by a brutal loss of innocence following the uncovering of Pokey's moral corruption and avarice, and the realisation of impending unemployment; 'imagine being so suddenly useless' (Ryan 2012, p.15).

The pastoral image of rural Ireland singularly collapsed in September 2008 when the Irish government officially acknowledged the country's descent into recession, and the symbiotic coexistence of village life and rapid transformation proved to be a romantic ideal far removed from the crumbling reality. The crisis stemmed from the collapse of the domestic property sector and subsequent contraction in national output. Approximately 8.7 million jobs were lost from February 2008 to February 2010, and real GDP contracted by 4.2% making the Great Recession the worst economic downturn since the Great Depression. Nearly forty thousand Irish people emigrated in 2011. Buchanan (2009, p.22) refers to the period preceding the economic collapse as 'an escape from Irish history' with Lewis (2011) further noting that the swiftness of the move from poverty to wealth in Ireland during that time was 'without precedent in economic history' (p.7). The economic boom was largely based on heavily inflated house prices and frantic over-borrowing as a result. When the economy collapsed it left thousands of people in unmanageable debt and tied to houses that they could no longer afford or, at best, in negative equity, paying for a house that was worth a fraction of what they had borrowed. O'Toole observed that 'Irish house prices had fallen more rapidly than any others in Europe . . . the average Irish family had lost almost half of its financial assets, whose worth had fallen from €95,000 at the height of the boom to €51,000 in mid-2009 — not counting the steep decline in the worth of its house' (O'Toole 1997, p. 229). Ryan's novel becomes decidedly anti-pastoral when a character's *heimat* is lost or under threat or when in enforced exile, and the anti-pastoral thus operates as a method of establishing tensions within the narrative, revealing the dynamic of personal displacement and consequent loss of *heimat* that prevails in the decimated rural village.

Slavin (2017) asserts that Irish recession literature can best be interpreted through the lens of melancholia, which is understood as an unarticulated and unconscious grief at the loss of what was perceived to be, in the height of the Celtic Tiger, a glorious neoliberal future. As Lavis (2014) observes 'melancholia is typified by the anti-pastoral mode… it functions here by constant juxtaposition to and hints at, its pastoral opposite' (p.73). In his essay 'Mourning and Melancholia', Freud distinguished melancholia from what he considers to be the healthier state of mourning, the suffering engendered by the loss of a loved one. In melancholia, Freud argued, the sufferer is experiencing the perceived loss of a part of the self, a narcissistic injury that results in heightened self-criticism, self-reproach, and guilt, as well as withdrawal from the world, and an inability to find comfort or pleasure. Freud outlines the distinguishing features of melancholia as a profoundly painful dejection, cessation of interest in the outside world, loss of the capacity to love, inhibition of all activity…and culminates in a delusional expectation of punishment' (Freud 2017, p.244). In The Spinning Heart Ryan captures this melancholia in careworn portraits of the collective trauma of individuals, their family and their fractured society as a result of the economic crash. The shifting landscape of people offers a microcosm of Irish society, a society far removed from the romantic idyll of pastoral convention. The isolation of the village emphasizes the powerlessness of the community as rapid transformation renders their environment unfamiliar and unforgiving, and people discover that the sense of power they felt during the Celtic Tiger years was imagined, real power resided elsewhere. *The Spinning Heart* acknowledges the nation's compliance in creating the economic collapse but reveals that the real damage has been done by the people holding the power. As O'Toole observes 'Ireland is a diaspora, and as such is both a real place and a remembered place…Ireland is often something that happens elsewhere' (1997, p.199). The multiple perspectives are rooted in the national identity crisis in twenty-first century Ireland and reveal to the reader a complex and traumatized Irish ethnoscape that disrupts pastoral conventions.

In pastoral literature, alienation between characters typically ends with a reconciliation. In Ryan's novel, however, Frank's death forecloses the possibility of reconciliation between father and son. The novel conveys the complexity of Irish masculine norms in different contexts but also the complexity of the relationship between father and son. Most of the filial relationships in the novel are profoundly dysfunctional and the impact of this dysfunction is revealed in the character's monologue. Bobby tells us 'My father still lives back the road past the weir in the cottage I was reared in. I go there every day to see if he is dead and every day, he lets me down'. We learn of the cruelty of Frank's treatment of Bobby and his mother and how he alienated them from each other. Ryan reveals the collateral damage of this dynamic as Bobby and his mother silently and tacitly agree to become strangers to each other rather than leave him: 'We were mad about each other, my mother and me, but he made us afraid to look at each other' Frank's posthumous monologue reveals that he too was cruelly treated by his father revealing an intergenerational pattern of abuse and neglect, what d'Hoker (2004, p.107) refers to as 'psychic shocks passed on from generation to generation', a pattern at odds with the pastoral ideal of filial affection and contentment.

In *The Spinning Heart*, all the characters are trying to come to terms with the sudden economic downfall and most are despairing and melancholic. Ryan's novel offers a sober and unremitting reflection on the family unit and the symbiotic relationship between the breakdown of society and the breakdown of the family. The rapid development of society and its impact on the socio-cultural fabric of rural Ireland is manifested in the social and cultural ways of living that are no longer compatible with collective memory. The superfluity that characterised the Celtic Tiger is incompatible with pastoral ideals which focus on simplicity and sufficiency. As Bobby observes 'I had a right swagger there for a couple of years, thinking I was a great fella. Foreman, I was, clearing a grand a week…And now I can't pay for the messages' (Ryan 2012, p.13). Irish male identity is particularly affected as the monologues of the male characters reveal a mostly internalised response to external disasters. The 2008 recession was termed a male recession because it was male-dominated occupations, such as construction and manufacturing, that were most badly affected. For young men who subscribe to hegemonic ideals, there is a loss of identity and emasculation as a result of the recession and there are several isolated males in the text, all of whom experience what Freud referred to as 'a lowering of the self-regarding feelings to a degree that finds utterances in self-reproach' (2017, p.244) as they contemplate the lack of a sustainable future in rural Ireland. The impending emigration of Brian to Australia and Rory to London represents the loss of the connective tissue between a land and its people in the pursuit of excessive wealth and economic progress. Young male characters such as Brian, Rory and Seanie Shaper are all presented as disconnected in some way from society, the land, or themselves:

> because we have created an environment for us which isn't what it should be. And we're out of our depth all the time. We're living exactly on the borderline between the natural world from which we are being driven out, or we're driving ourselves out of it ....
> (Sebald, cited in Lavis 2014, p 56)

The novel thus testifies to the collapse of normality in people's everyday lives, most profoundly felt within the family unit.

Anti-pastoral landscapes may be physical or psychological spaces or represented by a character's psychological mood or psyche. *The Spinning Heart* is preoccupied with trauma, and Bobby Mahon, as the novel's central figure, represents the intersection of Ryan's two primary concerns within the interior landscape; the personal trauma that occurs within the family unit, and the communal trauma associated with the traumatic rupture of the recession. Bobby's narrative arc is driven by his attempt to come to terms with his father Frank's abuse and his loss of employment, and this plot connects the other fractured narratives within the novel, both in representations of Bobby as the focal point of the narrative, and in thematic preoccupations with abuse, unemployment and other anti-pastoral realities. In the intersection of personal and communal traumas in the novel, Ryan suggests that the cultural impact of the economic crash is particularly traumatic in a masculine culture with limited resources for engaging in healing or overcoming the impact of the recession. The aftermath of the economic crash is described as the sudden loss of an entire narrative framework; as Seanie observes in an anti-pastoral image of conflict and misery:

> You can kind of lose yourself very quick, when all about you changes and things you thought you always would have turn out to be things you never really had, and things you were sure you'd have in the future turn out to be on the far side of a big, dark mountain that you have no hope of ever climbing over'.
> (Ryan 2012, p.94)

The relationship between Josie and his sons, and Denis and his father, are similarly full of alienation, conflict and complexity. Indeed, Mulrennan (2016) refers to the novel as a multi-layered deconstruction of the internal exile of the Irish male identity in post-

Celtic Tiger rural Ireland. The pastoral model typically offers refuge to the troubled and the grief-stricken. In *The Spinning Heart,* there is no such consolation for the suffering or fabled Arcadian setting, there is only escape or annihilation.

Depopulation of the countryside due to poor agricultural yields and economic migration to urban centres are concerns common to anti-pastoral literature, and Ryan traverses familiar ground concerning emigration and economic collapse, contrasting the idyll with the apocalyptic in Denis's narrative as the anti-pastoral contingencies of modern life begin to overwhelm him; 'I haven't a snowball's chance in hell of a job. I'm owed a small fortune. The sky is falling down' (Ryan 2012, p.120). Denis embodies Kalotay's observation about many of the townspeople: 'These people have been left in a rut, spinning their wheels as well as their hearts' (Ryan 2012, p.14). The impact of recession on family life is directly transmitted through job and income loss and depression has caused many of the characters in the novel to lose their former sense of themselves. Job loss ranks in the upper quartile of stress when compared with other major life changes and often leads to detrimental outcomes for families. A significant outcome of unemployment is the deterioration of the psychological well-being not only of the unemployed parent but also of other family members experiencing the stressful adjustment to a lower standard of living and uncertainty about what the future will hold (Appel and Holden 1998, p.18). In *The Spinning Heart,* Ryan exposes the characters' difficult relationships with displacement both physically and psychologically, offering them no possibility of the pastoral retreat and return (Gifford 1999) but an unstable present and dystopian future.

If the pastoral derives its identity from a particular perspective on human experience (Marx 2000), the anti-pastoral too can be identified as a perspective on man's nature and situation. As Lindenbaum (1986, p.17) observes 'an anti-pastoral attitude marks a commitment to talk about man as he is and not as he might be in some perfect moral state either in the past or in the future'. When Bobby reflects on the 'pain in my heart for the man I thought I was' (Ryan 2012, p.15), he may be speaking about the loss of identity and self-reproach that accompanied his loss of employment, nonetheless the reason this loss is felt so acutely is that Frank has been similarly undermining his identity throughout his life, leaving Bobby 'like an orphaned child, bereft, filling up with fear like a boat filling with water' (Ryan 2012, p. 20) imprisoned in a traumatic past which perpetually repeats itself. Frank explains, 'I had to prepare him for the hard world... He'd have gotten some hop if I'd left him off out thinking he was the boy that his mother told him he was' (Ryan 2012, p.142). Frank's violent language, like the physical violence inflicted elsewhere in the novel, leaves its victim without the linguistic resources necessary to recover from the trauma of abuse. Bobby, who as a child 'stopped talking, not to be drawing his father on' him (Ryan 2012, p. 148), is unable to narrate a new identity to replace the one taken from him, first by his father, then by the recession as he negotiates his way through an unfamiliar cultural and economic landscape.

The trauma of the recession reveals the prevailing narratives of economic progress and commercial success as profoundly incompatible with the socio-economic reality of this unnamed village in rural Ireland and by extension, all villages suffering the same fate across Ireland. Ryan conveys the palpable loss felt by the workers when they discover that their boss has not been paying their pension contributions through haunting imagery: 'Mickey's left hand was outstretched. It held the invisible weight of what he should have been given but wasn't' (Ryan 2012, p.10), the loss of an imagined future of prosperity. In *The Spinning Heart*, Ryan presents us with an array of troubled characters devoid of pastoral sentiment and forcedly immersed in the realities of rural recession, a place where the nostalgic bonds of the familiar rural community are broken, replaced by an unforgiving reality.

The Spinning Heart uses the image of the family home to discuss traditional narratives of family which are disrupted, devalued, and threatened by the collapse of the housing market. As aforementioned, there is a direct correlation between the anti-pastoral mode and a character's loss of *heimat* and the novel employs the symbolism of the ghost estates as poignant *loci* of anti-pastoral tension that pervaded the Irish landscape in the aftermath of the recession when 'one home in every five was an empty shell' (O'Toole 1997, p. 224), a combination of actuality and concept. If the pastoral mode is invoked when *heimat* is stable as in idyllic episodes from the past, the anti-pastoral is characterised by individual displacement. Osborne (2010) notes that 'experiences of disorientation and displacement are bound in particular to the effects of encroaching urbanization and industrialisation' (p.300) and the novel portrays the impact of the 'inhumane agricultural change that altered the land itself' and 'represents what people have done to people' (Gifford 1999, p.122) moving from an inspirited to a dispossessed landscape that renders the familiar *unheimlich*, disrupting the sense of space and the unity of place and destabilizing our sense of belonging and identity:

> More and more it is hard to dismiss [in Irish culture] the sense of internal exile, the sense that Irish people feel less and less at home in Ireland, that Ireland has become somehow unreal. In one way or another, very many Irish people have experienced a sense of the familiar becoming unknown, unrecognizable. Ireland has become so multi-layered, so much a matter of one set of images superimposed on another, that it is hard to tell home from abroad.
> (O'Toole 1997, p. 89)

Ghost estates serve as a metaphor for the economic collapse of 2008 and the loss of an imagined future of prosperity. They have thus become powerful signifiers of melancholia in the post-recession Irish landscape (Slavin 2017), a sere landscape alienated from pastoral ideals. The ghost estates, one of Donal Ryan's sites of trauma in *The Spinning Heart*, serve as a concrete testimony to the follies of the Celtic Tiger. Empty houses became ruins, a spectre of unbridled development in a society where 'you could build houses out of cardboard and masking tape and they'd be sold off the plans' (Ryan 2012, p. 26) Mulrennan (2016) refers to the ghost estates as monuments to the people we thought we were, a post-religious state with a foot in the door of the global markets. Ghost estates embody 'the haunting legacy of the property boom' and have a significant emotional impact as 'the ruin of an ordinary home strikes many chords in our sensibility' (Ginsberg 2004, p. 370). In Ireland, where ruined great houses once belonging to the Anglo-Irish aristocracy coexist alongside famine cottages, each carrying the weight of a troubled history, the emotional load of a ruined house is considerable, in physicality and affects the conflation of past and present associated with the ruin materializes the sense of loss, the grief of displacement and the woe of exile:

> The symbolic ruin has a public dimension coloured with the content of loss, pride, identification, continuity, suffering, and survival: moral experiences. By becoming a symbol, the ruin gives aesthetic expression to shared moral values.
> (Ginsberg 2004, p. 109)

The ghost estates thus bear witness to the vanity and corruption that characterised the Irish political system, constituting a silent reproach to those who built them. Realtín tells us in melancholic phraseology:

> There are forty-houses in this estate. I live in number twenty-three. There's an old lady living in number forty. There's no one living in any of the other houses, just the ghosts of people who never existed. I'm stranded, she's abandoned.
> (Ryan 2012, p.42)

Réaltín's words can be effortlessly allied with Gifford's definition of the anti-pastoral mode, in which 'the natural world can no longer be constructed as a land of dreams, but is, in fact, a bleak battleground for survival without divine purpose' (1999, p.145). The ghost estates function as the 'location of memory, in which trauma took place and continues to be inextricably bound with that location in both an affective and evidential manner' (Trigg 2009, p.88). The pastoral/anti-pastoral tensions continue in descriptions of the interior of Réaltín's house; 'the loose skirting boards, the unpainted bannister, the badly hung door, the wobbly kitchen tile, the lumpy garden, the missing fence panel' demonstrating Réaltín's awareness and passive acceptance of her displacement, her psychological disempowerment further complementing the physical disempowerment of the landscape. In this way, the ghost estates symbolise the endless encroachment upon nature that characterised the Celtic Tiger era, an era that represents a deeply anti-pastoral period in

Irish history as industry flourished with the commodification of nature, and landscapes were plundered in the pursuit of progress:

> Ghost estates have become symbolic spaces in the national narrative capturing the transition from boom to bust, unprecedented growth to almost unfathomable collapse.
> (O'Callaghan 2016, p.12)

Ryan's fiction is geographically and psychologically rooted in the Irish landscape and Ryan represents the crash of the Celtic Tiger as a traumatic rupture, what Kristeva refers to as a 'non-communicable grief' (1989, p.3), about our ways of thinking about memory, the land, and identity. The fractured structure of the novel can then be read as an anti-pastoral strategy to reflect the disruptive and multifaceted condition of contemporary Ireland, reimagining traditional places, and charging them with a new symbolic value that disrupts the pastoral ideal for 'our inherited symbols of order and beauty have been divested of meaning' (Marx 2000, p.365) in this changed landscape.

Irish literature has a preoccupation with place and landscape, and writers like Ryan offer incisive engagement with the landscape of the national psyche. *The Spinning Heart* delves deep into the Irish *weltanschauung*, the marginal voices of rural Ireland and the weight of the recession on family life. The monologues traverse all the aspects of Irish culture that shape Irish identity and the Irish landscape, and Ryan's characters speak their truth and contradict each other's narratives to reflect the fractured state of rural Ireland after the recession (Mulrennan 2016). The many voices of Ryan's novel offer the reader a way of experiencing and interacting with the world the novel inhabits; a rural village marred by ghost estates and the trauma of looming emigration. The myriad monologues function also as an anti-pastoral strategy, railing against the alienating authority of a single voice or simplistic mode of pastoral representation, kindling the consciousness instead with the cultural reality of rural Ireland as an interrupted idyll (Marx 2000, p.253). Ryan's engagement with contemporary Ireland through a disembodied landscape and people thus reflects the emergence of anti-pastoral literature as a response to embedded pastoral ideals in Irish literature.

Works Cited

Alpers, P. (1976) *What is Pastoral*, Chicago: University of Chicago Press.

Appadurai, A. (1996) *Modernity at Large: Cultural Dimensions of Globalizations*, Minnesota: University of Minnesota Press.

Appel, A.E. and Holden, G. (1998) 'The co-occurrence of spouse abuse and physical child abuse: A review and appraisal', *Journal of Family Violence*, 12(4), 578-599

Bakhtin, M. (1982) *The Dialogic Imagination*, Texas: University of Texas Press.

Buchanan, J. (2009) 'Living at the End of the Irish Century: Globalization and Identity in Declan Hughes's Shiver', *Modern Drama*, 52(3), 300.

Clifford, J. (1994) 'Diasporas.' *Cultural Anthropology*, 9(3), 302-38.

d'Hoker, E. (2004) *Visions of Alterity: Representation in the Work of John Banville*, Cologne: Brill Press.

Frawley, O. (1998) 'Nature and Nostalgia in Irish Literature.' *Proceedings of the Harvard Celtic Colloquium*, 18, 268-277.

Ginsberg, R. (2004) *The Aesthetics of Ruins*. New York: Rodopi Press.

Freud, S. (2017) *Mourning and Melancholia*, New York: Routledge.

Gifford, T. (1999) *Pastoral*, London: Routledge.

Goldsmith, O. (1996) *The Deserted Village*, London: Everyman

Jordan, J. (2013) 'The Spinning Heart by Donal Ryan — Review', *The Guardian*, November 28, http://www.theguardian.com/books/2013/nov/28/spinning-heart-donal-ryan-review.

Kalotay, D. (2014) 'Was It Any Use? Donal Ryan's Spinning Heart.' *The New York Times*, 21 March, pp. 12-13.

Kermode, F. (1952) *English Pastoral Poetry from the Beginnings to Marvell*, New York: Norton and Co.

Kristeva, J. (1989) *Black Sun: Depression and Melancholia*, New York: Columbia University Press.

Lavis, G. (2014) *Pastoral Modes in the Poetry and Prose Fiction of W.G. Sebald*, London: University of London Press.

Lindenbaum, P. (1986) *Changing Landscapes Anti-Pastoral Sentiments in the English Renaissance*, Georgia: University of Georgia Press.

Lentin, R. (2001) *Racism and Anti-Racism in Ireland*, Belfast: Beyond the Pale Publications.

Lerner, L. (1972) *The Uses of Nostalgia, Studies in Pastoral Poetry*, New York: Chatto & Windus.

Lewis, M. (2011) 'When Irish Eyes are Crying.' *Vanity Fair*, March, http://people.ucsc.edu/~hutch/When%20Irish%20Eyes%20Are%20Crying%20_%20Business%20_%20Vanity%20Fair.pdf.

Lloyd, D. (2003) 'The Spirit of the Nation', *Theorizing Ireland*, London: Palgrave Macmillan.

Loughrey, B. (1984) *The Pastoral Mode*, London: Macmillan.

Marx, L. (2000) *The Machine in the Garden: Technology and the Pastoral Ideal in America*, Oxford: Oxford University Press.

Marx, L. (1969) 'Pastoral Ideals and City Troubles', *The Journal of General Education*, 20 (4), 251-271.

Morisson, V. (2011) 'A People's Sense of Belonging: Dislocation in Post Celtic Tiger Art', *The Canadian Journal of Irish Studies*, 20 (11), 178-207.

Mulrennan, M. (2016) 'Post-Celtic Tiger rural Ireland, internal exile and male identity in the fiction of Colin Barrett and Donal Ryan', *The Honest Ulsterman*, February, https://humag.co/features/post-celtic-tiger-rural-ireland-internal-exile-and-male-identity-in-the-fiction-of-colin-barrett-and-donal-ryan.

Murphy, G. (1932) 'Vergilian Influence upon the vernacular literature of Medieval Ireland.' *Studi Medievali*, 5, 372-381.

O'Callaghan, C. (2016) 'Ghost Estates: Spaces and Spectres of Ireland', *Spacing Ireland*, Manchester: University of Manchester Press.

Osborne, D. (2010) 'Topographical Anxiety and Dysfunctional Systems' *W.G. Sebald and the Poetics of Travel*, Zisselsberger,M. ed., London: Camden House, pp. 299-32.

O'Toole, F. (1997) *The Lie of the Land: Irish Identities*, London: Verso.

Ryan, D. (2012) *The Spinning Heart*, Dublin: Lilliput Press.

Schama, S. (1996) *Landscape and Memory*, New York: Vintage Books.

Schwartz, L. (2007) *The Emergence of Memory: Conversations with W.G. Sebald*, New York: Seven Stories.

Slavin, M. (2017) 'Ghost stories, ghost estates: melancholia in Irish recession literature.' *C21 Literature: Journal of 21st-Century Writings*, 5(1), p.7.

Synge, J.M. (1002) *The Aran Islands*, London: Penguin Classics.

Trigg, D. (2006) *The Aesthetics of Decay: Nothingness, Nostalgia and the Absence of Reason*. New York: Peter Lang.

Trigg, D. (2009) 'The place of trauma: Memory, hauntings and the temporality of ruins.' *Memory Studies*, 4(2), 87-10.

White, T.J. (2010) 'Celtic Collapse, or Celtic Correction?: Ireland's Recession in Historical Perspective.' *New Hibernia Review*, 14 (4), 27.

Robinson, A. (2011) 'In Theory Bakhtin: Dialogism, Polyphony and Heteroglossia', *Ceasefire*, July 29, https://ceasefiremagazine.co.uk/in-theory-bakhtin-1.

Artificial Nature in 19th Century France: The Buttes Chaumont Park and Landscape Art

The Parc de Buttes Chaumont, designed by Jean Charles Alphande in 1863 as part of Napoleon III's plan of urban renewal for Paris, is a unique park both in its complex, scenographic settings and in its commitment to the production of pictorial vistas. Featuring extensive cement builds, an artificial cave and elaborate waterworks, the Buttes Chaumont has been considered by scholars as marking the beginning of an era that produced a form of artificial, technological nature, a sort of industrial sublime. A close read of the distinctive aesthetic choices made in the design of the Buttes Chaumont allows us to build broader considerations on the 'new nature' that emerged from the larger cultural framework of 19th-century Paris. This chapter will draw parallels between the aesthetic of the Buttes Chaumont and contemporary landscape art, as well as consider how the park falls within a social and urban re-design that deploys 'nature' — both physical and imagined- as a political tool.

Human habitat in the 19th century was coming off of a century of unprecedented change. In the wake of the Industrial Revolution, a massive wave of migration had invested the cities, creating a ripple effect of consequences, among which three are crucial for this discussion: the depopulation of the countryside, the overpopulation and consequential expansion of the cities, and the birth of a new human experience of the environment. As we will see, not only did the material formation of the city create a new form of human habitat, but the experience of this new habitat changed the existing conceptualizations of space in general, and nature in particular.

In her writing on Jean Francois Millet, art historian Griselda Pollock tells us that "perhaps today we are too accustomed to urban life to appreciate the full force of its alien quality to a man reared in a small community" (1977, p. 9). After millennia of human society consisting of small, rural communities that operated in direct relationship with the land, industrialization saw a move to comparatively monumental, new modern cities, that promised social mobility and unprecedented economic emancipation through wage labour. The change in environment was drastic and often traumatic: Paris was polluted and overcrowded, with confined living spaces and under the constant threat of political unrest and the spread of disease due to the lack of hygiene and infrastructure (Eisenman, 1994, p. 238). Countrymen arriving in the city would find its occluded pattern, noise pollution and intense smell shocking. Parsons describes the new industrial city of Paris as "a leprous growth, transforming the remnants of unspoilt nature that surround it into a wasteland of mud, brick and human degradation" (1983, p. 49), while Eisenman writes of 1850 Paris as decrepit, stricken by epidemics of cholera and claustrophobic by the overcrowding of people and buildings (1994, p. 238). At the same time, the countryside was changing for the worse also: the rapid process of drastic urbanization left it abandoned, impoverished, and depopulated. Robert Herbert argues that "the loss was even greater because it was the oldest and the children who remained on the land" (1966, p. 44). Landscape as man had known it had been completely transfigured by the Industrial Revolution, and the previously unbroken link to nature was no longer part of the urban citizen's daily experience, a change that was leaving many city-dwellers feeling alienated. This feeling of alienation was enhanced by the fact that many of the inhabitants of Paris were first-generation migrants—former countrymen, coming from the province around Paris to find jobs and fortune (ibid).

At the time that the Buttes Chaumont was commissioned, therefore, these factors all concurred to create the conditions for "a wholesale reinvention of nature" (Green, 1992, p. 72). The unprecedented experience of urban life altered city-dwellers imagination as well as memory of nature and created an unprecedented public demand for artistic representations of nature: landscape art, bucolic trompe l'oeils and frescos, floral motifs in furniture and fashion became highly requested commercially. Green tells us that 19th-century France is distinctive for its "extraordinary proliferation of texts and practices that evidence interest in the countryside" (1992, p. 3). This market for landscape art, he explains, should not merely be explained as an inheritance of Romanticism but rather observed within a brand-new dynamic of private offer and demand (ibid). Paris was permeated by "overlapping and sometimes competing images of the natural world" (Green, 1992, p. 72). Paintings were the most in-demand media, with the pictorial being a constant theme (ibid). Green well articulates the experiential function of these images: "For metropolitans, pictures and prints were not just reminders of a nature already visited and enjoyed. Like urban gardens and walks in the country, they present a structured space through which the Parisian viewer could live out, briefly, *natura naturans*" (1992, p. 70). In creating these artificial natural spaces for city-dwellers, artists and park designers participated in world-building, creating many coexisting imagined geographies that often worked to either deny or affirm the reality of 19th-century nature. This imagined natural multiverse reflects a fragmented cultural image of nature, one loaded with personal and political yearnings and in the flux of dramatic conceptual -as well as material- transformation. One of these versions was the one offered by Realists such as the previously referenced Jean Francois Millet.

In *The Angelus* (1859) earthy, sombre palette tints two field workers in a potato field at dusk. They have presumably stopped to pray at the sound of the Church bells marking the end of the day. Their clothes and features are as rough as the land they are standing upon. The shrubbery at their feet creates an entangled carpet of rocks, earth and harvest. The painting is permeated by a sense of duty and morality; poverty and hardship assume biblical qualities, as the countrymen and women pray in the field. Millet's works fall within the artistic movement of Realism: he is not preoccupied with fabricating a new or escapist fantasy of nature but rather with documenting its reality and drawing attention to its current hardships. Millet's paintings are about land rather than landscape. Nature is not domesticated and recreational, not a decorative accessory or a spectacle—rather, it is a powerful and indifferent force that man continuously struggles to survive in. *Le Printemps* (1873), a later, slightly more positive painting, sees the human figures reduced, leaving more room for the natural landscape. Here, the awakening of nature in the triumph of Spring is beautiful but still sober. The sky is tinted by a rainbow, but dark clouds reveal the thunderstorm that has preceded it. The ground and trees are scattered with colourful petals, but the soil is still rocky, rough, and uneven. The countryman in the distance seems to have found refuge from the rain after a tree; a strenuous balance is found between the pleasure of nature and its overpowering abilities. Griselda Pollock tells us: "The fact that Millet was born on the land is the single most important factor in his life and work, for by realising the full significance of it, one can resolve most of the contradictions" (1977, p. 8). Millet "knew the land", and he especially knew "what it meant to leave the land" (ibid). In a letter to his friend and biographer Alfred Sensier, Millet described the countryman's life as charged with a reassuring feeling of belonging that the alienating, capitalist city remained unable to replace: "he is in some way an integral part of Nature, like a tree, or an ox" (cited in Pollock, 1977, p. 18). Millet's nature is coded as a working-class experience and is, in a sense, a picture of the nature of the past struggling to survive in the present. These images were not well received by most Parisians. Millet never declared himself political, but his paintings were interpreted as such anyway, and often incurred harsh reactions from art critics. Positive images of the countryside by Rosa Bonheur, for instance, were favoured by some over Millet's dignified yet starving peasants. Parisians appreciated Rosa Bonheur's soothing images of unrealistically florid, oversized farm animals and always sunny fields. Considering Realism and its public response helps us understand that even at a time in which 'nature's' popularity was peaking, this popularity was conditional: 'real' nature was not in demand. Faced with the pollution and claustrophobia of city life, and struggling through a century of class war, Parisians did not wish to be reminded of the working-class struggle that the countryside was presently hosting. Parisians had already started to reshape nature into artifice, at least as fantasy: nature was becoming an idealized, pastoral and pleasurable *locus amoenus*, an unreachable yet useful fantasy, and a commodified leisure destination.

The Buttes Chaumont certainly responds to this desire for escapism and artifice. With a one-hundred feet waterfall, a grotto with stalactites, a 1.5-hectare lake and a fifty-meter cliff (all artificial) the park is a triumph of well-camouflaged concrete—it is exceedingly technological, yet entirely masqueraded as natural. To Weiss, one of the goals of the park's extensive waterworks was to naturalize the very recent acquisition of potable water within the city, perhaps in an attempt to wash clean a century of disastrous public health (2020, pp. 747-748). A demonstrative -if not boastful- element is certainly palpable if slightly mitigated by the dominant atmosphere of escapist, fairytale fantasy. The park features a dense, somewhat kitsch mixture of exotic references: an Alpine cottage, a Roman temple; South Asian plant species as well as sequoias and cedars from Lebanon. Here it is useful to consider Malcolm Andrews's description of the locus ameonus as above all "insulated from the world of public affairs" (1999, p. 53)—in other words, an apolitical space. But how does one go about planning an apolitical space? Green tells us that "the interleaving of artifice and naturalness, illusion and reality, was to be an overriding priority in the later state-planned parks of Haussmann's administration...as one utopian planner, Hippolyte Meynadier was already insisting in 1843, what the capital required was... 'a real countryside in the town'" (1992, p. 69). For the park to solve a social purpose of recreation and relief, however, this countryside could not be real nor realistic—that is, it could not come to reflect the reality of what Nature had come to be in the land outside Paris, lest it became a depressing reminder with the potential to incite a political uprising.

In reality, life in the countryside, in proximity to non-artificial nature, was linked to labour rather than recreation—much more similar to Millet's paintings. It is clear then that a successful aesthetics of landscape construed as a refuge from the pressure of the city needed to create a new sort of natural space, an "ahistorical, timeless changeless land" (House, 1992, p. 584). Only then could it be "insulated from public affairs" (Andrews, 1999, p. 53). In this sort of mind-frame, the more artificial, escapist—even exotic—a park could be, the better its goal of relief could be achieved. The Buttes Chaumont's Swiss Chalet, Roman ruins and Alpine reliefs give the impression to the spectator to be not just outside of the city but outside of France itself, far from agrarian recession and into a world where nature was urbanized and recreational yet without any signs of labour and struggle—that is, nature that was industrialized but did not signal to any of the negative consequences of Industrialization. Consider the Buttes Chaumont in light of Realism and the political realities of nature of its time reveals a precise intention for escapism behind its aesthetic choices. Parisians preferred to think of the countryside, and of nature in general, in pastoral terms: the urban audience and patronage expected image of nature which consolidates "a myth of natural order from which humanity had strayed" (Andrews, 1999, p. 151). A fantasy life in the country seemed simpler, less subject to rapid and convulsive change, free from crowds, noise and pollution, and in tune with natural processes. The stylistic intention of the Buttes Chaumont is in line with Rosa Bonheur's florid oxen: it's essentially a soothing, perhaps even consolatory fairytale.

This kind of stylistic decision seems to indicate a mirroring ideological intention—the setting of a particular scene to achieve a particular mood in its visitors. Both Prendergast (1992) and Pinkney (1958) argue that the parks of Paris mended certain issues of the working class: green spaces could provide relief from the crowded slums, a sort of substitute for improved housing. As Strohmayer writes, nature was deployed "as a pedagogical vehicle aimed at undermining class conflicts" (2006, p. 564). Antoine Picon argues that the creation of urban parks reflected "this desire for rebalancing, a concern for social pacification… bringing all social classes into contact with nature should make it possible to attenuate their confrontation" (2010, p. 37, translated). The idea was to create a shared, public form of private life where the good habits of the upper classes would spread to the working class by proximity. This feature—the blurring of the line between private and public space—is emblematic of modernity and comes with its own set of preoccupations: the more the private entered public space, the more it invited regulating and moral intervention—a useful example is the many unsuccessful attempts within 18th and 19th centuries cities to regulate and suppress sex work. To Strohmayer, the idea behind the creation of urban parks had an explicit intention to create a moral landscape, one that would not require policing and legislation the way such other attempts to stomp out 'unwanted' behaviour within the working class had, but that rather relied on a philosophical faith that "the dangerous classes should learn from nature while being provided with 'fresh air'" (2006, p. 564).

Despite its moralizing mission being aimed at the lower classes, the reality was that the park did not predominantly host working-class visitors. Pre-union workers' hours and the park's opening hours clashed, and as a result, workmen and women would only be able to visit the park on Sundays and holidays. It would be the middle class who would use it daily (Pinkney, 1958, p. 99). Despite intentions, then, one of the primary reforming effects of the park towards the working class was not one of influence through inclusion but rather one of befalling exclusion, as their presence in the area was displaced.

Here, it is useful to provide a brief history of what spatially preceded the Buttes Chaumont. Previously known as Mountfaucon, from the middle of the 14th century to 1789 the area was used as a site of execution, with as many as 80 gallows operating simultaneously (Susik, 2009, p. 68). Corpses of the deceased would not be properly disposed of, creating a spectral reputation for the area. Once the execution area was deposed, the quarry became the primary équarrissage area of Paris. Susik writes: "Corpses of dead livestock animals and horses could be legally dumped and left to decompose... roughly fifty thousand animal corpses could be found at the site at any given time during the first half of the 19th century" (ibid). These centuries of health hazard led to "rat infestation of apocalyptic proportions" (ibid), with Theophile Gautier detailing apocalyptic visions of Paris "being devoured by the rats of Montfaucon" (cited in Strohmayer, 2006, p. 561). The pungent smell from the équarrissage was so prominent and far-reaching that "Montfaucon acted as an olfactory weather vane for the whole of Paris" (Susik, 2009, p. 68). The area, in other words, was a sanitary and reputational hazard for the 'new Paris'.

The surrounding area was predominantly working class, with Strohmayer characterizing the local population as "those that were no longer able to afford the ever-increasing rents of the centre, as well as newly migrant labour from the countryside and from abroad" (2006, p. 561). 85 expropriations were demanded for the construction of the park, effectively displacing large portions of the area's working-class residents (ibid). It should be noted that 19th-century 'gentrification' is not to be uncritically read through the contemporary lens of social critique. Modern cities undoubtedly faced infrastructural and sanitary emergencies that made urban transformation a necessary concern. The transformation of the abattoir as a park was beneficial to the public health of the area and Paris at large. Nonetheless, within a broader discussion of the use of nature as a correctional and reforming tool, we can address either incidental or intentional population overhaul that accompanied the building of the Buttes Chaumont.

Second Empire Paris had undergone a transformative wave of deliberate, strategic improvements set to elevate the capital "from the medieval city into modern metropolis" (Strohmayer, 2006, p. 559). As well as the introduction of potable water and efficient sewage systems (see Weiss), the city enjoyed improved transportation through the creation of large boulevards and the introduction of the railway. Efficient traffic (of people, of water, of goods and waste) is an essential asset to public health. To achieve this, however, large slum quarters had been torn down. Green helps us understand how large working-class areas were perceived by middle and upper-class Parisians during this time: "The unhealthiness of Paris" he writes "could be physically distanced, allocated to the decrepit old quarters of the centre and south bank—so ripe for infection—and their 'vicious' inhabitants" (1992, p. 51). In this way, vice and disease could be othered into a separate, alien city, segregation that simultaneously fueled class conflict and reassured the ruling classes. The result was that political violence itself was conceptualized as a "plague infecting the capital" (Green, 1992, p. 50), starting of course from the working-class barracks. As noted by Green, Victor Hugo's terminology of "'insurrectional virus' oozing from the 'entrails of the city'" is a prime example of this rhetoric (ibid). Slum areas were seen as inherent public health hazards, not exclusively from a pragmatic standpoint—overcrowding and poverty- but also a moral, classist standpoint.

The Montfaucon posed particularly troubling concerns. So embarrassing was the Montfaucon's wasteland to the city of Paris that Strohmayer reports "most of the pre-Haussmannian maps of Paris strategically place their index somewhere or another in close proximity to the area" (2006, p. 561). The destitute neighbourhood was increasingly out of place in Second Empire Paris. In Aragon's *Le Paysan de Paris,* a group of young men adventurously and enthusiastically enter the Buttes Chaumont at night, only to find themselves weighed down by its buried dark history. Susik interprets the novel as a parable about the inability of Paris to bury its turbulent past, a critique naturally extends to the park itself: "The concerted societal effort to attain a pure and timeless zone in the renovated guise of Buttes Chaumont instead renders the lurid patina of this locations history all the more conspicuous to the three friends" (Susik, 2009, p. 65). To Susik, "the renovated Buttes Chaumont subliminally broadcasts the residues of its troubled history", despite its valiant attempts "to function as a protective screen against sordid mnemonic traces" (ibid).

The reforming task of the park, therefore, was not just one of spiritual pacifiers but also repurposing of land. The park vanished undesirable sights and displaced undesirable subjects, replacing a wasteland with a technological marvel, and potential troublemakers with middle-class families. In other words, artificial nature here solved a double function: should the ideological plan to have all social classes find harmony in the escapist vistas has fallen short, the material presence of the Buttes Chaumont would at least have succeeded in repurposing the area, sanitizing the quarry. Picon argues that the Montfaucon quarry stood as a symbolic threat to bourgeois social order: "In the imagination of the bourgeois elites, the subsoil and the people seem united by multiple links. Both are characterized by their hostile obscurity" (2010, p. 37). He links this to Victor Hugo's choice, in *Les Miserables,* to set the confrontation between Jean Valjean and Javert in Paris' sewers, as a symbolic battleground between order above and unlawfulness below (ibid). While symbolic, this concern was also literal: Strohmayer reports that many fugitives "sought refuge in caves and tunnels" thus "adding to a perception of danger and the eerie quality of the area" (2006, p. 561).

These fugitives were not necessarily private criminals: for a century, Paris had been the site of political resistance. Prendergast notes that parks have the peculiar ability to inoffensively convert a rather large amount of public space, that could otherwise be utilized for protests or gatherings, into innocuous, leisure-based areas (1992, p.165). In other words, the urban renewal plan for Paris included a vested interest in turning all large, clear, flat public areas into hilly greenery that might get in the way of guillotine assemblage. This is essential in understanding the multiple ways in which artificial nature, both conceptually and materially, was being deployed by the government as a political tool. Strohmayer aptly speaks of the moral landscape of the park as "a political theatre" (2006, p. 564).

For those who were able to frequent parks, nonetheless, urban greenery did provide several unprecedented opportunities and experiences of social mobility. The park was a space within which the barriers between different classes would be spatially suspended. While this was true of many public spaces of the city, parks would add a quality of shared intimacy due to the kind of activities carried out by *promeneurs in* comparison to *flaneurs*. Its visitors could experience nature separately while being in the same space at the same time. In unadulterated nature, this would have never been the case, both for the abundance of space and for the physical barriers and distancing between the countryside mansions of noblemen and peasants' houses (Green, 1992, p. 95). In parks, instead, families from different classes might come to sit on the grass and enjoy the sun and vegetation at a relatively close distance from each other. Furthermore, they could practice these collective intimate activities, such as eating and watching children play, while remaining strangers, a typically modern experience.

One of the crucial new experiences the Buttes Chaumont offered was expanding the confines of which social classes got to experience and enjoy the pastoral — which as we have seen is defined as a safe, pleasurable, labor-less, apolitical, natural space. Previous to urbanization, the only ample natural spaces that had been enhanced and domesticated to the point of becoming a space of pure leisure had been the exclusive privilege of aristocratic mansions. A firm exclusionary distinction existed between those carving out and maintaining the Renaissance and Italian style gardens, and those who were able to regularly enjoy them. With the creation of public parks within cities, both the new bourgeoisie and the lower classes were for the first time able to experience the pastoral through spaces of artificial nature. This is especially true in a park as spectacular, technological and intentionally exotic as the Buttes Chaumont, which allowed its dwellers to mimic the experience of travel—sitting as a Swiss Chalet, promenading around a Roman temple or picnicking under a tulip tree. To the "increasingly leisure-conscious bourgeoisie" (Strohmayer, 2006, p. 564), the multitude of paths, the difference in sceneries, and the escapist motifs could all substitute the need for the much more exclusive *maison de campagne* as well as foreign travel. In this experiential sense, therefore, the Buttes Chaumont undoubtedly enacted social mobility. While spatially displacing certain groups, the park also opened up previously exclusive spatial experiences to larger parts of the population.

The bourgeois enjoyment of public parks is a recurrent theme in Impressionist paintings, which are populated by various images of "breakfasts, picnics, promenades and boating trips" (Eisenman, 1994, p. 244). Green reads these pictorial scenes as "the mundane process of leisure and pleasure, as part of an uneven field of discourses constituting nature" (1992, p. 3). While different in aesthetic, the park comes closest in atmosphere and use to Impressionist depictions of nature. The nature painted by Impressionists is aptly defined by Meyer Schapiro as" urban idylls of bourgeois recreation" (cited in Eisenman, 1994, p. 244). In Manet's Luncheon on the Grass (1862), the ancient topos of river nymphs bathing are urbanized and modernized. Water divinities become elegant bourgeoises, the mythological woods a secluded corner of a park. Nature is being rewritten from a venerable entity to a democratic background for middle-class leisure. Many of Monet's paintings cover similar themes, with fashionable groups of men and women enjoying wine and food on the grass. Both Monet and Manet often painted parks, such as in Manet's Music in the Tuileries (1862) and Monet's Park Monceau (1878). In the former, men and women are shown enjoying each other's company and the unique cultured experience of music in nature. The natural space has been entirely colonized by urban culture and activities: chairs have even been brought in to make the concert more comfortable. The painting is a testimony to the use of parks during this time. Nature is no longer a force to be reckoned with and painstakingly laboured to gain sustenance from, but rather a domesticated and pleasurable frame for human life, that appears emancipated from its environment. This can be seen even artistically — an interest in en plen air painting made parks a convenient, nearby standpoint for an artist to observe and depict nature in different lights, while simultaneously saving on rent for studio spaces.

Ann Komara has noted in her essay on the Buttes Chaumont how the application of science to the creation of parks (in the form of concrete, artificial waterfalls, and landscape architecture) also comes to signify the triumph of modernity (2004, p. 10). "The creation of the park", she writes, "applied the conquest of science and art to the conditions of the city" (ibid). Industry had enabled the production of the park, and industry was visible in it and from it: "Upon reaching a panoramic viewpoint, the visitor could then see an industrial landscape of train yards, factories and slaughterhouses beyond the borders of the park" (ibid.). Impressionist art perfectly reflects this hybridization of nature and industry. In Monet's *The Bridge at l'Argenteuil* (1874), the golden afternoon light cloaks the countryside. A boat sails silently on the water, a symbol of leisure ; equally included in the atmosphere is the bridge of the railway. The image seems to celebrate technological progress and its convenience: perhaps the very people enjoying sailing have reached the countryside thanks to the railway. Technology and nature both harmoniously serve the pleasure of human leisure. Picon argues that the suspended railway bridge crossing the Buttes Chaumont "constitutes one of the clearest expressions, in France of the second half of the 19th century, of the theme of the "machine in the garden" which the historian of technical culture Leo Marx showed the decisive importance in the United States" (2010, p. 42).

Despite its many modern aspects, however, from a stylistic perspective, the aesthetic of the Buttes Chaumont most closely recalls older aesthetics of Romanticism and the Picturesque. Its rocky reliefs are similar to the stormy peaks of traditional Romantic landscapes. The belvedere, isolated in the lake, offers through its bridges and natural terraces the view of a dramatic precipice, garnished by white spiraeas and ivy. On the top, the temple of Sybil, designed after Tivoli's ruins (a favourite subject by the Romantics) suggests isolated meditation, a sanctuary to reflect on emotion. The rocky waterfall and artificial grotto, made gothic by the sculpted stalactites, show a taste for sensational, climactic landscape; a taste emphasized by the popular renaming of the park's main bridge "the Bridge of Suicides". The bridge itself can be compared to one of Salvator Rosa's natural arches. Indeed, the park reflects and appeals to gothic, romantic sensibilities. It is easy to see the resemblance with the popular works of Caspar David Friedrich: the panoramic standpoint, the precipice and mountainous soil, the oak trees and the ever-present contemplating figures can easily be compared to various standpoints of the park. The temple on the Belvedere, in particular, is remarkably similar to paintings of the subject such as *The Temple of Vesta* by Christian Wilhelm Ernst Dietrich (1750) and Friedrich Nerly's *The Temple of Vesta and the Sybils at Tivoli* (1834).

Designing a modern, technological park after the Romantic landscape is a peculiar attempt, in so far, that Romantic nature focuses on the concept of the sublime. The idea of the sublime is strictly connected with wild, uncultivated nature, and it is meant to stem from witnessing the overpowering force of nature (Andrews, 1999, p. 129). A volcanic eruption, the ice of a glacier, and a stormy peak all fall under this category. On the one hand, it might seem that an urban park could hardly satisfy these standards. However, as Andrews reminds us, "for the sublime to be an attractive experience there needs to be some reassurance that the person is not actually in mortal danger" (1999, p. 134). Paintings were emblematically successful at this, and I would argue that as an artificial landscape, the park recreates the sublime in the same way — it certainly provides the ability to stare from safety at a turbulent view. The precipice, the waterfall and the ruins can all be contemplated in safety in the park: no matter how strong the illusion and emotion, the spectator only has to turn around and take in the identity of his fellow visitors, and the surrounding city roofs, to assure himself of his safety. Rather than by bards and historical figures, the park is populated by ordinary citizens, by governess and children. Moreover, as Picon notes, the Buttes Chaumont marks the introduction of an industrial sublime, one that showcases such innovative technology that it is sublime in its way of defying natural elements: "The art of the engineer and the art of gardens also share aesthetic codes based on the categories of the sublime and the picturesque. The work is sometimes sublime in its way of defying natural elements (Picon, 2010, p. 41)".

In conclusion, the Buttes Chaumont is a productive example of how artificial nature was being shaped and deployed as a tool within 19th century France. The design choices of the Buttes Chaumont have close ties with contemporary landscape art. Its aesthetics are strongly reflective of the urban demand for a particular view of nature. The spectacular and the artificial were both instrumental in giving Parisians a sense of relief and insulation from spatial, political and social pressures. Both the material space of the park and its aesthetic atmosphere worked together as tools for urban reform against social unrest and class tensions. The picturesque qualities of the park make it possible to consider it not solely as influenced by pictorial landscapes of the time, but rather as its form of three-dimensional landscape artwork. Produced within a time of profound cultural preoccupation towards creating new natural spaces, the Buttes Chaumont was designed, much like pictorial representations, to offer city-dwellers the opportunity to live out a fantasy of nature that catered to their specific, unprecedented understanding of nature as artificial destination. The Buttes Chaumont is a direct product of modern, urban re-conceptualizations of nature, and a return to the pastoral through the aid of technology.

Works Cited

Andrews, Malcom. *Landscape and Western Art*. Oxford University Press, 1999.

Eisenman, Stephen. *Nineteenth-Century Art: A Critical History*. London: Thames & Hudson, 1994.

Green, Nicholas. *The Spectacle Of Nature*. Manchester University Press, 1992.

Herbert, Robert L. "Millet Reconsidered." *Art Institute of Chicago Museum Studies*, vol. 1, 1966, pp. 29–65. JSTOR, www.jstor.org/stable/4104371.

House, John. "Renoir's 'Baigneuses' of 1887 and the Politics of Escapism." *The Burlington Magazine*, vol. 134, no. 1074, 1992, pp. 578–585. JSTOR, www.jstor.org/stable/885312. Accessed 30 Aug. 2021.

Komara, Ann. "Concrete And The Engineered Picturesque". *Journal Of Architectural Education*, vol 58, no. 1, 2004, pp. 5-12. Informa UK Limited, doi:10.1162/1046488041578158.

Parsons, Christopher and McWilliam, Neil. "'Le Paysan de Paris': Alfred Sensier and the Myth of Rural France". *Oxford Art Journal*, vol 6, no. 2, 1983, pp. 38-58. Oxford University Press (OUP), doi:10.1093/oxartj/6.2.38.

Picon, Antoine. "Nature Et Ingénierie : Le Parc Des Buttes-Chaumont". *Romantisme*, vol 150, no. 4, 2010, p. 35. CAIRN, doi:10.3917/rom.150.0035.

Pinkney, David. *Napoleon II and the Rebuilding of Paris*. Princeton University Press, 1958.

Pollock, Griselda. *Millet*. Oresko Books, 1977.

Strohmayer, Ulf. "Urban Design And Civic Spaces: Nature At The Parc Des Buttes-Chaumont In Paris". *Cultural Geographies*, vol 13, no. 4, 2006, pp. 557-576. SAGE Publications, doi:10.1191/1474474006cgj375oa.

Susik, Abigail. "Aragon's 'Le Paysan De Paris' and the Buried History of Buttes-Chaumont Park." *Thresholds*, no. 36, 2009, pp. 64–71. JSTOR, www.jstor.org/stable/43876389. Accessed 30 Aug. 2021.

Prendergast, Christopher. *Paris and the nineteenth century*. Blackwell, 1992.

Pinkney, David. *Napoleon III and the Rebuilding of Paris*. Princeton University Press, 1958.

Weiss, Sean. "Making Engineering Visible: Photography and the Politics of Drinking Water in Modern Paris". *Technology and Culture*, Volume 61, Number 3, July 2020, pp. 739-771. Published by Johns Hopkins University Press. DOI: https://doi.org/10.1353/tech.2020.0072

'Schrödinger's Pedestrian': The (ab)History & the (ab)Pastoral in Miéville's *The City & The City*

As the title indicates, China Miéville's *The City & The City* (2010) focuses on an urban imaginary. Fittingly, the opening scene implies the anti-pastoral with an "open ground between the buildings" (Miéville, 2010, p. 1). Instead of "wood" with a "pond," "[t]here is a corpse but the saplings were dead" (Miéville, 2010, p. 1). Despite an open space with the potential for cultivation, it is barren and lifeless. Residents in the surrounding apartments dump garbage there. Later in the novel and contrast to this image of urban blight is the cities' park: "An up-down treed and flowered landscape, some parts wilder, some coiffed" (Miéville, 2010, p. 144). It corrals the image of a countryside cultivated to suggest a pastoral landscape. Rather than nymphs and satyrs romping through forests and streams, however, city dwellers walk their dogs and have occasional picnics. Unlike the anti-pastoral, the pastoral exists only as a suggestion with a referent just out of reach in a Golden Age that remains unwitnessed. This essay investigates how the former is topographically locatable while the latter is not. In Miéville's novel, these open spaces offset urban construction and become sites of violation. Whereas a murdered corpse is found "between the buildings," the park enables the smuggling of artefacts (Miéville, 2010, p. 1). Each incident obscures agency. A 'before' needs reconstruction. Who committed the murder, for example? How were the artefacts smuggled? In *The City & The City*, the pastoral merges with the historical to similar effects.

The City & The City's mixed genres evade a single categorization in the same way modernity does. At the same time, the novel evokes the tendency toward globalization in its imposition of myth in place of history, of foreign investments ignorant of local culture, and of the pull towards cosmopolitanism that leaves individuals untethered. The cities, Besźel and Ul Qoma, sport recognizable images representative of any urban arena in the globalized landscape.

Empty buildings littering Besźel indicate urban decay in "ruins of industry" (Miéville, 2010, p. 9). In contrast to Besźel, Ul Qoma hosts a Hilton, "an ugly fountain," "faux pagodas," and neon-lit nights (Miéville, 2010, p. 137). For housing, Ul Qoma favours concrete while Besźel retains brick (Miéville, 2010, p. 137). Each city seeks Western investment, but the flashiness of Ul Qoma suggests it is more successful than Besźel. As in many cities, crime occurs to tear their social fabric. The novel's plot pivots on a detective's quest to find a murderer bound up with a graduate student's quest to discover the historical origins of both cities. For the residents, however, the cost of belonging depends on curtailed perceptions. In keeping with several essays written on this novel, my argument focuses on "seeing," but especially on the ways curtailed perception determines civic identity. Although dissidents exist within the cities, the cost of having a home is not seeing what is empirically evident because such seeing violates boundaries. In these cities, 'unseeing' is a condition of citizenship with implications not only for those native to the cities but also immigrants.

The cities' precise location is as indeterminant as their history (Freedman (2013) makes the point that the cities sometimes seem to be placed outside Europe, in an "irreducible margin of indeterminacy" (Freedman, 2013, p 21). Among scholars who note their differences, Gomel (2018) considers Besźel to "vaguely" indicate an "Eastern European city, modelled after Budapest, with a Cyrillic-based language, shabby and economically depressed," while Ul Qoma suggests an "avatar of Istanbul, prosperous, architecturally striking and rather oriental" (Gomel, 2018, p. 146) (Gomel (2018) clarifies the word ' Besźel' means speak in Hungarian", although "not Slavic language" but influenced by Russian (Gomel, 2018, p 46). Occupying the same geographical space, their point of origin relies on ambivalence in keeping with the word 'cleave,' meaning both to cling to and to separate. Since no one knows how their situation came about, a gap exists between the knowledge of the cities' origins and their spatial organization. Among the facets of this novel, the absence of historical origins suggests a connection between efforts to globalize and the suppression of historical identity as if one depends on the other: '"The situation was never helped by

Besźel's idiotic willingness to sell what little heritage it could dig up to whoever wanted it'" (Miéville, 2010, p. 168). Miéville relies on the word "abhistory" to indicate a void, that which is not, meaninglessness (Miéville, 2010, p. 283) (Pike (2019) defines the "abcanny" and "abcity" as "That which is at once viscerally material and impossible to know, that nevertheless can be located within the space of his cities" (Pike, 2019, p 250)). It designates a conceptual space, like the idea of the pastoral, left open to the imagination yet suggested through a material actuality and complicated by the need to find meaning.

Despite global ambitions or perhaps because of them, each of the cities creates its insularity vis-à-vis the other. Inhabitants, trained to 'unsee' the other city, reinforce firm but intangible borders. As Wilcock (2020) notes, the narrative "explores the way in which borders are cognitively based, and how they are maintained and policed through ideological rather than purely physical or rational means" (Wilcock, 2020, p. 534). Trained from birth, the cities' residents, going about their daily business, observe borders in order not to see across them. Although they know people pass them in the other city, they validate only those within their city. The trope of seeing with all its figurative meanings, such as understanding and visiting, investigating, and considering, dominates the metaphor that is the narrative. As Schimaski (2016) notes, "Topography and epistemology work together in the lives of denizens and visitors" (Schimaski, 2016, p. 112). Given the restrictions on 'seeing' in the cities, the trope invites readers of the novel to reflect on the limits of perception and knowledge even as the narrative hinges on the violation of the boundaries in open spaces.

To elucidate how 'seeing' maps onto the cities, the following provides a summary. Whereas some city sections are "crosshatched" allowing the citizenry of both states to pass next to each other, other sections indicate their separate governments. Burdened by bureaucracy, police patrol each city to maintain their respective laws, but the shadowy authority named Breach watches both cities to arrest any inadvertent 'seeing' and trespassing by one citizenry onto the other's land. The organization of Breach disappears those who violate their mandate. Its power, however, depends on the community's compliance. As Ashil, one of Breach's avatars, explains, "'It's everyone in the cities who does most of the work. It works because you don't blink. That's why unseeing and unsensing are so vital. No one can admit it doesn't work. So, if you don't admit it, it does" (Miéville, 2010, p. 210). The fabrication of limited sight and ideological borders highlights an unwritten contract between citizens and authority in addition to the criminal laws within the jurisdiction of each city. The inhabitants comply because they fail to recognize Breach's mandate as an unnecessary actuality. The threat of 'disappearance' unites the community in fear just as it reifies the difference between the cities. 'Seeing' determines civic identity that, in turn, determines the permissible object of sight. Although dissidents exist within these cities, the cost of belonging, of having a home, depends on curtailed perception. It is a condition of citizenship. Their curtailed perceptions keep them from knowing a contextual actuality beyond their designated borders.

As this summary indicates, the novel mixes genres. It has been categorized as Science Fiction and Police Procedural, as a combination of fantasy and realism. Scholars have explored its implications in terms of social-political identity (Gomel 2018), colonialism (Nediger 2014), capitalist and socialist economics (Freedman 2013), and common and natural law (Hourigan 2011). Bould and Vint (2011) discount the category of Science Fiction "since [the novel's] bizarre, alternative geography is the product of ideological rather than material difference" (Bould and Vint, 2011, p. 202). Related to the trope of seeing, Kuehmichel (2014) relies on Foucault's comments on Bentham's Panopticon as a model for surveillance so that "seeing the unvisible, or taking on the authoritative gaze, is the definitive act of resistance" (Kuehmichel, 2014, p. 350), which challenges the citizens of the cities. Since the combination of genres forces the narrative across literary borders, Wilcock (2020) argues for the reader's liminality (353) while Schimanski (2016) aligns readers' experience of disorientation with that of the cities' inhabitants due to their limits on 'seeing.' Undisclosed plot details further curtail the reader's understanding as one genre slides into another. At the same time, awareness of Miéville's strategies urges the reader to find a stable perspective along the lines of the plot.

To some extent, the figure of Inspector Borlú of Besźel's Extreme Crime Squad provides that stability. Miéville terms *The City & the City* "a crime novel" that nods to noir conventions (Miéville, 2010, p. 316). In keeping with this genre, the primary detective conforms to expectations as he follows clues. The plot hinges on the discovery of the murderer of an American visiting graduate student, Mahalia Geary, who studies archaeology and history. The process generates confusion in part because the corpse, found in Besźel, results from a murder in Ul Qoma. Unravelling the cause of her murder, Borlú reconstructs Geary's recent activities and ferrets through her academic notes. His efforts demonstrate the fiction of logic akin to puzzle-solving and in keeping with police procedurals. As any typical detective in an urban setting, he knows his city of Besźel. But in his pursuit, he needs to travel to Ul Qoma. Crossing city borders challenges his expertise because it strips him of his authority as a detective and of his familiarity with neighbourhoods and topography. Crime disrupts the social fabric. But in this narrative, not only are there two social fabrics, but the respective residents are forbidden from 'seeing' across their boundaries. Borlú's single-minded pursuit, of course, eventuates in identifying and apprehending the killer. The status quo returns. In keeping with many modern detective fictions, Borlú moves on to the next crime where he will apply similar strategies.

Miéville, however, complicates the resolution. Whereas such conclusions usually reassure the reader that urban chaos can be controlled, the solution to Geary's murder occasions the inspector's transformation and displacement — he is lost to the city of his origin and joins the shadowy avatars between the cities. Likewise, solving the crime offers only a minor solution that sanctifies the inspector's logic without affecting the city's layout and the cultural framework it has instituted. As Freedman (2013) notes, "the genres of crime fiction…tend to be deflationary (and opposed to the idea of utopia)" for "the main tendency of crime fiction has been to assume that there is generally less, rather than more, to reality than may first meet the eye" (Freedman, 2013, p. 15). By reducing the narrative to crime fiction, the empirical confusion based on allowable 'seeing' becomes a plot device rather than a phenomenological condition of the citizens. In other words, while Inspector Borlú demonstrates the fictional logic of ratiocination, the rift in the social fabric effectively turns out to be elsewhere. His way of knowing, however useful, fails to reach problems deep inside the cultural framework other than the current murder receiving his attention. He merely puts a finger in a kaleidoscopic dike.

Given the various meanings of 'seeing,' the narrative implies different levels of comprehension based on the same word. As a metaphor, sight lends itself to analogies applicable to any urban centre. In modern cities, for example, people live on top of each other without 'seeing' each other. Economic stratification further enables separation within the same location. Native-born citizens, for example, may 'other' immigrants as those who do not belong. Crossing borders, however ideological, entails abiding by that country's laws with actual consequences for violating them, however ridiculous they may seem. Refugees and visitors to the novel's cities, therefore, need to undergo indoctrination into its systems before their entry. They learn and change the way they think. A Kurdish taxi driver who emigrated to Ul Qoma reports he spent one year in a refugee camp in addition to three years of study to learn not just the language but also '"to unsee the other place"' (Miéville, 2010, p. 227). With the enthusiasm of a convert, he declares Ul Qoma the "best city in the world,'" and when Borlú points out that '"Not everyone's welcoming to foreigners,"' the immigrant notes the presence of fools everywhere (Miéville, 2010, p. 227). To enter Ul Qoma, Inspector Borlú undergoes a training simulation to prepare him for crossing the border from his home in Besźel (Miéville, 2010, p. 133). The scenario of the two cities, then, exaggerates the experience of any visitors to any foreign city in the negotiation of unknown streets and unfamiliar inhabitants. Borlú experiences 'unseen' neurological changes accompanying exposure to the foreign. The necessity of such neurological changes within the novel, however, bumps against a modern actuality resulting from global capitalism. If we seek corporate icons such as MacDonald's or Starbucks in other countries, we defeat changes that travel would otherwise engender. In effect, the novel paradoxically suggests a neurological change is lost because the familiar curtails perception by promoting urban uniformity, including a space for the greenery of a park and for the refuse of a neighbourhood.

Although Besźel and Ul Qoma offer only a few recognizable structures like the Hilton in Ul Qoma, their language mirrors the way referents adjust to any urban environment. The same word even in the same language changes meaning based on context. The urban "estate" where Mahalia Geary's corpse is found differs economically from an estate located out in the countryside. The luxuriousness of the latter falsifies the public housing in apartment blocks of the former. Residents are privy to the implications of terms. Likewise, the "park" refers to sculpted concrete for skateboarding "ringed by big drum-shaped trash bins" as well as a tree-lined landscape for picnicking (Miéville, 2010, p. 1). At another remove, Canadian efforts to establish economic ties with Besźel call their efforts "the New Wolf economy" (Miéville, 2010, p.92). The project title derives from starving wolves roaming through the Besźel's streets. But it also reveals the Canadian attitude toward the citizenry as if they "were a street mongrel, maybe, or a scrawny milkrat" (Miéville, 2010, p. 92). The investment company's name for the project suggests an attitude vacant of all but superficial knowledge of the community. Implied is the willingness of those in wealthy countries to impose a sense of superiority on those with less capital. Another familiar example refers to the term "camp" wherein the meaning changes depending on purpose. On the outskirts of each city, the camps house refugees rather than open spaces for bucolic relaxation. The designation of "camp" fails to capture its impact on its respective residents. The politicians within Besźel are equally guilty of playing with referents. Aiming to attract foreign investment, Besźel exaggerates to the point of misrepresenting itself. A river running through the cities and stretching to the sea, for example, enables "Besźel's fatuous recent self-description as a 'Silicon Estuary'" (Miéville, 2010, p. 14). The advertising slogan distorts the actuality as if to invite theft of its rich resources. In summary, the urban environment demands a negotiation of linguistic referents as the actual referents change depending on perspective, which in turn, depends on location.

In addition to ambivalent referents, however, there is a lack of any referent. For these cities, the historical and the pastoral find no actuality. An urban environment easily highlights the anti-pastoral because it depends for its meaning on space visibly overtaken by either activity or construction. However, the pastoral is more difficult to locate not because of the urban setting but because it lacks an objective correlative. The open space beginning of the novel, for example, contains recognizable material. The trees in the park, however, suggest rather than present a Golden Age of pastoralism. Lacking any surrounding wilderness, it is an organic oasis among the inorganic structures of roads and buildings. The seams of human manipulation show in the park's cultivation. The novel's focus on urbanization excludes the countryside, except for refugee camps located on the cities' outskirts. Any fertile ground surrounding the city logically offers a place for farming, for work to feed an urban population. *The City & The City* relegates the pastoral and the historical to an absence, to that which is not present except in the imagination.

The citizenry of Beszel and Ul Qoma are unable to 'see' their foundational history. Although the origin of the two cities is suppressed, the topic dominates the search for Geary's murderer. The story of origin known as the "Cleavage" binds the cities together but also implies a space between them. Within the novel, no living memory exists to recount the way these two cities came about. There is an "Old Town" in Beszel and "the historic, famous Ul Maidin Avenue" in Ul Qoma. But such references limit history to a sense of the old rather than to the events which placed them there: the cities house remnants rather than foundations. History fails to interest most of the citizens in each city, as if 'unseeing' the city and the people next to them limits curiosity. Yet the retrieval of the immediate past and the cities' foundational one is thematically crucial to solving Geary's murder. As a graduate student, she associates with the few foreign students working at an archaeological dig. One of the guards speculates that they frequently breach: '"You can't avoid all breach, not in a place like this, and not with kids like these"' (Miéville, 2010, p. 186). While trained to 'see' according to each city's protocols, they are outsiders, foreign to the cities' culturally ingrained customs. For them, violation risks revocation of their Visas, and deportation, but not the loss of their citizenship and homes. Some, like Geary, exercise their curiosity.

According to the narrative, the past belongs, on one hand, to the oral imagination. The legend of Orciny arises as a "fairy tale," "children's standards" (Miéville, 2010, pp. 50-1). Accordingly, "'Orciny's the third city. It's between the other two. It's in the *disensi,* disputed zones, places that Beszel thinks are Ul Qoma's and Ul Qoma Beszel's'" (Miéville, 2010, p. 50). Not only is its location secret, but it allegedly "runs things" (Miéville, 2010, p. 50) because it derives from an "old commune" of inhabitants who did not want to be in the other cities. Instead of exiles, they are *insiles.* According to the poets, "Orciny is where the Illuminati lived" (Miéville, 2010, p. 50). Like the idea of the pastoral, Orciny becomes the subject of academic discourses and folk literature. The novel, Boden's *Between the City and the City* exemplifies a spurious history banned in each city. In the folktale, the legend stems from an imagined idealism complete with wise inhabitants. It fits into the mythical underpinnings of what Charles Taylor (2003) terms the "social imaginary," the "common understanding that makes possible common practices and a widely shared sense of legitimacy" (Taylor, 2003, p. 23). As a fairy tale passed along, it is shared between the cities. It crosses the borders, and that shared knowledge turns out to be fantasy, that is, geographically unlocatable. Like the idealized pastoral, the record of Orciny is academic, that is theoretical and irretrievable.

Yet the mystery of Orciny parallels that of Breach. They are both 'unseen.' At times within the novel, they are equated with each other. Mahalia's American mother notes "'It sounds like that Orciny was like the Breach'" (Miéville, 2010, p. 80). Borlú instils Orciny with substance when he thinks Breach fears Orciny's existence despite their denial of it (Miéville, 2010, p. 246). Mahalia's friend Yolanda "thought [Breach] was Orciny'" (Miéville, 2010, p. 246), "'the name Breach calls itself'" (Miéville, 2010, p.211). Yet Breach, whatever it calls itself, is a presence. Even as a child, Inspector Borlú senses the interference of Breach. Feeling watched as an adult, he "notes an old woman" barely discernible in the dark; he fails to figure out "which city she was in" (Miéville, 2010, p. 198). In other words, empirical evidence based on shadowy people attests to Breach's existence. They disappear inhabitants who violate by 'seeing'; the organization relies on a tactic common in modern autocratic governments. They erase their people.

On the other hand, and in contrast to the legend of Orciny, Ul Qoma houses an archaeological dig alongside the park. The site exposes "the remnants of a material culture" that is unclear in terms of identifying a singular original people (Miéville, 2010, p. 150). Yet even this site generates a mythical history. As Professor Nancy explains, "'We've never found written records from the Precursor Age except a few poems fragments to make sense of any of it'" (Miéville, 2010, p. 150). As a result, stories ensued. One group posited a "'hypothetical civilization before Ul Qoma and Besźel that systematically dumped all the artefacts in the region,...mixed them all up and buried them again'" (Miéville, 2010, p. 150). The explanation aims to account for objects indicative of different millennia but found next to each other (Miéville, 2010, p. 150). The thesis titles of graduate students provide no better idea as to what precisely is in the dig. One belongs to the murdered victim; "*A Hermeneutics of Identity* stems from the layouts of gears" (Miéville, 2010, p. 88). Her graduate colleague was working on "*Representing Gender and the Other in Precursor Age Artifacts*" (Miéville, 2010, p. 170). The recovered items include an "opaque rubble of bottles, orreries, axe heads, parchment scraps" (Miéville, 2010, p. 261), and "Precursor lingams and ancient pipettes" (Miéville, 2010, p. 262). Instead of illuminating history, the confusion of objects invites further speculation. Even archaeology fails to contribute to the knowledge of foundational origins.

Given the restrictions on the citizens within their respective cities, a minority of dissidents arise. Political identification leads to identity politics both for and against the ideology constitutive of the borders. On one hand, are the Unificationists who advocate for merging the two cities. They covertly communicate with each other across their borders. They take on Breach's authoritative gaze using demonstrations and graffiti aiming to resist the separation of the two cities. On the other hand, are the militaristic Nationalists, who insist on the entitlement and integrity of their city, ready themselves to defend its borders and war against their neighbouring city. They aim to support Breach by becoming paramilitary. In contrast to the Unificationists, they favour weapons. The result of such divisions, however, makes all groups vulnerable to manipulation by those holding either political power or concealed resentments. Thus, the council member Buric, responsible for stealing artefacts, relies on Besźel's nationalists for protection against his citizens as he affiliates himself with a foreign corporation. In other words, belief in the rightness of their causes exposes all the dissidents to exploitation and associates them with criminality, the Unificationists I Breach and the Nationalists I their police forces. The damage spirals outward. In an anticlimactic incident, the Unificationists stage a revolt. Two buses crash and breach. Collateral damage are the refugees who were being taken to camps. Other citizens in each city become victims when chaos ensues in what will be termed "Riot Night" (Miéville, 2010, p. 309). In short, the few undermine the many.

In summary, the obfuscation of origins suggests the irretrievability of history except in an idealized vision of myth and the incomprehensible detritus left behind. By way of comparison, urban parks hint at a pastoral landscape without actualizing it. The pastoral and Orciny are constructs of the mind. Since sight is curtailed, the citizens' memories only go back to their separate locations, after the Cleavage that separates and binds them together. Their collective memory is insular excepting the fantasy of Orciny. Rather than a mainstream history vying against an alternative version, a historical foundation is absent and replaced with an "abhistory" (Miéville, 2010, p. 283). Without historical events, residents are vulnerable to ideological manipulation complementing their restricted vision. Without evidence that verifies the historical past, the narrative opens a doorway to creating fatuous ones. Authorities whether with global economic goals or in defence of their borders can impose a fiction such as a communal Orciny in a pastoral Golden Age.

Mahalia Geary exemplifies the ways such fictions work as she falls victim to a conspiracy that leads to her murder. She illustrates belief as a way of knowing based on Bowden's book written in his youth. Although he has renounced the book's claims, Bowden's

Between the City and the City fuels her search. Her belief in the existence of Orciny somewhat aligns her with the dissident groups she pursues for information. The lack of historical knowledge, however, allows her to fall victim to an economic scheme. Thinking she returns objects that belong to the *insiles* of Orciny, she smuggles artefacts from the archaeological dig where she works. Located alongside a parkland, the dig "looked at first like a wasteland, …scrub punctuated with old stones of fallen temples" (Miéville, 2010, p. 144). Yet it is precisely this landscape, the dig leading into the park, that allows Geary to smuggle artefacts. Borlú reconstructs her crime by walking through a gate into "not much of a park this close to the excavation, but scrub and a few trees crossed by paths" (Miéville, 2010, p. 263). It is located "only slightly in Besźel" with a "little stretch of totality cutting the Ul Qoman sections off from each other" (Miéville, 2010, p. 263). Although Breach supervises such "crosshatches," the border allows Geary to stand near it and drop the artefact through a hole in her pocket from Ul Qoma onto the soil of Besźel. Either the council member Buric or one of his minions can then pick it up with neither Geary nor Buric breaching. By the parkland, a historical object is translated, and carried 160 cross, merging legal and geographic violations. Yet the object remains un-decoded, not understood, and destined to end up in foreign hands that have no interest in its origin but only in the artefact's mechanics.

Like the dissidents, Mahalia Geary believes she does the right thing. Yet in addition to violating legal boundaries, her theft contributes to obscuring any reconstruction of a historical culture based on objects. She eventually realizes her victimization. Although her epiphany remains undisclosed in the narrative, Borlú deduces her realization in his efforts to solve her murder. The narrative finally reveals that she steals for a corporation conducting research and development aimed to support their investment in Besźel. Believing the disgraced historian Bowden is also under threat from the conspirators, Geary confronts him with her knowledge, and he arranges her murder to protect himself. Ultimately Geary's trespass across borders is an intellectual one: she figures things out just as detective Borlú does. Their 'seeing' combines knowledge with understanding. Each seeks information:

Geary as a scholar and Borlú as a detective. Each pays a price. Borlú's efforts and Geary's interests inadvertently suggest the danger of mistaking fiction (Orciny) for fact (unknown), a mistake partially resulting from the obfuscation of historical origins. Each violates the permissible object of sight. Borlú will breach and break the condition of his citizenship, but Geary's violation stems from challenging the official story which is, after all, concocted to deceive her.

The insularity of the cities surfaces when Borlú realizes that the foreign investors do not have "the fear," "[t]hat Breach freeze, that obedience reflex shared in Ul Qoma and Besźel" (Miéville, 2010, p. 273). Without fear, the CEO dismisses Borlú's attempt to arrest him: "'You think anyone beyond these odd little cities cares about you?'" (Miéville, 2010, p. 286). His words dismantle Breach by invoking the force of his home government: "'It's funny enough the idea of either Besźel or Ul Qoma going to war against a real country'" (Miéville, 2010, p. 287). With this statement, the narrative self-reflexively identifies its fictionalization. Its metaphoric aspects — that these are two different cities that may not see each other — seem to halt with the CEO's reminder of actual capitalist colonialism. The economically deprived become victims of corporate investment. Their local identities do not matter. The constraints imposed on their citizens fail to obtain in the global economy. Although the dissidents focus on borders — either their elimination or protection — the actual threat is the corporation aiming to take their resources and actively take their artefacts. The cities' strict ideological boundaries evaporate; the CEO takes off in a helicopter. He simply flies away leaving a criminal and political mess behind.

While the narrative casts the global capitalists as opportunistic at best, the mundane reasons for Geary's murder undercut the narrative's noire elements. The representation of Breach steps into the gap, figuratively and literally. Breach's gaze is always outward as if in denial of their own space. Whereas disorientation signifies the citizens' perceptions, Breach occupies a liminal place that defies an exact location. Borlú breaches as a result of doing his job. He hunts a man who shot Mahalia's friend, Yolanda, as she tries to leave Ul Qoma. To aim his gun, he must see into Besźel from Ul Qoma. While the very borders let the criminal escape, the detective needs to break Breach's mandates regarding those borders to stop the criminal. Taken by Breach, Borlú is interrogated according to their justice of unknown punishments. In their custody, he works on solving the crime, which allows Breach to investigate him as he investigates Geary's murder. Accompanied and guided by the avatar Ashil, Borlú now moves between the cities and among the citizens. Within Breach's headquarters, however, Borlú "could not tell where [he] was" (Miéville, 2010, p. 242). He leaves and returns several times, but descriptions usually place him within a room with little reference to the organization's physical placement amid the cities. For Borlú, "The Breach was nothing"; "The Breach is a void full of angry police" (Miéville, 2010, p. 248). Once with them, he becomes a displaced person. In short, he is in a camp similar to that of the refugees.

In the process of apprehending Geary's murderer, Borlú takes on the temporary authority of Breach. He aims to arrest Bowden who attempts to escape through the interstices of the city. Once in between the cities, Borlú's orientation devolves from the restrictions of seeing he had been subject to. He asks Bowden, "'Where's here?'" (Miéville, 2010, p. 297). Unable to locate himself, Borlú becomes topographically lost. His loss, however, extends further than the narrative specifies. As the phenomenologist, Gaston Bachelard has argued space determines identity and memory that enables a sense of being and meaning. The narrative suggests that space locates us and provides form, a kind of border responsible for definition. Without such a definition, we slip from actuality.

Without a border to engulf him in one of the cities and without trespass into one of the cities, Borlú labels Bowden "Schrödinger's pedestrian" (Miéville, 2010, p. 295). When Bowden finally surrenders to Borlú and turns over to Breach, Borlú does not know what happens to him. In being between the cities and then disappearing, Bowden occupies the box with Schrödinger's cat. He is either dead or alive, neither dead nor alive until located and seen. He becomes like Orciny and the pastoral, conjured through imagination. Both Bowden and Borlú share the consequence of disappearance, no matter their different motives. Although what happens to Bowden remains undisclosed, Borlú keeps asking "'When can I go home?'"

(Miéville, 2010, p. 310). Even after he solves the crime, he cannot leave. His longing to return home, to what seems the squalor of Besźel, attests to the way memories and habits claim people to inform their personal history, however limited it may be to others. An avatar of Breach explains that once you see, "'You'll never unsee again'" (Miéville, 2010, p. 310). In other words, the limitations on 'seeing' have been lifted, and once lifted, cannot be reversed.

Once taken by Breach, Borlú gains knowledge that disenfranchises him from citizenship. Although he had sensed Breach and had even spotted some of their avatars patrolling the cities, he now joins their shadowy existence, "[h]iding like books in a library" (Miéville, 2010, p. 248). And like Geary when she realized Orciny did not exist, his knowledge circumscribes him and his ability to act. The detective pays for this knowledge with the loss of his home and friends because once he can see beyond the borders, he must relinquish his former self, an identity rooted in relationships and place. Even his name changes from Tyador to Tye (Miéville, 2010, p. 253). His position of liminality allows him to see both cities as long as he remains virtually unseen. Breach allows him one letter to say goodbye, ostensibly to let his friends know he is still alive. Without borders, Borlú remains displaced. He becomes at once cosmopolitan and invisible. As one of Breach's avatars, his allegiance is to liminality. His identity maintains consistency only through his occupation: "'I'm a detective'" (Miéville, 2010, p. 311) just as Bowden maintained "'I'm an archaeologist and a historian'" when he walked in-between the cities "rootless and untethered, purposeful and without a country" (Miéville, 2010, p. 298). In making such claims, Bowden draws attention to the problem of being a historian without a verifiable, witnessed history while Borlú remains in that "untethered" space.

With its emphasis on dislocation, the novel evokes actuality throughout its fantasy. The status of modern refugees provides a salient example. Syrians fleeing from interminable war or Bangladeshis fleeing climate change leave homes. Whatever the situation which forced them to do so, whatever the condition of that home, they may suffer the same longing for it Borlú expresses. As a displaced population, they frequently dwell in the shadows as Borlú does once he breaches. They occupy a liminal position between the past they left and the future they face, between the native inhabitants and a new culture. While Borlú demonstrates the advantages of liminality in enabling a change in consciousness resulting from a change in perspective, it is as ambivalent as the definition of cleave. Borlú, after all, survives, but his experience of displacement transforms him as it does for refugees who are victims of war and climate. Sometimes they move a short distance in terms of miles. Yet they cross borders and into a bureaucracy different from what they left. Unlike Borlú, many need to either give up their profession or retrain in it. Like Borlú, they leave everything behind and often end up in camps. As the taxi driver in Ul Qoma exemplifies, they need to learn a new language and with it, a unique way of 'seeing,' if the offer of staying is even possible.

Without a sense of either geographical or historical place, how do we make meaning? Reading Miéville's "abhistory" in tandem with concepts of pastoral and anti-pastoral highlights the construction of the pastoral as a void similar to that of Orciny. Designating the anti-pastoral by a lack of green space, the label paradoxically involves substance because, like Breach, it offsets a city's construction and announces either the remnants of activity or the blatant absence of it. The anti-pastoral may contain material objects that offer analyses. The opening image in the novel and this essay indicates a lack of nurturing with its dead trees and its garbage. It is comparable to the archaeological dig, which uncovers indeterminant artefacts. Each location offers a surplus. These visible scenes enable the label of anti-pastoral as if it had an empirical landscape for comparison. But it does not. The pastoral, like Orciny, remains a literary construct, the fantasy of a Golden Age unseen in actuality. Like Schrödinger's pedestrian, the pastoral is unlocatable and non-geographic. Unlike the 'uncanny,' it has no history. We might imaginatively locate it between the cities as an environment unrepresented in either urban or rural settings. Finally, Miéville's concept of "abhistory" within the novel invites the acknowledgement of an 'abpastoral' because the pastoral occurs fictionally rather than topographically.

Works Cited

Bachelard, Gaston (1958) *Poetics of Space*. Trans. Maria Jolas. NY: Penguin, 2014 edition.

Bould, Mark, Sherryl Vint (2011) *The Routledge Concise History of Science Fiction*. London and New York: Routledge.

Freedman, Carl. (2013) "From Genre to Political Economy: Miéville's *The City & The City* and Uneven Development." *CR: The New Centennial Review*, 13:2, pp. 13-30.

Gomel, Elana. (2018) "' Divided Against Itself': Dual Urban Chronotopes." Ed. Meyrav Koren-Kuik. *Cityscapes of the Future: Urban Spaces in Science Fiction*. Leiden: Netherlands; Boston, MA: Brill Academic Publishers, pp. 139-150.

Hourigan, Daniel. (2011) "Breach! The Law's *Joissance* in Miéville's *The City & The City.*"

Law, Culture, and the Humanities. 9.1, pp. 156-68

Kuehmichel, Shannon. (2014) "Thriving in the Gap: Visual and Linguistic Meaning Unmaking in *The City and The City*." *Extrapolation: A Journal of Science Fiction and Fantasy*. 55.3 (fall), pp. 349-367.

Miéville, China (2010) *The City & The City*. NY: Ballantine, Random House.

Nediger, Will. (2014) "Whorfianism in Colonial Encounters from Melville to Miéville." *Mosaic*.47.3, pp. 19-34.

Pike, David L. (2019) "China Miéville's Fantastic Slums and the Urban Abcanny." *Science Fiction Studies*. 46.2, pp. 250-266.

Schimanski, Johan. (2016) "Seeing Disorientation: China Miéville's *The City & the City*." *Culture, Theory, and Critique*, 57.2 (April), pp. 106-120.

Stackniak, Alexander (2014) "Progressing from Definition to Heuristic: The Uncanny and the Abcanny." *Berfrois*. 21 January. Available from https://www.berfrois.com/

Taylor, Charles. (2003) *Modern Social Imaginaries*. Durham and London: Duke University Press.

Wilcock, Simone. (2020) "Seeing is Believing: Perception and Liminality in China Miéville's *The City & The City*. *Critique: Studies in Contemporary Fiction*. 61:5, pp. 534-44.

Irish Protestant Poets and the Dichotomy of Urban Belfast and Rural West

The thematic importance and ubiquity of "place" in modern Irish poetry cannot be overstated. Ireland's history of cultural and religious conflict has a particular bearing as it relates to place, having been the site of land confiscation, settler colonialism, and political partition. As a place, culture, and identity are closely interconnected concepts in Ireland, where "cultural identity has often been interpreted as bound up with place" (Kennedy-Andrews, 2008, p. 1), writers of Protestant background have especially been given to expressions of ambivalence in their work. In part, this is a testament to the endurance of late 19th- to early 20th-century Irish cultural nationalism's precepts establishing authentic Irishness as being Catholic, Gaelic, and rural. For those of supposedly alien culture, ethnicity, and faith, one's notion of belonging was subject to disputation. Irish identity was symbolically bifurcated following partition and the founding of separate political entities in 1921. Thus, another aspect exacerbating anxieties about belonging in Ireland for the poets in this chapter has to do with the distinguishing features of the dominant culture of the region from which they came.

For the arbiters of Irish authenticity, the North bore the added ignominy of industrialization and urbanization, quintessentially represented by Belfast and its surrounding suburbs. This is part of Ireland where the poets whose work is to be examined hail from constitutionally British, geographically Irish, and culturally divided. The poetry of Louis MacNeice (1907-1963), the first major Northern Protestant poet post-partition, and Michael Longley (1939–), whose career coincided with the violence of the Troubles, exhibits a shared struggle to come to terms with one's sense of place in Ireland. For many nationalists and Catholics, Belfast was regarded as "an overt symbol of British colonization on Irish soil" (Pelaschiar, 2000, pp. 118-119). Cultural nationalism conceived of Gaelic Irish identity as essentially rural (Potts, 2011, p. 175) and insisted on "an immanent and natural link between the peasantry and the land" (O'Toole, 1985, p. 111). Ireland's West had assumed a preeminent position in nationalist formulations of true Irishness as the region connoted cultural survival, racial purity, and traditional pastoral. For much of the twentieth century, this idealized interpretation of Irish identity rooted in the primordial West held sway.

It is of added significance then that MacNeice and Longley have each used the West as a site of exploration for mitigating an unsettled sense of place. Both poets engage in reproducing elements of traditional pastoral, giving rise to a discernible dichotomy in the way that the poetry treats Ireland's North and West. The textual tension between images of peace and rural refuge on the one hand and images of conflict and urban threat on the other is a notable pastoral convention (Hunt, 1992, p. 15). So too is the textual awareness of the town/country divide, wherein certain limits of the bucolic world are acknowledged and rustic identity bespeaks an important sign of differentiation from that beyond it (Fairweather, 2000, p. 279). As an urban setting is much less likely to be assimilated into the national imaginary than the rural landscape (Bradley, 2017, p. 97), the city, as a site of commerce, heavy industry and sectarian violence, offers little in the way of offering communion with a desired sense of Irishness. Thus, their work might be said to perpetuate common literary representations of the city as a "negative center of meaning," of "power and possession," and in the case of Longley, "a slaughterhouse" (Scherpe and Roetze, 1992-1993, p. 139).

Bucolic poetry has been a means for coming to terms with war and cultural crisis since Virgil (Potts, 2000, p. 2). Both MacNeice and Longley make the physical and spiritual departure from city to country in a similar attempt to attune to, or attain, an unqualified Irish identity, often in the context of violent conflict. Yet, the conditions of Irishness under which they do so are ones laid down by the tenets of cultural nationalism, playing an important role in how the poetry treats its two primary Irish settings. The Northern city is typically characterized by its most unattractive stereotypes and defects while the Western countryside acts as a locus of desire and fulfillment. This dichotomized manner in which urban Belfast and rural West are represented attests to a tendency among Protestant poets to abide by established territorial assumptions when it comes to the notion of identity and place in Ireland.

The Two Poles of Politicized Culture

For poets invested in mitigating an uncertain sense of Irishness, Belfast may have presented the least accommodating grounds on which to pursue such mitigation. As the Protestant state espoused supremacist and prejudicial attitudes towards the Catholic minority, affiliating either too closely or comfortably with Belfast risks an unwanted association with the more objectionable elements of Northern Protestant identity. In a period when Catholicism had become a "vital binding force" expressing "the core of what it meant to be Irish" (Townshend, 1999, p. 44), any gestures of attachment to the capital of a state founded on the "core values of Protestantism and Britishness" (Brewer and Higgins, 1998, p. 88), could be interpreted as compromising one's right to any claim of Irishness. Northern Catholics shared their sense of cultural identity with their co-religionists in independent Ireland, but the establishment of Northern Ireland left them "defined as outsiders … positioned in a social structure that rendered them 'second-class citizens'" (Brewer and Higgins, 1998, p. 88). Perceptions of Belfast have themselves been subject to dichotomization:

> Protestants consider it as their own creation … the tie they have to it is often tinged with pride in the achievements of its founding fathers, who are their ancestors, men who 'invented' and created the city through hard work, labour, patience and endurance, reclaiming land from the sea and from the bog, building industries and shipyards, creating civilization and progress where there was nothing but unproductive land. The relationship that Catholics have with Belfast, on the other hand, is complicated by these very origins, by the Protestant ethos that generated it… (Pelaschiar, 2000, p. 118)

Exhortations of Protestant achievement and productivity carry an implied indictment of stereotypical Catholic incompetency and idleness. Nationalist ideology, with its "combination of Catholic social values" and "territorial claim to the whole island" (Townshend, 1999, p. 147), further complicates the matter since the popular perception of the city has been created in the Protestant community's exclusivist self-image. For the later poet Longley, the destructiveness of the Troubles compounds Belfast's differentiation from the rural Irish ideal by its violent transformation to an inner-city wasteland (Kirkland, 2009, p. 27).

Idealization of the West had both cultural and political motivations that were synthesized in the early decades of independence. The West's natural features lent themselves to a romantic ideation that seemed to topographically embody nationalist aspirations. The Young Irelander Thomas Davis' ballad "The West's Asleep," in which he celebrates "That chainless wave and lovely land/Freedom and Nationhood demand," is probably the most notable early example of this type of politicization. The myth of the West was both a reaction against colonial stereotypes and a response to the Irish people's need for a national identity:

> They [nationalists] sanctified the Irish people as heroic and noble with a glorious Gaelic past and propagated the west as intact and authentic because it was distanced from the Anglicised, corrupted east and thus retained its Gaelic-speaking, old-fashioned lifestyle. In this way, an idealised west was created by cultural nationalism: as the preserver of the Gaelic language and culture, the west represents the Irish national identity, characterised by a timelessly noble peasantry and an idyllic countryside. (He, 2017, p. 1)

As this version of true Irishness is oppositional to every aspect of colonial identity, with its accompanying language (English), religion (Protestantism), and laws (British), one would be forgiven for assuming that Western mythologization was a primarily Catholic concern. Davis was Protestant, as were other leaders of the Young Ireland movement of the 1840s, and much of the literature of the later Revival venerating the West was the work of writers of Protestant background like Lady Gregory, W.B. Yeats, and J.M. Synge. Marie Bourke (2000, p. 30) comments:

> Apparently untouched by progress or political turmoil, people lived in close communities, led primitive lifestyles and preserved customs and traditions from generation to generation [...] Artists discovered that by using imagery associated with the West in a new

and inventive manner, they were able to develop a body of work that looked distinctively Irish.

As the societies on both sides of the border post-partition became increasingly defined by the cultural dictates of their respective majorities, attempts by writers of Protestant background to appear "distinctively Irish" came under greater scrutiny. For MacNeice and Longley, their poems set in the part of the island that was figured to have retained the last vestiges of the essence of Irishness (Hanrahan, 2004, p. 95) would often be read as explorations into the extent to which the poets themselves could be said to manifest that essence.

Louis MacNeice

Though MacNeice was born in Belfast and brought up in a northern suburb called Carrickfergus, his connection to his place of origin would be complicated by disturbing memories of childhood and repressive religious culture. Carrickfergus has been described as MacNeice's "first world" underlying the rest of his poetry set in Ireland, "a vivid microcosm, an underworld or unconscious, stained by his mother's death and other unhappiness" (Brearton and Longley, 2012, p. x). When combined with sectarian history and Protestant religiosity, the effect is one of alienation and repulsion. As MacNeice (1965, p. 216) states:

> The human elements of this world need not be detailed: guilt, hell fire, Good Friday, the doctor's cough, hurried lamps in the night, melancholia, mongolism, and violent sectarian voices. All this sadness and conflict and attrition and frustration ... so that from a very early age I began to long for something different, to construct various dream worlds which I took were on the map.

The West indeed figures as a constructed dream world, but the North of greater Belfast is quite literally a nightmarish landscape. The more complex social dimensions of his surroundings possibly lost on MacNeice as a child are recognized by the poet in adulthood, and when his Northern home is recalled, it is done so in a way that ideologically and spiritually distances him from it.

MacNeice often emphasizes Belfast's commercial and industrial characteristics to negative effect. "A city built upon mud … veneered with the grime of Glasgow … wet/Pavement … dripping shrubbery … smoking chimneys" (*Autumn Journal* "XVI"); "Belfast, devout and profane and hard … hammers playing in the shipyard, /Time punched with holes like a steel sheet, time/Hardening the faces, veneering with a grey and speckled rime" ("Valediction"). Far from being a testament to Protestant achievement and enterprise, industrialization and urbanity are seen to have dehumanizing effects, contrasting greatly with the colourful vitality of the Western peasantry. In the Northern city, existence is boiled down to the exertion of labour in dirty and drab environs. The values of "A culture built upon profit" where "the money that comes in goes out to make more money" are undermined by the presence of "Thousands of men whom nobody will employ" ("XVI").

The city's sectarian religious and economic dynamics are given a sustained critical treatment in "Belfast." MacNeice (1990, p. 60) admits, "My conception of Belfast, built up since early childhood, demanded that it should always be grey, wet, repellent and its inhabitants dour, rude, and callous." Yet as "a poet who always cherished long-term hopes for unity" (Longley, 1994, p. 145), his conception carries political connotations, evidenced in his assertion that "the North was tyranny" (MacNeice, 1990, p. 60). The poem applies several stereotypes that align with a nationalist perspective. MacNeice (1990, p. 62) deems the city's personality harsh, and his poem depicts Belfast in exacting terms:

> The hard cold fire of the northerner
> Frozen into his blood from the fire in his basalt
> Glares from behind the mica of his eyes
> And the salt carrion water brings him wealth.

The opening stanza evokes stereotypical Northern Protestant "dour determination," "solidity," and "hard-headedness" (O'Halloran, 1987, p. 41). As the poem progresses, one might add hard-heartedness and cold-bloodedness to this list of attributes. "Belfast" envisions a city "only known under the guise of tyranny" (Brown, 1998, p. 21), having both its superficial and spiritual ugliness highlighted:

> Down there at the end of the melancholy lough
> Against the lurid sky over the stained water
> Where hammers clang murderously on the girders
> Like crucifixes the gantries stand.
>
> And in the marble stores rubber gloves like polyps
> Cluster; celluloid, painted ware, glaring
> Metal patents, parchment lampshades, harsh
> Attempts at buyable beauty.

These stanzas impugn industry and consumerism in a manner that mirrors the nationalist sentiment that held Belfast to be alien, materialistic, unromantic, and spiritually deficient (O'Halloran, 1987, p. 13). The city's "despondent mode and mood" is brought on by "the religious noise of Ulster and the sounds of the Belfast shipyards, [and] shops full of manmade materials" (Cunningham, 2012, p. 95). The commodities are likened to polyps, suggesting a cancerous nature, a further indictment of the city's modern bourgeois values which could not be more at odds with the folkways of the Western Irish hinterland. As the gantries in the lough are likened to crucifixes, politicized religious symbolism takes on a more sinister complexion in the increasingly violent closing stanzas:

> In the porch of the chapel before the garish Virgin
> A shawled factory-woman as if shipwrecked there
> Lies a bunch of limbs glimpsed in the cave of gloom
> By us who walk in the street so buoyantly and glib.
>
> Over which country of cowled and haunted faces
> The sun goes down with a banging of Orange drums
> While the male kind murders each woman
> To whose prayer for oblivion answers no Madonna.

In a nationalist gender paradigm (Cathleen Ni Houlihan, the Shan Van Vocht, Mother Ireland) (Kennedy-Andrews, 2008, p. 6), there is little doubt as to the Protestant identity of the murderous "male kind." The shawled woman recalls traditional depictions of the Virgin Mary, making a clear political statement. As Edna Longley (21994, p. 189) comments, "To characterize Irish nationalism ... as archetypally female both gives it a mythic pedigree and exonerates it from aggressive and oppressive intent." As the woman is an innocent corollary for nationalist Ireland, her murder to the backdrop of triumphalist Orange Order drumming reads like a condemnation of the Northern Irish state and a lament for unrealized unity, with her status as a factory worker underscoring urban debasement.

In poems set in the West, where notions of authenticity, mythology, and national essence persist (Duffy, 1997, pp. 68-69), MacNeice treads more respectfully. E. Longley (2000, p. 126) notes, "An implicitly Protestant poetic entry into western Catholic communities tends to walk on tiptoe." There is an undercurrent in MacNeice's work of a sincere longing to identify with the part of the country that would render the assertion of one's Irishness unassailable. Cultivation of a Western identity has its roots in childhood, as the poet's sister (Nicholson, 1974, p. 14) explains:

> Our parents had both been born and spent their childhoods in Connemara ... my mother spoke of it so constantly and with such love and such longing that I think it was she who really made it come alive for Louis and myself ... It became for us ... where we thought that by rights we should be living ... We were in our minds a West of Ireland family exiled from our homeland.

Thus, MacNeice relied on his parents' connection to the region to foster a sense of Irishness. As he did not visit the West until his twentieth birthday, his conception of the region is underlined by two decades of youthful fantasy and "nostalgia for somewhere I had never been" (MacNeice, 1965, p. 217). While nostalgia serves as a bridge between memory and longing (Frawley, 1998-1999, p. 270), we might ask ourselves what it is that the poet is longing for. In the Irish pastoral mode, the loss of culture, rather than nature, is lamented (Frawley, 1998-1999, p. 272), and the poet's romantic pretensions tend to mesh with nationalist constructs of the region's synonymity with Irish roots, identity, and origins (Boey, 2008, p. 28). For example, in "Auden and MacNeice: Their Last Will and Testament," the poet claims kinship with the Western peasantry, "my own in particular," crediting them for his "peasant vitality and ... peasant's sense of humour," evoking Irish republicanism's social ideal of the rural and pious peasant-family utopia (Gellner, 1983, p. 91).

Utopian imagery drawn from traditional pastoral frequently appears in MacNeice's Western poems. In "Sligo and Mayo," from "The Closing Album" sequence, natural features are described in a manner that registers pastoral escapism and nostalgia; "the country was soft ... shadows of clouds on the mountains moving/Like browsing cattle and ease ... twilight filtered on the heather/Water-music filled the night air ... night came down on the bogland/With all-enveloping wings." Observation of the land and its natural beauties in a self-conscious return to nature constitutes an identity-forming process in Irish pastoral (Frawley, 1998-1999, p. 273). However, Sukanta Chaudhuri (1989, p. 4) notes that the characteristic achievement of pastoral is also its characteristic danger; "The artifice is often too patently artificial or trivial: pleasant and untaxing, deliberately confined to superficialities instead of penetrating to the primary impulse." This is paradigmatic of the artifice inherent to politicized constructs of "place." What to Irish nationalists was a green unspoiled landscape was to British imperialists an untamed wilderness justifying their control (Potts, 2011, p. 7). In as much as the West is figured as a site of escape, the unreality of this "dream world" is recognized in light of the then-erupting Second World War:

> Salmon in the Corrib
> Gently swaying
> And the water combed out
> Over the weir
> And a hundred swans
> Dreaming on the harbour
> The war came down on us here.
>
> The night was gay
> With the moon's music
> But Mars was angry
> On the hills of Clare
> And September dawned
> Upon willows and ruins:
> The war came down on us here. ("Galway")

Neutral Ireland's "self-contained world" is "a good dream that he knows must end when he returns to the nightmare of war-threatened England" (Brown, 1975, p. 101). The tenacious refrain that closes each Yeatsian stanza unsettles the litany of pastoral imagery preceding it, making timeless Ireland and the impending future seem incongruous (Johnston, 1985, p. 221). However, just as war is a reminder of an inability to escape into the dream world, the pastoral depictions are a reminder of there being no escaping from the desire for a mythic home grounded in his Irish origins (Kennedy-Andrews, 2008, pp. 45-46).

Notes of desire are registered in poems that recollect MacNeice's parents. In "The Strand," a vicarious homecoming takes place that dramatizes the way that MacNeice had, since childhood, identified with his mythic home. He admits, "All the time my reactions to the West were half my father's. That is, I was not seeing the West for the first time; I had been born there sixty years before" (MacNeice, 1965, p. 111). "My father," the speaker states, "So loved the western sea and no tree's green/Fulfilled him like these contours of Slievemore/Menaun and Croaghaun and the bogs between." His love for the landscape reflects that of his father's; the strand's "mirror of wet sand," where "my steps repeat," is the same "mirror [that] caught his shape which catches mine." However, while MacNeice's father "has always been at home in the West … the son knows that his wish for such reciprocity is hopelessly paradoxical" (Longley, 2000, pp. 123-124). As he writes of himself in "Carrick Revisited," "Torn before birth from where my fathers dwelt … the pre-natal mountain is far away." He is to remain like those who "find their dream's endorsement/In certain long low islets snouting towards the west/Like cubs that have lost their mother" ("Last Before America"). It is telling that a dream of wedding Irish identity place is not imagined in the North, the place of his birth that has made him a bastard/Out of the West by urban civilization" ("Western Landscape"). When deciding on the place where the sense of one's Irishness can find its greatest fulfilment, it is "the West" that is "all the world … The chosen … The Best," not the inimical cityscape of Belfast.

Michael Longley

Longley's poetry of "place" is indelibly linked to concepts of "home." The two distinct homes in his work are Belfast, where he was born and raised, and Carrigskeewaun in County Mayo, which he has frequently visited since 1970. While Longley has resided in Belfast for most of his life, a greater sense of attachment is expressed towards his Western home. His poems set in the region participate in a type of discourse alluded to by Peter McDonald (1992, p. 65):

> 'Home', as a word simultaneously private and public in its connotations ... The resonance of 'home' in Irish poetry is due partly to its potency in the discourses of sentiment and nostalgia, its emotional pull on the individual back to something larger than his identity.

More recently, Longley has embraced dual identity, stating in 2009, "Because I was born and bred in Belfast, I'm Irish. Because m*y mother and father were English, I'm British. I have been both British and Irish all my life" (M. Longley and E. Longley, 2009). However, statements made earlier in his career reveal a greater sense of uncertainty. In 1969, the year of his first book's publication early in the Troubles, he reflected, "I see that I have been schizophrenic on the levels of nationality, class and culture ... it is personally uncomfortable for me to question continually my own identity" (Pierce, 2000, p. 765).

Longley's Western home gradually takes precedence over his original. For the poet, "the notion of home is not based on birthright or divine sanction ... home always has to be constructed, built up through a process of personal, emotional and imaginative attachment" (Kennedy-Andrews, 2008, p. 141). Yet as home functions as both "a place to escape to and a place to escape from" (George, 1999, p. 9), where the poetic persona attaches itself through such processes is significant. The politicized cultural currency of the poetry's preferred landscape cannot be overlooked. In Longley's case, the West does not conform to a traditional understanding of home as the place of one's ancestors and origin. It does, however, maintain its status as the bedrock of Irish identity, shaped by nationalist narratives involving racial purity, rural simplicity, and Catholic familialism. While some have read Longley's West as "a personally imagined world, freed of territorial significance and national meaning" (Kennedy-Andrews, 2008, p. 139), one cannot ignore the region's reputation as the repository of "the true sense of Irishness" that "remained unsullied by Anglicization, which had infested the north-east and caused the Ulster Protestants to forget their Irishness" (Nagle, 2016, p. 100). As "home" is "the desired place that is fought for and established as the exclusive domain of a few" (George, 1999, p. 9), an Ulster Protestant poet of English parentage seeking rootedness in the locus of Irishness is immensely symbolic.

In Longley's early work (four volumes between 1969 and 1979), Belfast weighs heavily on the poet's conscience. The advent of the Troubles forces him to confront its jarring effects and question the feasibility of maintaining a "home" in Belfast. Concern for his endangered city appears in the epistolary sequence, "Letters," which is dedicated to fellow Northern poets James Simmons, Derek Mahon, and Seamus Heaney. The opening poem, "To Three Irish Poets," considers them Irish with none of the qualifications typical of Northern Irish identity discourse. At a time when "Irish" was a byword for nationalist political sympathies, Longley's confident label distances him from his community. The typical Northern Protestant "has no difficulty, no identity crisis. He knows he is British" (Harkness, 1988, p. 130), making the title a meaningful statement of dissociation. His son's birth causes him to reflect on the volatile home that the child inherits, "About his ears, our province reels/Pulsating like his fontanel":

> Blood on the kerbstones, and my mind
> Dividing like a pavement,
> Cracked by the weeds, by the green grass
> That covers our necropolis,
> The pity, terror... What comes next
> Is a lacuna in the text

Belfast's casualties transform the city into a cemetery. The Troubles divides the poet's mind in a way that reflects the conflict's dynamic as one of competing identities. The letter ends on a fearful note, "I who have heard the waters break/Claim this my country, though today/*Timor mortis conturbat me.*" In the city, birth is haunted by the spectre of death. The Latin phrase, "fear of death disturbs me," alludes to the Scottish poet William Dunbar's "Lament for the Makaris," a roll call of names of dead poets. The line iterates their mortality, showing how the northern home is epitomized by "pity" and "terror." The poem precipitates Longley's Western pastoral impulse, as in the face of a threatened social structure, "place and nature can be conceived of as a steady and unaltered realm" (Frawley, 1998-1999, p. 270):

> To Seamus Heaney" is written, "From Carrigskeewaun ... Offering you by way of welcome/To the sick counties we call home." The expatriate addressee is welcomed in language that recalls the explosion of bombs, "Hoping this fortnight detonates/Your year in the United States.

While Longley chooses to "take my stand" in the isolated West, "That small subconscious cottage where/The Irish poet slams his door," he is self-critical of the retreat's implicit escapism, "A tempting stance indeed ... Except that we know the old stories." Longley has recalled how he and his contemporaries were constantly expected to offer their take on the Troubles (Longley and Wilmer, 1994). Psychic pressure to respond to public events is mirrored in the way that public violence invades private confines and domestic spaces:

> He collapsed beside his carpet-slippers
> Without a murmur, shot through the head
> By a shivering boy who wandered in
> Before they could turn the television down
> Or tidy away the supper dishes.
> To the children, to a bewildered wife,
> I think 'Sorry Missus' was what he said. ("Wounds")

Senseless violence is a "strangely intimate, everyday actuality" (Peacock, 2000, p. 271). The killer's apology reads like a colloquial absurdity. "The Civil Servant," from the sequence "Wreaths," "was preparing an Ulster fry for breakfast/When someone walked into the kitchen and shot him/A bullet entered his mouth and pierced his skull." In humiliating fashion, the victim "lay in his dressing gown and pyjamas" as police dust for fingerprints, a reminder that there is no inviolate space in the Northern home of Longley's poetry (Brearton, 2006, p. 145). Whereas the West offers the possibility, Belfast represents futility. Longley has described how some of his poems "attempt to define my Irishness" (Hanna, 2015, p. 59), so his work unsurprisingly dislocates from a place where an assertion of Irishness might get one killed.

His Western poetry engages in self-conscious processes of negotiation, acclimation, and affiliation. These poems demonstrate Longley's pastoral tendencies of depicting the human relation to the natural world, contrasting city and country, and examining the underlying tension between civilization and nature (Potts, 2011, p. 2). A desire to assimilate completely with the West intensifies the longer the poetry imaginatively disconnects from Belfast. An early poem "The West," still frames identity concerning both places as the speaker continues to "listen for news through the atmospherics … news from home." Yet it is in Carrigskeewaun where he imagines himself "finding my way for ever along/The path to this cottage." Belfast threatens destruction, as alluded to in an image of moths incinerated by firelight; the Western "home from home" offers continuity and perpetuity. This theme of eternal association becomes a trope in Longley's later work where death is comprehended much differently.

Unlike the irrational deaths taking place in Belfast, death in the West is envisioned as a means of integrating oneself "for ever" in the region. Acts of immersion and disappearance have positive associations and outcomes, usually denoting a subject's complete assimilation. In "Landscape" the speaker is:

> … clothed, unclothed
> By racing cloud shadows,
> Or else disintegrate
> Like a hillside neighbour
> Erased by sea mist.

The speaker's sense of identity and place oscillates, but there is an option to "disintegrate" or be "erased," thereby localizing him and affirming belonging. As McDonald (1992, p. 68) comments, "… the voice, and the observing self behind it, are drawn closer and closer to the landscape… the distance between the observer and observed is reduced to almost nothing." Strategies of assimilation are pursued to close that distance with none being more effective than dying.

This evokes traditional pastoral, as death's inevitability, its effect on nature, and hopes for immortality are among the genre's common themes (Potts, 2011, p. 78). In the West, death has the power to merge identities and bond individuals to places. In "Between Hovers," written in memory of Joe O'Toole, a friend whose family once owned the Carrigskeewaun cottage, Longley links his friend's death to his return to a Western homeland. At O'Toole's burial mound:

> Encircled by a spring tide and taking in
> Cloonaghmanagh and Claggan and Carrigskeewaun,
> The townlands he'd wandered tending cows and sheep,
> I watched a dying otter gaze right through me
> At the islands in Clew Bay, as though it were only
> Between hovers and not too far from the holt.

The place-names are comfortingly familiar, O'Toole's burial is a natural transition that affirms the dead man's habitual association with them (Harmon, 2012). They also link Longley to the Gaelic tradition of *dinnseanchas*, "which imbues place-names with spiritual significance that resonates beyond the temporal" (Potts, 2011, p. 92). This practice signals a typically nationalist, conscious reclamation of the Irish landscape through verbal mapping (Frawley, 1998-1999, p. 273). As the burial mound is the poem's vantage point, it appropriates for the speaker those places with which his friend was "habitually associated." A connection to nature is tokened by the dying otter; death will transition the animal to a holt (den) of a different kind, ending its suspended state "between hovers," paralleling the early poetry's sense of being caught between two homes, with death now being the means through which one of them can be perpetually inhabited.

In "Petalwort," set on the Mayo coast, the speaker echoes his friend's desire to blend his ashes with elements of nature, "You want your ashes to swirl along the strand... Around the burial mound's wind-and-wave-inspired/Vanishing act... Self-effacement in sand." Man, invisibly merges into the landscape after death (Brearton, 2006, p. 240), making him inseparable from the terrain. As to the afterlife:

> There's no such thing as heaven, so let it be
> The Carricknashinnagh shoal or Caher
> Island where you honeymooned in a tent
> Amid the pilgrim-fishermen's stations

The poem implies that "the only heaven there is exists in this world" (Kennedy-Andrews, 2008, p. 145), and its location in the West speaks to the later poetry's conception of the region as a place of ideal conditions, supreme bliss, and everlasting life. This glorification of the West "places it in the realm of imagination and defines it as pastoral paradise: with balmy nights, resplendent constellations, dazzling moon, smiling shepherds, bountiful salmon, men relaxing in the fields ... deliberately pastoral and idyllic imagery" (Potts, 2011, p. 92). Thus, Longley participates in extending the romantic myth of cultural nationalism's conception of the West as a rural idyll (Kockel, 1995, p. 243). Far from the strife-ridden city from whence he came, the Ulster Protestant poet can therefore only resolve a conflicted sense of Irish identity and place through physical and spiritual coalescence within the pastoral heartland of nationalist Irish essence.

Concluding Statements

MacNeice and Longley write from the experience of having come from a community whose sense of identity was antithetical to that of nationalist Ireland. While their work extends a literary tradition of Protestant writers being drawn towards the West, the poets' Northern background, in the context of their respective eras, dealt with added pressures that many of those earlier writers did not have to confront. However the poets may have conceived of their sense of being Irish, their native city of Belfast proved unsuitable for reflecting on Irish identity, much less embracing it. The West's allure as a site of untainted and unchallengeable Irishness persists to the present day, albeit in a less politically charged form. For both places though, their culturally imposed qualities and politicized historical dimensions remain hard to shake. Twentieth-century Belfast could be dissociated from neither past nor contemporary bigotry; decades of domineering and discriminatory Protestant political and religious culture contributed to the eventual outbreak of a conflict that would obliterate a secure sense of being "home" in the North completely. Belfast's industrial character and sectarian elements presented a disturbing departure from the idealized Ireland of cultural continuity, pastoral quietude, and spiritual purity as embodied by the West. The region, as a place of escape and refuge, was still the most desirable grounds on which to resolve a problematic sense of belonging in Ireland and alienation from an Irish identity to which there was a contested right to claim. The dichotomy of urban Belfast and rural West witnessed in the poetry of MacNeice and Longley stands as a testament to the endurance and entrenchment of cultural nationalist dictates in both their consciences and the popular consciousness which only in more recent times Northern Protestant writers have felt less compelled to keep in mind.

Works Cited

Boey, K.C. (2008) 'Sailing to an Island: Contemporary Irish Poetry Visits the Western Island', *Shima: The International Journal of Research into Island Cultures*, Vol. 2, No. 2, pp. 19-41.

Bourke, M. (2000) 'A Growing Sense of National Identity: Charles Lamb (1893-1964) & the West

of Ireland', *History Ireland*, Vol. 8, No. 1, pp. 30-4.

Boyce, D.G. (1982) *Nationalism in Ireland*, Croom Helm, London.

Bradley, A. (2017) 'Changing Places: Locations of Contemporary Irish Poetry', *New Hibernia Review/Iris Éireannach Nua*, Vol. 21, No. 4, pp. 89-105.

Brearton, F. (2006) *Reading Michael Longley*, Bloodaxe Books, Tarset.

Brearton, F. and Longley E., eds. (2012) *Incorrigibly Plural: Louis MacNeice and his Legacy*,

Caracanet, Manchester.

Brewer, J.D. and Higgins G.I. (1998) *Anti-Catholicism in Northern Ireland, 1600-1998: The Mote and the Beam*, Palgrave Macmillan, London.

Brown, T. (1998) 'MacNeice and the Puritan Tradition', in K. Devine and A.J. Peacock (eds.) *Louis MacNeice and His Influence*, Colin Smythe, Gerrards Cross.

Brown, T. (1975) *Northern Voices: Poets from Ulster*. Gill and Macmillan, Dublin.

Chaudhuri, S. (1989) *Renaissance Pastoral and its English Development*. Oxford University Press, Oxford.

Cunningham, V. (2012) 'MacNeice and Thirties (Classical) Pastoralism' in F. Brearton and E. Longley (eds.) *Incorrigibly Plural: Louis MacNeice and his Legacy*, Caracanet, Manchester.

Davis, T. (1844) 'The West's Asleep', *The Spirit of the Nation*. James Duffy: Dublin.

Dawe, G. and Longley E., eds. (1995) *Across a Roaring Hill: The Protestant Imagination in Modern Ireland*. The Blackstaff Press, Belfast and Dover.

Duffy, P.J. (1997) 'Literature and Art in the Representation of Irish Place' in B. Graham (ed.) *In Search of Ireland: A Cultural Geography*, Routledge, London and New York.

Fairweather, C. (2000) 'Inclusive and Exclusive Pastoral: Towards an Anatomy of Pastoral Modes', *Studies in Philology*, Vol. 97, No. 3, pp. 276-307.

Frawley, O. (1998-1999) 'Nature and Nostalgia in Irish Literature', *Proceedings of the Harvard Celtic Colloquium*, Department of Celtic Languages & Literatures, Harvard University, Cambridge.

Gellner, E. (1983) *Nations and Nationalism*, Basil Blackwell Publisher Limited, Oxford.

George, R.M. (1999) *The Politics of Home: Postcolonial Relocations and Twentieth Century Fiction*, University of California Press, Berkeley.

Hanna, A. (2015) *Northern Irish Poetry and Domestic Space*, Palgrave Macmillan, New York.

Hanrahan, S. (2004) 'Reading the West', *Irish Arts Review*, Vol. 21, No. 4, pp. 92-97.

Harkness, D.E. (1988) 'Nation, State and National Identity in Ireland: Some Preliminary Thoughts', *Irishness in a Changing Society*, Barnes and Noble Books, Monaco.

Harmon, M. (2012) 'Michael Longley and the West of Ireland', *About Place Journal*, Vol. 1, Issue 3.

He, C. (2014) 'Nationalism and the West in Brian Friel's "The Gentle Island" and Martin McDonagh's "The Beauty Queen of Leenane"', *Nordic Irish Studies*, Vol. 13, No. 2, pp. 1-17.

Hunt, J.D. (1992) 'Introduction: Pastorals and Pastoralisms', *Studies in the History of Art*, Vol. 36, pp. 10-19.

Johnston, D. (1985) *Irish Poetry after Joyce*. University of Notre Dame Press, Notre Dame.

Kennedy-Andrews, E. (2008) *Writing Home: Poetry and Place in Northern Ireland, 1968-2008*, D.S. Brewer, Martlesham.

Kirkland, R. (2009) 'Ballygawley, Ballylynn, Belfast: Writing about Modernity and Settlement in Northern Ireland', *The Irish Review*, No. 40/41, pp. 18-32.

Kockel, U. (1995) '"The West is Learning, the North is War": Reflections on Irish Identity' in U. Kockel (ed.) *Landscape, Heritage and Identity: Case Studies in Irish Ethnography*, Liverpool University Press, Liverpool.

Longley, E. (1994) *The Living Stream: Literature and Revision in Ireland*, Bloodaxe Books, Newcastle.

Longley, E. (2000) *Poetry and Posterity*, Bloodaxe Books, Tarset.

Longley, M. (2006) *Collected Poems*, Jonathan Cape, London.

Longley, M. and Longley, E. (2009) 'Edna and Michael Longley — The SRB Interview', *Scottish Review of Books*, Vol. 4, Issue 3, 29 October.

Longley, M. and Wilmer, C. (1994) 'In Conversation with Michael Longley', *PN Review*, Vol. 20, No. 4.

MacNeice, L. (1965) *The Strings are False: An Unfinished Autobiography*. Faber and Faber, London.

MacNeice, L. (1990) *Selected Prose of Louis MacNeice*, Clarendon, Oxford.

MacNeice, L. (2007), *Collected Poems*, P. McDonald (ed.), Faber and Faber, London.

McDonald, P. (1992) 'Michael Longley's Homes' in N. Corcoran (ed.) *The Chosen Ground: Essays on the Contemporary Poetry of Northern Ireland*, Seren Books, Bridgend.

Nagle, S. (2016) *Histories of Nationalism in Ireland and Germany: A Comparative Study from 1800 to 1932*, Bloomsbury, London.

Nicholson, E. (1974) 'Trees Were Green' in T. Brown and A. Reid (eds.) *Time Was Away: The World of Louis MacNeice*, Dolmen Press, Dublin.

O'Halloran, C. (1987) *Partition and the Limits of Irish Nationalism*, Gill and Macmillan, Dublin.

O'Toole, F. (1985) 'Going West: The Country Versus the City in Irish Writing', *The Crane Bag*, Vol. 9, No. 2, pp. 111-16.

Peacock, A.J. (2000) *The Poetry of Michael Longley*, A.J. Peacock. and K. Devine (eds.), Colin Smythe, Gerrards Cross.

Pelaschiar, L. (2000) 'Transforming Belfast: The Evolving Role of the City in Northern Irish Fiction', *Irish University Review*, Vol. 30, No.1, pp. 117-31.

Pierce, D., ed. (2000) *Irish Writing in the Twentieth Century: A Reader*, University of Cork Press, Cork.

Potts, D.L. (2011) *Contemporary Irish Poetry and the Pastoral Tradition*, University of Missouri

Press, Columbia.

Scherpe, K.R. and Roetzel, L. (1992-1993) 'Nonstop to Nowhere City? Changes in the Symbolization, Perception, and Semiotics of the City in the Literature of Modernity, *Cultural Critique*, No. 23, pp. 137-164.

Stallworthy, J. (1995) *Louis MacNeice*, Faber and Faber, London.

Townshend, C. (1999) *Ireland: The 20th Century*, Arnold, London.

Jamaica Kincaid's *Among Flowers: A Walk in the Himalayas* as a Black Pastoral

Whereas Kincaid's considerable body of work has received a lot of attention, *Among Flowers: A Walk in the Himalayas* has not received as much scholarly attention. Postcolonial critics foreground Kincaid's ambivalent positioning as the colonized subject and privileged American garden owner. Ricia Anne Chansky argues that *A Small Place* and *Among Flowers* should be read together because their interconnecting themes of movement and belonging are indicative of the doubled identity of diasporic subjects. Sarah Casteel (2007, p. 131) reads her gardening and botanical activity as interrogating the cultural politics of "the plant theft of colonial botanists, ironically reproducing the botanical conquest of the New World." Jill Didur (2010, p. 184) suggests that Kincaid's bifurcated positionality "allows her to turn the colonial garden inside out, offering a subversive view of its origins, even while she attempts to redirect and decolonize its ongoing creation in the present." Along similar lines, Zoran Pećić (2011, p. 153) interprets *Among Flowers* as "in relation to the British colonial enterprise, for seed and plant collection was a significant part of the colonial project and the creation of London as the colonial centre."

Rather than situating her work about the colonial travel narratives invoked above, I want to place *Among Flowers* in an environmentalist and Black diasporic framework. In the US, the Black movement is always already surveilled and policed; furthermore, there is a widespread belief that Black people do not belong in the natural environment. This erroneous notion has a long history, as access to parks, public green spaces, and natural recreation areas has been restricted for African Americans and other minorities of colour (Floyd and Stodolska, 2019). A consequence of this expulsion is that "black geographic subjects differently produce space within this context of domination and objectification: specifically, the seeking out of alternative geographic options, and the coupling of geography with black matters, histories, knowledges, experiences, and resistances" (McKittrick, 2006, p. 92). Black geography thus conceptualizes the forms of constraint, policing, and regulation that Black people must evade, contest, and confront in white supremacist spaces. J. T. Roane and Justin Hosbey's (2019) concept of Black ecologies builds on these arguments about the interlocking nature of racial and geographic violence, marking the spaces of the wretched as environmental sites of "ongoing injury, gratuitous harm, and premature death," and also "sites wherein ordinary Black people articulate alternative maps — dissonant and heterodox ecological grammars as well as a vision for a different order."

The chapter utilizes these intersecting theories of the Black outdoors, geography, and ecology to argue that Kincaid's travel book might be conceptualized as a pastoral work. To explore the radical potential of Black gardening, journeying, and seed collecting, the essay draws on Black feminist practices of conjoining beauty and joy against the incessant and insistent pull of racialized violence and terror. It argues that the "uncharted" Himalayan landscape opens up otherwise possibilities of geographic presence, expression, and movement, as well as new relationships to land, plant life, and local people. It also shows that her seed-collecting hike cultivates reciprocal, grounded, and nondominating relationships to the land/scape. These emergent relationalities radically disrupt prevalent modes of living and logic anchored in conquest, theft, property, ownership, and dispossession that underwrite chattel slavery, settler colonialism and their afterlives.

As this collection evinces, the pastoral has become an increasingly debated term. The traditional pastoral may be understood as an idealized representation of country life, focusing on the life of shepherds. As Brian Loughrey (1984, p. 8), editor of *The Pastoral Mode* explains, however, the pastoral is not dead, as there is an "almost bewildering variety of works" to which contemporary critics attribute the term, ranging from anything to do with nature or the rural, the bucolic appeal, or a retreat from city life. For ecocritic Lawrence Buell (2005, p. 32), pastoralism cannot be avoided in our search for a more mature environmental aesthetics, as "pastoralism is a species of cultural equipment that western thought has for more than two millennia been unable to do without." He says the pastoral "has become almost synonymous with the idea of (re)turn to a less urbanized, more "natural" state of existence" (p. 31). Accordingly, the "ideological grammar" of the pastoral cannot be pinned down, the Euro-American pastoral has always been dualistic, capable of assuming a "luminous ideal" and retaining "oppositional forms" (p. 51). For instance, the author of the classic *The Machine in the Garden* Leo Marx (2000, p. 5) somewhat problematically distinguishes "between two kinds of pastoralism—one that is popular and sentimental, the other imaginative and complex." The longing of the culturally dominant, popular pastoral for a "more natural environment" (p. 5) and its "continuing appeal of the bucolic" (p. 6) is a willfully escapist ideal in the service of industrial capitalism. In contrast, the complex pastoralism of canonical Euro-American writers embodies a more complicated pastoral politics. Along similar lines, ecocritic Terry Gifford theorizes two developments in modern Anglophone literature that revise the traditional pastoral: the anti-pastoral and the post-pastoral. Whereas the anti-pastoral is a "corrective" of the traditional pastoral's idealization, post-pastoral literature inscribes a fundamental shift from the anthropocentric to the ecocentric view, "an awe in attention to the natural world" (2001, p. 264, 265). The latter is paradoxically cognizant that "retreat informs our sense of community," and of our "need to improve our relationship with our neighbours on this planet" (p. 303).

Building upon Gifford's theorization of environmentalism and multiple frames of post-pastoral literature, I propose the term Black pastoral for Jamaica Kincaid's nature writings. *My Garden (Book)* can be seen as a pastoral work, for it collects her writings on her activities as a gardener and the colonial legacy of botany, including a brief account of her plant-hunting trip in China. I also use the term to refer to *Among Flowers*, the chronicle of her three-week seed-collecting hike in the footfalls of the Himalayas in 2002. Simultaneously invoking and subverting the genre of colonial travel and botanical writing, she describes how she and her travel companions, botanists and nursery owners in the US and Wales, hunt for garden-worthy seeds in the unforgettably beautiful Nepalese landscape. Her Black pastoral centres her alienation, anxiety, and joy in the Himalayan landscape. The terrible irony that "plant hunters are the descendants of people and ideas that used to hunt [her]" does not escape her complex pastoral vision, which is haunted by the ideological and aesthetic ethos of the colonial pastoral (Kincaid, 2020, p. xxii).[19]

Pastoralism in/as the Black Garden

Kincaid's garden book might be called a pastoral work in multiple senses: it is an orientation of self to nature that is humbling at the same time as it is rejuvenating; it ironically and self-indulgently thematizes the privilege that allows her to be the owner of a garden. Throughout she exhibits awareness of the garden as the site of colonial conquest, settlement, and exploitation. According to Kincaid (2020, p. xvii), since Columbus, "the world of the garden changed" and "the way the world we now live in began." Reviewing the intertwining history of colonialism and transatlantic slavery, she defines gardening as the "act of possessing" (p. xvi), thus linking the gardener's possession to the interlocking systems of resource extraction, capital accumulation, and the plantation system. However, she also defines the "true nurseryman" as a gardener, "who at least once in the gardening year feels the urge to possess completely at least one plant" excluding mere buying (p. 32). Later, she explains that this urge is driven by a "complicated state of craving," namely, 'discovering' and claiming a flowering plant in its natural environment and subsequently taming it in one's garden (p. 32). Even though her pastoralism participates in the botanists' desire to pore over "[e]very square foot of terrain . . . so that not a single garden-worthy plant is missed" (p. 32), it also distances itself from their "classificatory and acquisitive" objectives (Didur, 2010, p. 179).

Kincaid's garden has not removed her from the world of capital, the market economy, or the commodity chain, her pastoral

---

19 Space constraints prevent me from discussing at great length how Kincaid's use of irony troubles colonial pastoralism, instead pointing toward a complex affective response to land. For an excellent discussion of her use of irony in her *My Garden (Book)*, see O'Brien (2002).

delight is laden with tensions. She readily admits that gardening is "an absolute luxury," and revels in "the deliciousness of complaining about nothing of any consequence" (Kincaid, 2001, p. 22). As she puts it, "I have joined the conquering class: who else could afford this garden—a garden in which I grow things that it would be much cheaper to buy at the store?" (2001, p. 123). If her botanical knowledge, seed catalogues, and gardening draw on the legacy of the imperial garden, we need to consider that her so-called "ignorance" of the botany of the enslaved "really only reflects the fact that when [she] lived [in the Caribbean], [she] was of the conquered class and living in a conquered place" (2001, p. 120). Disconnected from the Caribbean soil and her people's herbal knowledge, throughout I will be arguing that her reading of white botany is simply a reflection of Black and Indigenous landlessness and the precedence of colonial concepts of land in the US. Furthermore, this knowledge of imperial botany is complicated by the fact that botanical gardens, traditions, and knowledges of the dispossessed have been appropriated by the system of "ecological imperialism" as environmental historian Alfred Crosby (2004) calls it.

Critics who read her ambition, her power, her will, and her strength as colonial tropes disregard the Black ecofeminist tradition of gardening, including writers such as Zora Neale Hurston, Alice Walker, and Fanny Lou Hamer. Rather than a terrain to be regulated and governed to produce capital, I argue that her garden enacts a Black feminist "respect for the possibilities—and the will to grasp them" (Walker 2011, p. 470). Following Sylvia Wynter's "Novel and History, Plot and Plantation," the plot and plotting embody alternative possibilities for the survival, resistance, and cultural subsistence of enslaved people in the Caribbean. As Wynter (1971, p. 99) describes, "The planters gave the slaves plots of land on which to grow food to feed themselves to maximize profits." As she explains further, the "inbuilt confrontation between the plantation and the plot" is inevitable; "the market system and market values" of the Plantationocene[20] are against the plot system's

---

20 Plantationocene can be defined as a "devastating transformation of diverse kinds of human-tended farms, pastures, and forests into extractive and

cultivation of "traditional values — use values," the "values that had been created by traditional societies of Africa" (p. 99). Rather than authorizing the exploitation of nature, these traditional African values imbue her pastoralism with an ecocentric commitment to the land.

Her garden is a successor to what Wynter terms the plot. Echoing Walker's description of her mother's garden, Kincaid (2020, p. xv) identifies her mother as a gardener, whose careless, everyday way of cultivating fruit and crops as well as the "kind of godlike domination" to crops embodies a pastoral heritage grounded in Black cultural forms of labour and resilience. She stresses that her mother's garden is outside the regulated, managed, compulsory domestication characteristic of the plantation regime, "For her [mother] the wild and the cultivated were equal and yet separate, together and apart" (p. xiii). As a site of the production of biodiverse foods and plants, the feminist Black ecology of her mother's garden and plant collecting enact an intertwining praxis of love, sustenance, and healing: "Much of the love I remember receiving from my mother came during the time I was sick. I have such a lovely image and memory of her hovering over me with cups of barley water (that was for the measles) and giving me cups of tea made from herbs (bush) she had gone out and gathered and steeped slowly (that was for whooping cough)" (p. xii). Kincaid's lifelong pursuit of the pastoral experience, her habit of growing things is in search of "the place she came from," her mother's garden, its beauty, its care, and its ambition (p. xvi). A beautiful experiment in staging an otherwise relationship to Black ownership, desire, and land enmeshed in the dictates of racial capitalism. Gardening thus enacts rooting oneself in place, by way of counteracting the displacement and placelessness of the Afro-diasporic subject and making place as a practice of love and remembrance. As Roane (2018) significantly argues in "Plotting the Black Commons," the insurgent and fugitive practices of plotting by enslaved and post-emancipation Black communities articulate geographic identities full of

---

enclosed plantations, relying on slave labor and other forms of exploited, alienated, and usually spatially transported labor" (Haraway, 2015).

epistemological possibilities and horizons. In addition to such practices of plotting, I posit that her pastoral encounter with Nepalese nature—untouched or less touched by ecological imperialism than her birthplace or current home—develops a more intimate and conscious relationship with the environment.

Alienation, anxiety, and joy: pastoral experiments in beauty

Kincaid can afford to go on this expansive trip because she is funded by National Geographic to write a travelogue. This clinches her status as the privileged American traveller who can indulge in her pastoral passions for plant sighting. At the same time, for a Black woman, going on a journey to collect seeds in Nepal is highly unusual. Considering the risky, controlled, and constrained movements of African diasporic women, Kincaid's pastoral retreat and what Gifford (2001, p. 18) calls the "fundamental pastoral movement" within the Himalayan landscape are beautiful possibilities. While predicated on extraordinary ability and the ambivalent position of the Caribbean American writer, Kincaid's travelogue produces an outside to the colour line, a pastoral experiment in living otherwise—on the edge of the enclosure that is the global system of the racial capitalocene.[21]

Kincaid (2020, p. 7) claims that due to her love of things "far away," she would have gone on this trip, even without her obsession with her garden. At several points in the journey, the beauty of the Himalayan landscape causes her to exclaim and hush, to stop and get still: "Just to see the earth crumpling itself upward, just to experience the physical world as an unending series of verticals going up and then going down—... —made me quiet" (p. 77). Kincaid's mode of viewing the landscape is a deep leaning into place and the natural environment, a co-creation of the "exquisite uniqueness" of each moment, the beauty of what is in a respectful, reverent, and joyful way (p. 166). She expresses her unbounded love of things and expanded view of self, when she says, "I found

---

21 Taking a page from Anna Tsing's (2015) influential account of Matsutake mushroom gatherers, the edge of empire is a good place to begin our search for alternative versions of the pastoral.

each plant, each new turn in the road, each new turn in the weather, from cold to hot and then back again, each new set of boulders so absorbing, so new, and the newness so absorbing, and I was so in need of an explanation for each thing, that I was often in tears, troubling myself with questions, such as what am I and what is the thing in front of me" (p. 135). In contrast to the white botanist, whose world-making depends on the categorization and domestication of "exotic" fauna and flora, she opens herself up to an unattainable and indescribable form of beauty outside the limits of the human. I see this turn to new sensings and imaginings, passions and relationalities, modes and genres of living, as a pastoral continuation and expansion of what Saidiya Hartman (2020, p. 33) terms young Black women's radical urban experiments in beauty, where "[b]eauty is not a luxury; rather it is a way of creating possibility in the space of enclosure, a radical art of subsistence, an embrace of our terribleness, a transfiguration of the given. It is a will to adorn, a proclivity for the baroque, and the love of too much." In contrast to the white pastoral tradition, her experience of natural beauty may be a means of surviving the brokenness of the world and imagining a non-instrumental relationship to the earth.

Kincaid (2020, p. 136) is so overwhelmed with the singular and terrible beauty of each natural novelty that her tongue is "stilled," wondering whether it is real at all. For instance, when she sees the uncomplicated, unexpected, pristine beauty of the secret lake, "a hidden lake that could only be seen from the pass," she feels "as if [she] would dissolve" (p. 138). This sensation of dissolution does not trigger her fear or anxiety, however, only the prospect of self-transformation, "complete acceptance" of and love for everything (p. 102). When she feels that the "border" between herself and the objects of her perception, herself and her everyday life disappears, she realizes that she "loved [her] tent and would have probably died for it, and [is] now so glad things never came to that" (p. 20-1). More specifically, this infinite love of things, of beings, of people, of life emerges in her mutual encounters with plants and seeds and objects and humans, in what anthropologist Anna Tsing (2015) might call polyphonic assemblages. That is interspecies entanglements in which nonhuman and human entities collide. Enmeshed in such cross-species assemblages, Kincaid (2020, p. 102) loses herself as a self-possessed, possessive individual, and in that objectless and selfless state feels bliss: "I didn't long for anything; I felt quite lost and this feeling led to another feeling — happiness." She thus reaches for, practices, and cultivates joy, not the alienated, commodified, and Western satisfaction of pastoralism, but pastoral "joy that could only be had for [her] when shared with others, when common, when mundane and ordinary" (Crawley, 2020, p. 155).

Additionally, Kincaid's travelogue challenges affect theory pioneer Sianne Ngai's (2021, p. 247) concept of the ultimately gendered and disembodied nature of anxiety, which she connects to the "male knowledge-seekers distinctive yet basic state of mind" in works by Sigmund Freud, Herman Melville, Alfred Hitchcock, and Martin Heidegger. For Ngai, anxiety rescues the male subject from "horrible interspaces" or "sites of radical significance or negativity" (p. 245); this "act of aversively turning away" ultimately "restores and ultimately validates the trajectory of the analyzing subject's inquiry" (p. 247). In Kincaid's pastoral narrative, however, anxiety is not the mark of the white male intellectual's aversion, but the postcolonial subject's recognition of fear in the face of moving toward and practising alternatives to normative relationships to the landscape. Botanist, nurseryman, and long-time friend Dan Hinkley's e-mail, with its long list of suitable clothes for the trip, "made [her] bristle with anxiety, but anxiety is never any help at all, and so [she] took note of it and then ignored it" (Kincaid, 2020, p. 12). In Nepal too, her ongoing anxiety is linked to her bodily discomfort, exposure to the elements, and joy: "This was only a reflection of my anxiety, my unease, my sense of ennui, my fragility. I have never been so uncomfortable, so out of my skin in my entire life, and yet not once did I wish to leave, not once did I regret being there" (p. 27). In contrast to Ngai's identification of anxiety with the intellect, Kincaid characterizes her nervousness as an affective awareness of her corporeal vulnerability, the sheer animality and embeddedness of her living body in the landscape.

In contrast to postcolonialist Pramod Nayar (2021, p. 4) who argues that the "travelogue is dedicated less to pleasure than to anxiety, and given more to uncertainty rather than to confidence,"

I argue that Kincaid's anxiety does not stand in the way of her pastoral joy. Even when (or precisely because) she is uncomfortable, "[she] knew [she] was having the very most wonderful time of [her] life" (Kincaid 2020, p. 101). This conscious, intentional allowing, and accepting of discomfort as a way of orienting oneself toward and feeling with the land embodies Black Study scholar Ashon Crawley's (2020, 148-49) ongoing practice of joy as a daily sustenance, something toward which Black people aspire daily. Although joy is not something easily achieved, held, or narratable, Kincaid (2020, p. 101) chooses to participate in its constant unfolding, "not letting [her] fear stand in the way." Rather than reinforcing an idealized binary of anxiety and joy, she typically portrays a set of coinciding emotions. She sardonically notes, for instance, that her "poor eyes, influenced by a combination of the anxiety, wonder, and strange happiness . . . could not see the fruit bats" she so badly wanted to see (p. 22). Her feelings disrupt the "vital role" of the "colonial gaze" relegating the "native" "fauna and flora" and animals to "exhibit[s]," instead pointing to an affect-based pastoral response that includes her embeddedness in nature (Kochar and Khan 2021, p. 11).

Following advice from Dan, she begins to run, lift weights, and walk with a backpack full of stones in preparation for the physically challenging hike. Despite all this preparation (physical, mental, and emotional), she observes that "[she] just did not understand the kind of walking that was required of [her]" (Kincaid, 2020, p. 59). Reflecting on "the ease with which [she] was used to going anywhere and everywhere" in America, she readily concedes that modern modes of transportation, comfort, and spatiotemporality are inextricably intertwined (p. 58). [22] In contrast, the relatively uncultivated Himalayan landscape offers her a different sense of place and how she might move through it: "the idea that [she] had to get [her]self from one point to the other, through [her] own effort, was hard to take in" (p. 58). She must release the pastoral fantasy of the landscape's permeability, for she cannot "just walk through the

---

22 Surprisingly, she does not recognize any limits placed on her movements as a Black subject in the US.

hills and the trees . . . as if they would yield" (p. 107). Instead, she follows Sunam, the main Sherpa, who maps their route and decides where to camp for the night; she walks the local paths, moving over, around, and through the hills, the valleys, the forests, and fields on foot. Akin to the young woman passing through the village of Hedangna, who walked six days from her village to the big town and back with a bag of salt on her back (p. 70), the type of walking that she must perform models itself on indigenous life forms and modalities of movement. Ongoing land-informed practices teach her indigenous ontologies, epistemologies, and values, "the vast difference between my expectation, my perception, and reality; the way things really are" (p. 143). Her alienation from colonial modes of settlement thus allows her to unlearn land exploitation and to learn what Jobb Arnold (2018) terms land affect, a pastoral relationality grounded both in place and mobility.

Despite the map included in the volume, she cannot map, flatten, or totalize the opaquely dense non-western landscape. When Kincaid (2020, p. 63) asks Sunam what the name of the huge mountain in front of them is, he says, "That is not a mountain, that is a hill and it has no name." He reminds her that the landscape is not hers to categorize or name, which makes her become "truly silent" (p. 63). As she says, "The landscape at the foothills of the Himalayan mountains have left my tongue somewhat stilled, perhaps permanently so" (p. 136). Her silence is a sign of her affective attunement to the land, an extension of the land effect, "fleeting experiential and relational sensations grounded in land-based, embodied ways-of-being and knowing that exist between human and other-than-human agents" (Arnold, 2018, p. 98). Following Arnold's way of thinking about land affect, her embodied, energetic, relational encounter with the Nepalese landscape is linked with "the intellectual and political histories and traditions of Indigenous peoples whose values and practices have long centred on land-based relational ontologies" (Arnold, 2018, p. 102). From this perspective, her attachment to the land and the indigenous land-based knowledge is effectively organized: "There are no hills in Nepal, there are no meadows, there are no valleys, there are only things that might be called hills and meadows and valleys, all of them little interruptions, little distractions in a landscape that is all mountain" (Kincaid, 2020, p. 63). Rather than turning the land into pastoral mythology, property or territory, the Sherpas teach her Indigenous studies scholar Glen Coulthard's (2014, p. 60) ethics of "land as a mode of a reciprocal relationship . . .about living our lives to one another and our surroundings in a respectful, nondominating and nonexploitative way." In ecocritic Jonathan Bate's (2000, p. 264, 282) terms, the Heideggerian "letting-be of Being" allows for the pastoral representation of the earth, of which she is part, but which she does not possess.

In the beginning, Kincaid can still remember "the feeling of living in a village in the mountains of Vermont" (2020, p. 24), however, as the journey continues, she relates she has more and more difficulty retaining "a sense of who [she] was" (p. 20-1). Kincaid (2020, p. 2-3) surmises she "felt that thing called alienated," conceptualized by W.E.B. Du Bois as the psychic trauma of Black life, "but it was so pleasant, so interesting, so dreamily irritating to be so far away from everything I had known." Even though her alienation involves a form of pastoral retreat, it is neither a nostalgic escape into the past, nor a willful "retreat from politics into an aesthetic landscape that is devoid of conflict and tension" (Gifford, 2001, p. 11). Rather, the alienation inherent in the Black pastoral mode reflects a distancing of oneself from antiblack ecologies and claiming freedom: "freedom from the world, freedom from Humanity, freedom from everyone (including one's Black self)" (Wilderson, 2010, p. 23).

Upon leaving Topke Gole, a holy place with a Sacred Lake, Kincaid (2020, p. 155) opines, "I looked around for a last look with the thought that it would not be too long before I doubted that I had ever been in such a place."[23] As indicated earlier, the Black pastoral is an attempt to extend thinking about "the Black Outdoors," a mode of life that exceeds the binary of the inside and outside that

---

23 As seed gathering will show us, her affective relationship to the beauty of the landscape unleashes its speculative energies and makes her "truly feel as if [she] was in the unreal, the magical, extraordinary" (Kincaid, 2020, p. 18).

structures the brutal enclosure of settlement.[24] In Hartman's words, "part of what a critical tradition of abolition [does] is produce a thought of the outside while on the inside ... the enclosure is brutal but the practice is always finding a way to produce an outside within that space" (Hartman quoted in Carter and Cervenak, 2017). In this sense, Kincaid's pastoral produces a space "outside" the Plantationocene, or at the very least the "thought of the outside" while being held captive inside. However, as we can see, her pastoral does not simply narrate the outside from within the periphery and/ or inside of racial capitalism, but it also engages with the thought of the inside while on the outside. As her remark makes it all too apparent, it is impossible for Kincaid not to anticipate a limit to or the inevitable compromise of this pastoral outside, always already haunted by the African diaspora's forced movement: geographic rupture, irrecoverable loss, and psychic interruption. She is fully in the moment, embodying an affective state of relationality with the land, but her present is also entangled with concerns of the future, whence her present pastoral sanctuary appears to be unreal and irretrievably lost. As it will be clarified later, the Black pastoral mode is doubling and tripling temporality in ways that have the potential to multiply the land effect, producing different models of living beautifully and brutally in multiple time frames.

A pastoral community: collaborative forms of survival

When discussing Kincaid's relationship with the Sherpas, most critics focus on the moment when she not only lacks interest in the names of the locals but in her arrogance names them "Cook," "Table" and "I Love You" while claiming that, "This is not at all a reflection of the relationship between power and powerless," but "only a reflection of [her] own anxiety" (Kincaid, 2020, p. 27). Whereas Nayar (2021, p. 6) calls this "the most horrific manifestation of Kincaid's colonial legacy in the postcolonial world" that embodies her position as "the privileged Black First Worlder," I argue that her "carelessness, arrogance and authority" are complicated by

---

24 For an account of multiple meditations on the meaning of "the Black Outdoors," see Carter and Cervenak (2017).

her respect for and dependence on the local guides. Throughout the travelogue, Kincaid (2020, p. 27) makes it abundantly clear that the planters' personal Sherpas and the porters are "important to [their] safety and general well-being." Therefore, her pastoral vision refuses to "delete workers to enhance the idyll" and makes it clear that her "aesthetic pleasure" is predicated upon the labour of indigenous people who inhabit the land (Buell, 2005, p. 145). Without rehearsing here all the details of their service, suffice it to say that without the Sherpas they would have been lost in the unfamiliar landscape; they would not have been able to negotiate with the Maoists or known to dig trenches to keep the rainwater away from their tents. All in all, the guides supported the planters in trying circumstances, meeting their needs with generosity and kindness. More specifically, Sunam, the Sherpa guide whose name is Kincaid (2020, p. 135) has no difficulty recalling, and takes care of her "whenever the going was difficult." He made sure she would never be left behind or lost and shielded her from the microaggressions of locals by pretending not to speak their dialect. While Kincaid's descriptions of her relationship with the porters may seem naively simplified at first sight, her pastoral idealism is imbricated in the oppositional character of the anti-pastoral.[25]

Kincaid's candid representation of the porters' rebellion and their refusal to accommodate the entitled travellers is an important anti-pastoral moment in the narrative. Even though the irritable plant hunters angrily demand that the porters return to make their camp where they wish, the porters refuse to do so, thus upsetting the "beautiful relation between rich and poor" that is the "essential trick of the old pastoral" (Empson, 1935, p. 11). Kincaid (2020, p. 84) reflects that even as "they were used to being very comfortable . . . in [their] native societies," they could not fire the porters who were making them uncomfortable because the porters were irreplaceable, essential to their survival and purpose in Nepal. Using a characteristically ironic tone, Kincaid mocks the social inequality and

---

25 I do not have sufficient space to discuss other anti-pastoral moments included in Kincaid's Black pastoral, for example, the night in a field of leeches, the threatening presence of the Maoist guerrillas, or Dan's fear of death on the shaking bamboo bridge.

division of labour that the pastoral mode depends on. To use another one of William Empson's (1935, p. 210) terms, Kincaid refuses to feign the "ironical humility" characteristic of the old pastoral. In her own words, the European and American travellers "wished Sunam would fire the porters. But he couldn't even if he wanted to. There were no other porters around" (Kincaid, 2020, p. 84). She rather identifies herself with Western bourgeois forms of entitlement, holding up the old pastoral's sensibility to ridicule (Empson, 1935, p. 210). Her travelogue reveals the global hierarchies at the core of pastoral representation, "the created injustices ... led to [the hikers] being there, dependent on the Sherpas," while positioning the Sherpas as beyond the fungibility and the disposability of the neoliberal worker (p. 84).

Kincaid models something like genuine interdependence between buyer and seller, as she recounts "[their] little community of the needy, dependent, plant collectors and the Nepalese people, whose support [they] could not do without" (2020, p. 81). [26] While it is important that the Nepalese provide service, hospitality, and care for the travellers, these persons also insist on their daily routine, their needs, and wants. All along the journey, the reality of the locals remains distinct from that of the hikers. The indigenous population "seemed very absorbed by the reality of their lives" and, as Kincaid recollects, "we were not part of it" (p. 112). For instance, the travellers go to bed early and are not invited by the porters to "stay up and drink and sing and dance to music they made" (p. 154). In this sense, Kincaid's pastoral expresses an awareness of interethnic conflicts and tensions of the landscape; she refuses the pastoral "as the idyllic face of settler-culture expansionism" and exploitative postcolonial tourism (Buell, 1995, 35). She is seeking to reconcile her pastoral quest for beauty with tolerance and letting be of the inhabitants of the land. Even when the travellers' foreign—

---

26 At present I am unable to gauge the environmental impact of the trekking industry or the extent to which the local guides are forced to participate in it. Though the theory of the Himalayan eco-crisis was disproved, the area remains susceptible to weathering, soil erosion, glacier lake outburst floods, landslides, and other extreme weather events (for a helpful review on the subject, see Koirala 2017).

and particularly her racialized — presence subjects them to the scrutiny and invasive gaze of the local population, Kincaid (2020, p. 38) normalizes their discomfort instead of global inequalities, indigenous land and sovereignty: "It felt odd but also seemed fair: we were in their country looking at their landscape after all." Her pastoral writing thus offers to respect diversity and differences of both people and the environment versus the old/colonial pastoral that requires, romanticizes, and effaces particular forms of dis/possession.

The multitemporality of the Black pastoral

Based on her citation of plant hunters such as Joseph Hooker, Nayar (2021, p. 8) argues that Kincaid is a "cultural insider to planting — and Western plant-collection and planting" performing the pastoral domestication of the exotic in her Vermont garden. As discussed before, this reading erases the traumatic ripping away of Afro-diasporic peoples from the land as well as from the botanical legacy of enslaved people. We must also not forget that Kincaid is writing before contemporary popular movements uniting Black farmers and gardeners as well as the emergence of the discipline of Black Ecologies.[27] Undoubtedly, her collection of seeds can be seen to reproduce the movement of plants and animals precipitated by colonialism. Even so, I argue that her collection of seeds, a return to a closer relationship with nature, is an act of refusing or bypassing colonial seeding, and a continuation of the fugitive seed keeping and sharing by enslaved women and their descendants.

Her pastoral practice is deeply connected to the strategies of seed keeping, planting, and cultivating that contest the extractive and coercive monocrop necroeconomics of the plantation. As Christian Brooks Keeve (2022) explains in "Fugitive Seeds," seed keeping, plant breeding and botanic life are embedded in plantation-style agriculture, where "seeds are sown en masse in as systemic and replicable a process as possible. An entire crop of a single variety is often planted simultaneously, maintained along the same

---

[27] This at least partly accounts for why she cannot fully liberate herself from the individualism of the pastoral genre.

schedules and with the same methods, and harvested together." However, oral histories and anthropological studies suggest a counternarrative, linking rice planting in the Americas to enslaved women who carried grains of rice in their hair or snuck it into their children's hair before they were sold. Judith Carney and R. N. Rosomoff (2009, p. 125) call the fugitive growing of African crops, likely leftovers or stowaways from slave ship provisions, a "shadow world of cultivation." In part, because she does not have the knowledge to keep heritage seeds, the Nepali excursion allows her to be with/in the vibrant presence of the seeds in their natural habitat. As she says, "We were . . . looking for things that would give us pleasure, not only in their growing but also with the satisfaction with which we could see them growing and remember seeing them alive in their place of origin" (Kincaid, 2020, p. 83). In this way, her Black pastoralism follows her ancestors' tradition of keeping alive the past, the seeds, and their stories (Penniman, 2018).

Seeds contain the potential of multiple temporalities and spatialities; simultaneously anchoring her in the Himalayan landscape, "where seeds are being collected," and prompting the unfolding of future possibilities, "the place where the garden is coming into being" (Kincaid, 2020, p. 7). *Among Flowers* invokes what Moten calls the tradition (exemplified by Harriet Jacobs's *Incidents*) of being in two places at the same time (quoted in Moten and Hartman 2016, 22:37-23:05). She is firmly grounded in the landscape, and in the vibrant, beautiful, joy-giving Nepalese plants, where "every place we walked was something, every place we walked was important" (Kincaid, 2020, p. 40). At the same time, the life-giving quality of seeds prompted her to be in Vermont, to imagine what each plant would look like in her garden, and what it would be like to grow it: "And all the time I was walking around in Nepal I was mostly thinking of my garden" (p. 42). The multi-potentiality of the seed simultaneously lands her in the present moment and ushers her into possible futures where her seeds will eventually come alive and "become flower-bearing shrubs and trees and herbaceous perennials in [her] garden" (p. 1). The reason for this is that seeds are not inert, inanimate objects/commodities, but potential vegetable happenings "that contain and sustain life or even the potential for life" for several years (Keeve, 2022). We can, therefore, read seed collecting as a form of double alienation: a continuation of the Black tradition of being in multiple places at the same time, of not quite being in place and time. A temporal intervention that troubles the linear time of colonial dispossession and triggers a constant going back and forth between past, present, and future. As Kincaid (2020, p. 7) attests, gathering seeds calls for a double, if not triple or quadruple, consciousness, an exploration of what might be: "I always want to be someplace where seeds are being collected, I want to be in the place where the garden is coming into being." In imagining a future with and through the seeds, she "honours the work of [the] ancestors who braided seeds in their hair before being forced to board transatlantic slave ships, believing against the odds in a future on soil" (Penniman, 2018). The Black pastoral therefore endeavors to not only heal the diaspora's ongoing disconnection from nature but also to imagine a future in which the rift between land and people is healed.

Conclusion

Kincaid's overwhelming sensations of natural beauty, feelings of anxiety and joy, vulnerability and loss of self are all inextricably connected to the "constant movement and constant change" of the travellers' "routine" (Kincaid, 2020, p. 158). In contrast to traditional pastoralism, Kincaid's multisensory experience of and her affective identification with the ungraspable, diverse, and constantly shifting beauty of the biodiverse landscape opens her to new, unusual modes of relationality with the self, indigenous people, and the plant community. The interaction with the lively landscape blurs the boundaries between the human and the non-human, coalescing in environmental effects and multispecies assemblies. Even when she feels alienated, that alienation signifies her distance from the familiar logics of subjection and appropriation of the racial capitalocene and her non-coercive alignment with and attachment to otherwise ecologies. While deemed a luxury by many, Kincaid's pastoral retreat from the racially structured milieu of the US and Antigua, her freedom to move, to make and take up space in the

Himalayas, her joyous contact with nature and her collection of seeds remain experiments in living and writing the Black pastoral experience otherwise.

The Black pastoral emerges as a way of experiencing and narrating a beautiful and experimental outside to Black ecologies, that is, "sites of ongoing injury, gratuitous harm, and premature death" (Roane and Hosbey, 2019). Like Black ecologies and geographies, the epithet Black indicates the experimental ways in which the Black pastoral interrogates and revises the traditional pastoral engagement with the environment. As we saw, Kincaid's travelogue articulates an alternative landscape as well as different ways of relating to, inhabiting, and moving through that landscape. In this essay, I focused on how the Black pastoral model imagines *the outside that is forever haunted by the inside*. Further studies on Kincaid's *Garden (Book)* should be done to investigate how the Black pastoral plots *the outside from within the inside* of Black ecologies.

Works Cited

Arnold, J. (2018) 'Feeling the Fires of Climate Change: Land Affect in Canada's Tar Sands', in Bladow, K., and Ladino, J. K. (eds.) *Affective Ecocriticism: Emotion, Embodiment, Environment.* Lincoln: U of Nebraska P, pp. 96-115.

Bate, J. (2000) *The Song of the Earth.* London: Picador.

Buell, L. (1995) *The Environmental Imagination: Thoreau, Nature Writing, and the Formation of American Culture.* Cambridge, MA: Harvard UP.

Buell, L. (2005) *The Future of Environmental Criticism: Environmental Crisis and Literary Imagination.* Oxford: Blackwell.

Carney, J. A. and Rosomoff, R. N. (2009) *In the Shadow of Slavery: Africa's Botanical Legacy in the Atlantic World.* Berkeley: University of California Press.

Carter, J. K. and Cervenak, S. J. (2017) 'The Black Outdoors: Humanities Futures After Property and Possession', *Humanities Futures Blog of the Franklin Humanities Institute.* Available at: https://humanitiesfutures.org/papers/the-black-outdoors-humanities-futures-after-property-and-possession/ Accessed 1 August 1 2018

Casteel, S. P. (2007) *Second Arrivals, Landscape and Belonging in Contemporary Writing in the Americas.* Charlottesville: University of Virginia Press.

Chansky, R. A. (2015) 'Between Selves: An intertextual approach to Jamaica Kincaid's "Among Flowers', *Biography*, Winter, vol. 38, no. 1, pp. 135-151.

Coulthard, G. (2014) *Red Skins, White Masks: Rejecting the Colonial Politics of Recognition.* Minneapolis: University of Minnesota Press.

Crawley, A. (2020) *the lonely letters.* Durham and London: Duke University Press.

Crosby, A. (2004) *Ecological Imperialism: The Biological Expansion of Europe, 900-1900.* Cambridge and New York: Cambridge University Press; 2nd edition.

Didur, J. (2010) "Gardenworthy': Rerouting Colonial Botany in Jamaica Kincaid's *Among Flowers: A Walk in the Himalayas*', *Public*, vol. 41, pp. 173-185.

Empson, W. (1935) *Some Versions of Pastoral.* London: Chatto and Windus. Available at: https://quod.lib.umich.edu/g/genpub/AEH5661.0001.001?rgn=main;view=fulltext

Floyd, M. F., and Stodolska, M. (2019) 'Scholarship on Race and Ethnicity: Assessing Contributions to Leisure Theory and Practice', *Journal of Park and Recreation Administration*, vol. 37, no. 1, Spring, pp. 80–94.

Gifford, T. (2001) *Pastoral.* London and New York: Routledge. AppleBooks.

Haraway, D. (2015) 'Anthropocene, Capitalocene, Plantationocene, Chthulucene: Making Kin', *Environmental Humanities*, vol. 6, no. 1, pp. 159-165.

Hartman, S. (2020) *Wayward Lives, Beautiful Experiments: Intimate Histories of Social Upheaval*. Norton.

Keeve, C. B. (2022) 'Fugitive Seeds', *Edge Effects*. Available at: https://edgeeffects.net/fugitive-seeds/ Accessed 25 February 2022.

Kincaid, J. (2020) *Among Flowers: A Walk in the Himalayas*. New York: Picador.

Kincaid, J. (2011) *My Garden (Book)*. New York: Farrar, Straus and Giroux.

Kochar, S. and Khan, M. A. (2021) *Environmental Postcolonialism: A Literary Response*. Lexington Books.

Koirala, H. L. (2017) 'Myth and Reality of the Eco-crisis in Nepal Himalaya', *The Geographical Journal of Nepal*, vol. 10, pp. 39-54.

Loughrey, B. (ed.) (1984) *The Pastoral Mode: A Casebook*, London: Macmillan.

Marx, L. (2000) *The Machine in the Garden: Technology and the Pastoral Ideal in America*. New York: Oxford University Press.

McKittrick, K. (2006) *Demonic Grounds: Black Women and the Cartographies of Struggle*. Minneapolis: University of Minnesota Press.

Moten, F., and Hartman, S. (2016) "The Black Outdoors: Humanities Futures after Property and Possession" *YouTube*, uploaded by Duke Franklin Humanities Institute, 5 October 2016. Available at: https://www.youtube.com/watch?v=t_tUZ6dybrc

Nayar, P. K. (2013) 'Mobility and Anxious Cosmopolitanism: Jamaica Kincaid's Among Flowers', *Transnational Literature*, vol. 6, no.1, pp. 1-15. *ProQuest*. Accessed August 11, 2021.

Ngai, S. (2005) *Ugly Feelings*. Cambridge: Harvard UP. ProQuest. Web. 4 Aug. 2021.

O'Brien, S. (2002) 'The Garden and the World: Jamaica Kincaid and the Cultural Borders of Ecocriticism', *Mosaic: An Interdisciplinary Critical Journal*, vol. 35, no. 2, pp. 167–184.

Pećić, Z. (2011) 'Floral Diaspora in Jamaica Kincaid's Travel Writing', in Edwards, J. D. and Graulund, R. (eds.) *Postcolonial Travel Writing: Critical Explorations*. Great Britain: Palgrave Macmillan, pp. 138-155.

Penniman, L. (2018) *Farming While Black: Soul Fire Farm's Practical Guide to Liberation on the Land*. White River Junction and London: Chelsea Green Publishing. Ebook.

Roane, J. T. (2018) 'Plotting the Black Commons', *Souls*, vol. 20, no. 3, pp. 1-24.

Roane, J.T. and Hosbey, J. (2019) 'Mapping Black Ecologies', *Current Research in Digital History*, vol. 2, doi: https://doi.org/10.31835/crdh.2019.05

Tsing, A. L. (2015) *The Mushroom at the End of the World: On the Possibility of Life in Capitalist Ruins*. Princeton, NJ: Princeton University Press.

Walker, A. (2011) *In Search of Our Mothers' Gardens: Womanist Prose*. New York: Open Road. Apple Books.

Wilderson III., F. B. (2010) *Red, White, and Black: Cinema and the Structure of US Antagonisms*. Durham and London: Duke University Press.

Wynter, S. (1971) 'Novel and History, Plot and Plantation', *Savacou*, vol. 5, pp. 95–102.

Urban Pastoral and Collective Memory in Penelope Lively's *City of the Mind*

The pastoral often implies an idealisation of the countryside or celebration of nature, as well as a contrast with the urban. With the development of post-pastoral writing and critique in recent years, however, there arises "an awareness of both nature as culture and of culture as nature" (Gifford 1999, 161). Such an awareness is not limited to nature writing that views nature as culture. It is also prominent in city literature, especially in the poems or novels pastoralizing urban culture. As Kevin McNamara and Timothy Gray (2014, 246) point out, "the art of urban pastoral inheres in ways of seeing that find or create within the city spaces or images conducive to pastoral moods." In other words, what makes a literary work pastoral depends on the represented way of relating to and feeling about one's environment.

The city, though often criticized for alienation and isolation, is sometimes completely transformed through literary imagination. For example, in her classic city novel *Mrs Dalloway* (1925), Virginia Woolf imagines London to be a place evoking a "sense of invigoration, harmony with one's surroundings, and enrapturing aesthetic revelation that is traditionally associated with the green world of pastoral" (Alter 2010, 105). Despite its dark undertone, Woolf's pastoral vision manifestly celebrates London and offers the reader a much-needed boost of confidence in the renewed strength of the English society undergoing radical changes in the aftermath of World War I.

More than half a century later, another radical change altered not only the social space but also the material landscape of London. To counter the intense anxiety caused by the massive projects of urban redevelopment propelled by neoliberal policies and globalisation, a significant number of contemporary British writers consciously or unconsciously feature London in their works. Angela Carter, who turns the contemporary metropolis into a lively theatrical stage from the perspective of a pair of elderly twin sisters in her novel *Wise Children* (1991), puts particular emphasis on her Dickensian rendering of London in an interview: "I wanted to preserve the London I remember. [...] Because the city we were all born in is vanishing, it's like we're all writing in this frenzy of nostalgia" (quoted in Bradfield 1994, 93). The urge to "preserve" what London was like is certainly a mounting concern shared by writers like Peter Ackroyd, Iain Sinclair, Patrick Wright, etc. While writers remember the capital city in their words and contribute to the city's collective memory, London somehow grows, lives, and is grafted onto their bodies, as if becoming "the best organ of memory", to borrow Lewis Mumford's metaphor (1961, 562). In these London writings, the relations between the city and its inhabitants—fictional and non-fictional—seem to have acquired a reciprocal and corporeal, or rather, trans-corporeal dimension. Such thematised intertwining between the human and the environment echoes the imagination of the harmonious urban village offered by Woolf at the beginning of the twentieth century.

Penelope Lively's novel *City of the Mind* (1991), set in the late twentieth century, presents a pastoral vision of London from the perspective of collective memory. Through the protagonist's double role—as an architect professionally involved in the Docklands development project and as a *flâneur* habitually drawn into the collective past embodied by buildings and places, the novel interweaves individual consciousness into the collective memory of the city. It highlights the protagonist's sentient physical body intimately embedded in an urban landscape rich with historical references. In sharp contrast to the considerable uncertainty regarding the future of London at the turn of the twenty-first century, Lively resorts to the poetic convention of the pastoral and places her imagined city in a reassuringly perpetual cycle of decay and growth that has always been there. At the same time, by skillfully structuring the narratives and sub-narratives in the novel, the author avoids collapsing the present into the past or over-idealizing the harmonious yet homogeneous aspect of the urban pastoral.

Postmodern architecture and "semblance of place"

City of the Mind is mainly focalised through Matthew Halland, a forty-ish English architect who is involved in the construction of a skyscraper in the Docklands. The high-rise building with a distinctively postmodern style heralds the future of London, forming a strong contrast with its de-industrialised and derelict surroundings. As the Docklands project goes on, Halland imagines that the whole city is being transformed into a "glass city":

> Sometimes the façades were mirrors of silver or copper, throwing back their surroundings — the movement of traffic, the complexities of other buildings, the flowing clouds. Enigmatic, uncommitted presences; an architecture of deception. All around, glass was soaring above the old structures of brick and stone, dwarfing them, distorting them so that they swam shrunk and misshapen in the shining surface of the new city. (Lively 1992, 128)

To readers who have experienced the rapid gentrification of London in recent years, Halland's vision is realistic rather than imaginary. In his introduction to a volume of essays on contemporary London culture, Joe Kerr (2003, 20) remarks that since the 1980s London "has shed its drabness; the dinginess and dirt that once coated its every surface have been scraped away from its older structures, or else they have been replaced with sleek, hard facades of steel and glass." The city has become increasingly pleasant to the eye. While being hyper-visible and attesting to London's strong position in the global market, these shiny new buildings are not much connected with their immediate surroundings. Their glassy surfaces distort and reflect the onlookers and the urban landscape. Fredric Jameson (1991, 42), in his discussion on the Bonaventure, a characteristic postmodern building located in Los Angeles, points out, "the glass skin achieves a peculiar and placeless dislocation of the Bonaventure from its neighbourhood." Instead of fitting into the existing urban fabric, postmodern architecture "does not wish to be a part of the city but rather its equivalent and replacement or substitute" (Jameson 1994, 40). Or, as phrased in Lively's novel, such postmodern skyscrapers are "uncommitted presences" (1992, 128) — not committed or attached to any specific place. By personifying the buildings and accusing them of "deception", the novel draws attention to the increasing disjunction among different areas in London.

The construction of glassy skyscrapers not only creates place-less space but also goes against the traditional development pattern. While driving through East London, Halland contemplates:

> A city is an organic growth and here the profoundly arrogant assumption was being made that you can bulldoze the past, replace it with new constructions and expect the result to be anything other than the semblance of a place. (Lively 1992, 90)

Disagreeing with the new construction's elimination of the past, Halland appeals to the organic strength of the city. The notion of London as an autonomously growing entity that disregards the "arrogant assumption" is not rare. As far back as the early twentieth century, the Danish architect Steen Eiler Rasmussen in his study *London: The Unique City* (1934) praises London as an exemplar of the "scattered city", in contrast to the "concentrated city" filled with planned, monumental buildings like Paris (1960, 23). According to Rasmussen, the scattered and "wholesome" form of London originates with its inhabitants and with the concept of "precedent" in English Law that recognises the authority of what has already taken place. Neither London nor English law "conform to a coherent, logical system but are organically developed out of the life of the people" (Rasmussen 1960, 75). From this viewpoint, London's seemingly chaotic form has been gradually brought into existence by numerous generations of free-spirited Londoners. In this way, the material environment of the city embodies the victory of the ordinary people over the overbearing state.

In *City of the Mind*, however, London's organic character tends to be detached from its people and its cumulative development in history. On one hand, Halland expects the organically growing London to frustrate those arrogant land speculators. Halland does not conceal the intense distaste he feels for Rutter, a wealthy client who reminds the reader of the Cockney crime boss intending to invest in Docklands redevelopment in the John Mackenzie film *The Long Good Friday* (1980). To snatch a piece of land in Spitalfields,

Rutter conspires in an arson attack to scare away the recalcitrant tenants. Enraged by Rutter's heedless inconsideration for the local communities, Halland rejects his job work. On the other hand, as an architect, Halland cannot avoid working with real estate companies. He admits that what drives the city forward nowadays is "the unstoppable force of profit" (Lively 1992, 17). New buildings come into being all the time, despite his willingness or reluctance. Deeply involved in the development of London, Halland comes to understand "people as pawns" and "the city as some uncontrollable organic force" (Lively 1992, 13). London seems to have a will of its own, but it is no longer a will constituted by the common people. Rather, what dictates the growth of London is capital and the global market.

As if making up for his complicity in the Docklands construction project, Halland attempts to retain some trace of the city's past. He suggests the building be named "Frobisher House" and its main entrance decorated with a glass engraving of a ship (Lively 1992, 32). Martin Frobisher is a sixteenth-century privateer who sailed from Blackwall, the place where the fictional skyscraper is set. The novel includes a fictional account from the viewpoint of Frobisher during one of his journeys and relates his victorious return to London. With the name "Frobisher House", the skyscraper is endowed with an identity that relates to the history of the place. Nevertheless, the name and the glass engraving have little effect on other characters in the novel. The past embedded in these symbols is no more than private knowledge. It is "a sort of knowledge that remains silent. Only hints of what is known but unrevealed are passed on 'just between you and me,'" as Michel de Certeau (1984, 108) remarks concerning places with buried past. On hearing the suggested name, the investor calls it a "nice gimmick" and later mistakes the stars in the glass engraving for a kite (Lively 1992, 30). There is no doubt that most people are content with the superficial meaning or mere image of these symbols, and few would delve into the buried past.

Nevertheless, with the name and the engraving, the building is furnished with some "semblance of a place" that is lacking in its shiny façade. This fabricated sense of place only serves to increase the market value of the building, which is part of the general trend of selling places. In his discussion on place construction, David Harvey (1993, 8) argues, that nowadays cities and places endeavour to "differentiate themselves from other places and become more competitive to capture or retain capital investment." One crucial factor of differentiation originates in the past of a place. Therefore, the practice of selling places often involves concocting and promoting an appealing cultural image of the place with a distinct history or tradition, either through physical preservation, media representation, or literary imagination. This trend draws resources and inspirations from the urban past to attract customers, tourists and profitable businesses in the present. It leads to "constructed authenticity, invented traditions and a commercialized heritage culture" (Harvey 1993, 12). Consequently, Halland's efforts are easily assimilated into the commercialization of the city and its history, in which cultural symbols with a rich historical context are reduced to unique selling points, as part of a "constructed authenticity" to be marketed.

The novel's presentation of Halland's architectural practices and comments reveals a significant mode of relating to the city and its past. The Italian architect Aldo Rossi (1982, 130) once argued, "The city is the locus of collective memory." Collective memory, a concept made popular by Maurice Halbwachs and a key term in recent years' memory boom, indicates that memories are socially constructed through collective frameworks—opinions and values shared by a social group—and adjusted for the creation of an image of the group's past in light of the present (Coser 1992, p34). The physical landscape is one of the important facets of the collective framework of memory. By locating collective memory in the city, Rossi emphasises that the city as a physical landscape, where buildings, things, and people congregate, not only bears the city's past but also helps the individual recollect what they have experienced in the city or have heard about the city. In the 1990s, the time when Lively's novel as well as many other London books were written, London's physical landscape was going through changes. Not only do "uncommitted" and "placeless" postmodern skyscrapers take up the land, but also make Londoners feel alienated and threaten their memories of the city. Not in a position to stop the material and actual changes driven by money and profit, concerned writers' resort to literary imagination to strengthen the memories of London.

What Rossi proclaims can be understood as the "top-down" mode of memory. Unlike the architects who equate history with collective memory (Rossi 1982), the literary critic Aleida Assmann distinguishes between the two. Whereas memory is embodied and rooted in the recollection of concrete spaces, gestures and objects, history is disembodied and deemed to be abstract, objective and universal (Assmann 2008, p 60-61). Yet, the differences are not absolute. Memory and history are dialectical. Unlived history can be incorporated and turned into memory via external symbols and institutions such as monuments. This kind of memory is termed "top-down political memory", forming a contrast to a "bottom-up social memory" that relies on embodied everyday practices and lacks an endurable ground (Assmann 2008, 56). Rossi's understanding of the collective memory of the city belongs to the "top-down" mode. It inadvertently facilitates an official version of urban memory that suits the needs of the dominant power and excludes or suppresses the memories of other peoples. Given his position as a famous architect and theorist, it is no wonder that Rossi prioritises abstract grand urban plans over the embodied practices of ordinary urban dwellers. After all, it is the former that represents the interest of the urban elites, who hold the power of shaping the material cityscape and "(re)writing" urban history by designing monumental buildings, thereby influencing the way the ordinary inhabitants remember their city.

The mode of top-down urban memory is reflected in the protagonist's profession in Lively's imagined London. The novel drives home the limits and constraints placed on architectural practices by the global market and multinational companies. Because of his coalition with the top-down collective memory of London, Halland's relation with the city seems distanced, distorted and inauthentic, which is shown in his self-contradictory rumination over the "organic" nature of the city. At the same time, however, through another practice, the novel puts forward a more intimate way of relating to London's past and inhabiting the city in the present.

Flâneur and bottom-up urban memories

Apart from being an architect, Halland is also a habitual *flâneur* who often takes long walks throughout London, observes the cityscape, and picks up traces left by past Londoners. The main narrative focalised through Halland in contemporary London, is paralleled with several sub-narratives which are triggered by the various sensations felt by Halland in different places. For instance, while passing the Covent Garden market, Halland feels the inexplicable urge to buy a bunch of violets from the flower stall. In the next paragraph — separated by a space in the text — we are told: "She can smell violets. And dung and sewage and the strong pervading stench of unwashed humanity" (Lively 1992, p34). "She" is an orphan called Rose, living on the streets in Covent Garden in the Victorian age. The smell of violet, as a shared sensory experience, becomes a trace that connects the past urban lives with the present experience of Halland. Also, the present tense of the sub-narrative suggests what has happened more than one hundred years ago is not completely gone. The past and the present are put side by side in the textual space of the novel. This technique is repeatedly employed in the novel to insert other fragmentary stories about previous Londoners from different historical periods, including an air raid warden named Jim Prothero during the Blitz, the nineteenth-century biologist Sir Richard Owen, the Elizabethan privateer Martin Frobisher, as well as a nameless Inuit captured and brought back to London by Frobisher as a trophy. Various periods and historical figures are paralleled with Halland's life in the contemporary city, forming a juxtaposition of present and past in the narrative.

The unique structure of Lively's novel recalls the idea of "spatial form" proposed by Joseph Frank. (Frank 1991, p7-8) rebuts the categorisation of artistic forms in Gotthold Lessing's *Laocoon* (1766), in which painting is characterised as an art of space while literature is one of time, because in painting "the visible aspect of objects can best be presented juxtaposed in an instant of time" whereas literature is "composed of a succession of words proceeding through time." Frank examines modernist works by Marcel Proust, James Joyce and T. S. Eliot, arguing that in these texts, synchronicity overtakes the diachronic succession of words. To be specific, words or word groups referring to dissociated objects or non-consecutive events are often juxtaposed, which disrupts the linear reading process and requires "the reader to apprehend their work spatially, in a moment of time, rather than as a sequence" (Frank 1991, p10). As a result, temporality seems to be abolished in these modern literary works, and the high modernists, such as Joyce and Eliot, are shown to be nostalgic for the myth of eternal return. As Joseph Frank (1991, p63) claims, "Past and present are apprehended spatially, locked in a timeless unit." The spatial form affects the structure of temporality as we know it, not only in terms of reading experience but also within the imaginary world presented in the text.

The spatial form is flexibly adopted by Lively. The experiences of contemporary Londoners resonate with the past via similar sensations, but the present is not a mere repetition of some eternal prototypes. Instead, the novel juxtaposes the present with the past for various purposes. For instance, the Victorian street urchin's destitute life forms a sharp contrast with Halland's leisurely afternoon stroll and the happy life of his beloved eight-year-old daughter. Also, the bomb fires that severely damaged London and killed the warden's child during the Blitz are inserted as a critique of reckless contemporary redevelopment in Spitalfields. Rutter's arson attack leads to the death of a child in a Bengali family living in the local area. By paralleling the two fires, the novel makes active and inventive use of the past to express its disapproval of the contemporary situation. Lastly, the despair felt by the deracinated Inuit in sixteenth-century London—in "this terrible nowhere" (Lively 1992, 175)—reverberates in the feeling of the engraving artist Eva Burden, a German Jewish woman who has left home for London as a child via Kindertransport during the WWII. Unlike the Inuit who dies out of despair shortly after arriving in London, Burden manages to turn London from a "terrible nowhere" into an inhabitable place where she "becomes part of the urban stew and add[s] to it [her] own little bit of flavour" (Lively 1992, p177). Through these detailed and nuanced exercises of juxtaposition, the novel shows the urban past as a rich, but not deterministic, background. It integrates the past into the present urban lives to create new meanings, not to perpetuate the same pattern.

What is more, Lively's novel shows that the continuity of the urban past and the present requires material places. Most of the stories about past Londoners are re-collected during Halland's wanderings in markets and streets. These fragments of London's past are rendered palpable through the lived experiences of Halland in those material places. Michel de Certeau (1984, p108) proposes that inhabitable places are "fragmentary and inward-turning histories, pasts that others are not allowed to read, accumulated times that can be unfolded but like stories held in reserve, remaining in an enigmatic state, symbolizations encysted in the pain or pleasure of the body." Unlike Rossi's idea of "history", de Certeau's "inward-turning histories" are plural, fragmentary and subjective. They are memories lodged in local places, to be told in the form of stories and to be shared among an intimate social group, not spectacular monumental images to be visually registered by everyone and no one in particular. Also, what triggers the unfolding of memories is the experiencing and feeling body, in its "pain or pleasure". De Certeau's attention to the embodied and the subjective is echoed in M. Christine Boyer's criticism of Rossi. Boyer (1994, p188) points out that Rossi's theory "privilege[s] the position of the analyst and the definer of codes over lived experiences and subjective conditions." From the perspective of Halland the urban wanderer, *City of the Mind* presents London as a tangible place where the lives of past Londoners are retained in the material traces, which are later picked up by Halland's sentient body. The protagonist wandering through a wide range of places functions as a means of collecting past stories, which are unfolded in discrete passages and inserted into the main narrative of the novel.

Halland's double role—as architect and flâneur—signifies the top-down and the bottom-up aspects of the urban memory of London. Apart from revealing the tension between these two aspects, the novel opts for a more eclectic approach. It makes use of Halland's embodied, sensuous and authentic experiences of London's past to offset the sense of loss. With this reconciliation with the radical changes, the novel concedes that urban redevelopment and gentrification are unstoppable and instead suggests the best we could do is to cushion the pain of loss — remembering the urban past in each individual's daily practices. Admittedly, this turn towards a subjective engagement with the city is politically passive. Material traces might one day be completely wiped out and rendered inaccessible, and then there will be no sensory triggers for recollection.

On the other hand, the novel avoids fetishizing the urban past. Unlike the name and the glass engraving of Frobisher House Halland the architect proposes, which manifestly appeals to the official history of London and helps create some "semblance of a place", Halland the wanderer realises a deeper connection, or rather, "rootedness" with the collective memory of London. Making a distinction between being rooted in a place from having a sense of place Yi-Fu Tuan (1977, p198) points out: "The effort to evoke a sense of place and of the past is often deliberate and conscious. To the extent that the effort is conscious it is the mind at work, and the mind — if allowed its imperial way — will annul the past by making it all present knowledge." What Lively proposes in *City of the Mind* is a kind of "rootedness" that remains beyond the protagonist's "present knowledge" or consciousness.

Significantly, the protagonist is not always aware of the historical reference to his sensory experiences in London. Both the main story and sub-stories are focalised through their respective character's views and narrated by an omniscient, impersonal narrator, which precludes intersections of the present and the past. For instance, the association of the violet fragrance with the Victorian child is beyond Halland's consciousness, although the sensation is registered by his body. His corporeal body seems to "remember" more than his thinking mind does, so to speak. In his article on embodiment and collective memory, Rafael Narvaez (2006, p59) remarks, "we can 'naturally' carry, in our bodies, the strong presence of the past." Our habitual bodily practices such as gestures, pleasures and feelings are all layered with collective symbols and associated with a collective past. Our identity is inseparable from this embodied collective memory. In *City of the Mind*, Halland naturally, unconsciously, and daily carries the presence of the urban memory of London in his body: "Through him, the city lives and breathes" (Lively 1992, p3). Metaphorically, the city has been incorporated into Halland and become part of his embodied existence that is not always thematized. In the words of Tuan, Halland's semi-unconscious intertwinement with the urban memory of London represents a kind of "rootedness" which is distinct from an intentionally created "sense of place." By giving the corporeal experiences, a dimension of time and collectiveness beyond the grasp of the individual's subjective mind, the novel demonstrates a harmonious, reciprocal, and trans-corporeal relationship between the city and the individual, which has plenty in common with the pastoral mode.

The urban pastoral and ecological self

The pastoral often implies an idealisation of country life or celebration of nature, especially in contrast to the alienating and corrupt urban world. However, the distinction between the countryside and the city is not indisputable. In recent years there has been the notion of the urban pastoral, a mixture of two seemingly contradictory terms. As Kevin McNamara and Timothy Gray (2014, p12) point out, the pastoral is not just about the literary form or the content of a work; there exists a set of "attitudes and orientations transpose[able] from the pastoral to the city." The novel *City of the Mind* offers a pastoral vision of London, which is manifested in content and mood, and marked by an implicit anti-pastoral critique in its presentation of the urban past.

Despite the sense of uncertainty and disruption brought by the ongoing urban redevelopment projects, London in Lively's novel is presented as a largely invigorating place where the protagonist manages to cope with a failed marriage and finds a new love. Halland's encounter with a girl in a red coat at a street vendor is rather commonplace in city literature. Charles Baudelaire's poem "To a Passer-by" (1855) recounts the thrills and laments of seeing an attractive female stranger emerge from the urban crowd and walk past the speaker. The fleeting moment of passing captured in the poem exemplifies a crucial element in Baudelaire's definition of modernity, that is, "the ephemeral, the fugitive, the contingent" (Baudelaire 1964, p13). The fleeting encounter is extended to a brief stalking in *Mrs Dalloway*, where Peter secretly pursues a young woman through several streets and feels satisfied with playing a romantic "buccaneer" in a made-up "escapade" (Woolf 2000, 39-40). In both works, the urban space is characterised by unfulfilled or imaginary erotic potential. As Walter Benjamin (1973, 46) observes, "love itself is recognized as being stigmatized by the big city." The stigmatised love is lust, originating from the collision of the bodies rather than the communication of the souls. It is more physical and alienating than spiritual and rejuvenating. In *City of the Mind*, however, such an encounter is rewritten; love is redeemed. On seeing the girl in red for the first time, Halland feels like "seeing sunlight on a distant, inaccessible hillside" (Lively 1992, p18). The same pastoral scene shows up again in his dream. Their encounter is later developed into a romantic love, which recalls the idealised shepherd's love sung by ancient poets. The love story endows the imagined London with an unusually pastoral mood, where genuine communion with others is possible and human relationships can be salutary rather than disconcerting.

The protagonist's loss and regaining of love parallels the presentation of London, which goes through the cycle of decay and growth and yet remains enduring all the time. The image of London, as Christian Gutleben (2017) argues, is comparable to the concept of "urban palimpsests" raised by Andreas Huyssen. A palimpsest is a durable parchment on which its past is written, erased, and rewritten in historical sequence, but some marks and traces are still traceable, accessible or readable in the present. More importantly, in *City of the Mind*, the acts of reading the past—recombination and reinterpretation—are carried out via the omniscient narrator and presented to the reader on the textual level. Within the story, the urban past is revisited, albeit limited to the realm of unconscious embodied experiences. This differentiation allows for the protagonist to be propelled forward without being pulled back by the past, which generates a sense of certainty and stability for the reader. The novel does not advocate a return to or a restoration of an idealised past. Rather, it shows full confidence in the oncoming future.

Not only is the past temporarily and unconsciously visited, but the present also deposits its traces to form a new layer in the urban palimpsest. The novel itself offers a more interesting metaphor for the city other than the palimpsest. In the final chapter, Halland moves around London:

> doubling back and forth, navigating time and space. In Covent Garden there are no violets, but he hears Alice Cook tell him that she is pregnant, and buys her red carnations. The plane trees in Lincoln's Inn Fields rise up from the lake of their own leaves, but he sees an afternoon in June, shirtsleeves and Coke cans. [...] He sees his scattered hours—irretrievable, enshrined. (Lively 1992, 218)

Halland's experiences settle into the collective memory of London. They are turned into fragmentary life stories, as "scattered hours", and dispersed in different places. New memories symbolised by "red carnations" form a new trace, overlaying the "violets" that refer to a more remote one. Although the past is not completely absent—it is turned into a latent ground, like an annual growth ring that marks the passing of time. Indeed, the vitality of London is bodied forth by the London plane tree. The "city [that] lifts again and again from its decay, thrusting up from its detritus" is like the plane trees that "rise from the lake of their own leaves" (Lively 1992, p109- 218). In the novel's poetic depiction of London, the building and rebuilding of the city, though cultural and man-made, is understood in the form of the growth pattern of a tree. In this way, the novel pastoralises the urban landscape and crosses the boundary between culture and nature. To borrow Terry Gifford's (1999, 162) words, "the ebbs and flows of culture are natural flux in the post-pastoral sense."

Apart from envisioning the city as a pastoral world, the novel presents an ecological self in harmony with such a world. In his discussion on urban inhabitation, Lawrence Buell (2009, 84) argues that the eco-*flâneur*, the *flâneur* figure endowed with environmentalist consciousness, keeps "long-term reciprocal engagement with a place's human and non-human environments and welcomes the prospect of one's identity being moulded by this encounter." In *City of the Mind*, Halland interacts with the city constantly, by activating the memory traces of the city and by depositing his experiences into the collective memory of the city at the same time. As the individual story is blended into the collective memory of London, transient mortal life is elevated and "enshrined" as part of a grander, immortal unity. Whereas Halland's urban identity is reaffirmed in his engagement with the city, the engraving artist Burden's identity is positively moulded by her urban encounter. Overall, the natural accretion of a medley of individual and collective memories renders London an organic and natural collective body consisting of numerous living bodies and steadily progressing in a stable continuum.

While emphasising the sense of continuity with a rich past, Lively's novel avoids romanticising the urban past as a golden age. It conveys an anti-pastoral sentiment. The Elizabethan Sea exploration is counterbalanced with the painful uprootedness of an Inuit, and the Victorian scientific progress is set in contrast with the grinding poverty of the urban poor. These sub-narratives demonstrate that the collective memory of London includes not only the top-down political memory that conforms to British history but also the bottom-up social memories of people from heterogeneous backgrounds. By giving voices to the latter, the novel criticises the tendency to idealise or romanticise in the pastoral mode.

In response to the growing sentiments of uncertainty and nostalgia caused by urban redevelopment projects in London, *City of the Mind* imagines an urban pastoral where genuine communion with others is enabled, and the interrelation between self and world is reciprocal and harmonious. With an innovative structure of narratives, which juxtaposes the past with the present, and the individual with the collective, the novel demonstrates a natural mode of inhabitation and rootedness. While emphasising the steadily progressing continuum of the collective body of the city modelled after the London plane tree, the author makes clear that the pastoralised urban space consists not of restoring an idealised past, but of the daily interaction of Londoners coming from heterogeneous backgrounds and carrying in their bodies various memories of the city.

Works Cited

Alter, R. (2010) *Imagined Cities: Urban Experience and the Language of the Novel*. New Haven: Yale University Press.

Assmann, A. (2008) "Transformations between History and Memory." *Social Research* 75.1: 49-72.

Baudelaire, C. (1964) *The Painter of Modern Life and Other Essays*. London: Phaidon Press.

Benjamin, W. (1973) *Charles Baudelaire: A Lyric Poet in the Era of High Capitalism*. London: NLB.

Boyer, M.C. (1994) *The City of Collective Memory: Its Historical Imagery and Architectural Entertainments*. Cambridge, Mass.: MIT Press.

Bradfield, S. (1994) "Remembering Angela Carter." *The Review of Contemporary Fiction* 14.3: 90-93.

Buell, L. (2009) *Writing for an Endangered World*. Cambridge, Mass.: Harvard University Press.

Coser, L.A. (1992) "Introduction: Maurice Halbwachs, 1877-1945." In *On Collective Memory*, Maurice Halbwachs. Chicago: University of Chicago Press: 1-34.

De Certeau, M. (1984) *The Practice of Everyday Life*. Berkeley: University of California Press.

Frank, J. (1991) *The Idea of Spatial Form*. London: Rutgers University Press.

Gifford, T. (1999) *Pastoral*. London: Routledge.

Gutleben, C. (2017) "'Urban Palimpsests': When Novelistic and Architectural Languages Merge in Penelope Lively's *City of the Mind*." *Études Britanniques Contemporaines. Revue de La Société D'études Anglaises Contemporaines* 52. https://doi.org/10.4000/ebc.3545.

Harvey, D. (1993) "From Space to Place and Back Again." In *Mapping the Futures: Local Cultures, Global Change*, ed. J. Bird, B. Curtis, T. Putnan, G. Robertson, and L. Tickner. London: Routledge.

Jameson, F. (1991) *Postmodernism, or, The Cultural Logic of Late Capitalism*. Durham: Duke University Press.

Kerr, J. (2003) "Introduction." In *London: From Punk to Blair*, ed. J. Kerr and A. Gibson. London: Reaktion Books: 11-22.

Lively, P. (1992) *City of the Mind*. London: Penguin Books.

McNamara, K.R., and T. Gray. (2014) "Some Versions of Urban Pastoral." In *The Cambridge Companion to the City in Literature*, ed. K. R. McNamara. Cambridge: Cambridge University Press: 245-260.

Mumford, L. (1961) *The City in History: Its Origins, Its Transformations, and Its Prospects*. New York: Harcourt Brace Jovanovich Inc.

Narvaez, R. F. (2006) "Embodiment, Collective Memory and Time." *Body & Society* 12.3: 51-73.

Rasmussen, S. E. (1960) *London: The Unique City*. London: Penguin Books.

Rossi, A. (1982) *The Architecture of the City*. Cambridge, Mass.: MIT Press.

Tuan, Y.F. (1977) *Space and Place: The Perspective of Experience*. London: Edward Arnold.

Woolf, V. (2000) *Mrs Dalloway*. Oxford: Oxford University Press.

Paradise to Paradise Lost: Transforming Rural Scape in Bibhutibhusan Bandyopadhay's *Aranyak*

The Anthropocene has witnessed humans bring large-scale changes in the surroundings, and therefore now it is high time that humans introspect, and take responsibility for their actions. Well, warnings regarding adverse effects that callous human actions would cause on climate and surroundings are not recent. Bibhutibhushan Bandyopadhyay is a clairvoyant amongst many who raised concerns regarding sustainable development as early as the beginning of the twentieth century. His works have mentioned the insurmountable worth of natural resources and the repercussions of adopting an unsustainable lifestyle. The novel *Aranyak* explores the tranquil and pristine pastoral life of Phulkia-baihar, which is affected by the incoming changes brought on by rapid development and modern forces. In this novel, Bandyopadhyay extolled the beauty of Nature and showed human greed accompanied by corrupt malpractices and indifference infiltrating the paradise-like rural space. Amidst all this, he captured the protagonist's dilemma, whose consciousness about the conservation of natural surroundings makes him sensitive to the drastic changes occurring in Phulkia-baihar.

In *The Great Derangement: Climate Change and the Unthinkable*, Amitav Ghosh raises the pertinent issues of the present age, which are climate change and the ignorance of humans regarding it. Ghosh bemoans that climate change and climate crisis have minimal presence in contemporary literary fiction. He says this age would be called "the time of Great Derangement" because several factors like social, political and economic conspire to conceal the reality of climate change and how almost everyone has ignored the truth about climate change. He writes:

> In a substantially altered world, when sea-level rise has swallowed the Sundarbans and made cities like Kolkata, New York and Bangkok uninhabitable, when readers and museumgoers turn to the art

and literature of our time, will they not look, first, and most urgently, for traces and portents of the altered world of their inheritance? And when they fail to find them, what should they — — what can they — — do other than to conclude that ours was a time when most forms of art and literature were drawn into the modes of concealment that prevented people from recognizing the realities of their plight? Quite possibly then, this era, which congratulates itself on its self-awareness, will come to be known as the time of the Great Derangement. (Ghosh 2016, p.14-15)

Human beings have turned very ignorant about the role of nature in sustaining life on earth, and their self-pride makes them dismissive of the benevolence of Mother Nature. In recent years, the irreversible changes in natural surroundings and climate caused by the growing demands of human consumption have become more evident. If only humans had taken consequential note of warnings regarding climate change and considered the urgent need for preserving the natural surroundings, then the world would have fared better. This chapter will attempt to cover two ideas: first to look at Bibhutibhushan Bandyopadhyay's portrayal of the pastoral life in *Aranyak* where he shows a Paradise-like rural area constantly struggling to keep away the threats of modernisation. Apart from extolling the beauty of these rural areas, Bandyopadhyay has also shown the hardships of people residing there. Secondly, I will also locate examples in *Aranyak* to see Bibhutibhushan Bandyopadhyay as a forerunner who strongly spoke for sustainable development. *Aranyak* is replete with images which are close to Max Sutton's pastoral vision—which shows rural people "living in community as lovers, families, friends, neighbours, tending animals and the land, with time to celebrate what matters most in their lives." (Hardin 1979, p.ix) The simple rural folks are seen admiring their lives, fulfilling their minimalistic desires, and cherishing their limited possessions. The ordinary life of villagers was sometimes looked upon with derision or treated nonchalantly by the city folks. For example, we see Satyacharan's initial indifference to finding himself in a place like Phulkia-baihar and longing for his city life. Another example shows folks from the city coming to the forests of Phulkia-baihar only for a picnic and desire to return to the cityscape as soon as possible. *Aranyak* is a relevant read in the contemporary age, as it creates awareness about the adverse effects of our lifestyle on our surroundings and raises a concern regarding the future we would have if proper measures were not adopted for sustainable development.

The impact of modernisation has been felt everywhere fast cars, real estate, mining and industries have slowly replaced farmlands and forests. Natural resources are depleted, people are displaced from their homes, and rivers are polluted, yet all of these get ignored for rapid development. The research conducted by the National Institute of Technology Rourkela in 2009 cites an example from the Indigenous portal to show us the adverse effects of unsustainable growth in a few districts of Jharkhand, India. It notes:

> The rapid development of open-cast coal mining in the North Karanpura Valley in Hazaribagh and Chatra Districts of Jharkhand is destroying the resources of food and water of the original inhabitants of these areas, mainly of Adivasis (indigenous people), of more than 200 villages. The region has extremely fertile land which is now being converted into a mining site, taking away vital farming land and forests, and polluting the Damodar River, which is the lifeline of the area (Mishra 2009, p.25).

This example provides us with a picture of how we incur irreparable losses for development and the impact they have on rural lives. Rural areas have always been glorified in terms of beauty and innocence, which in turn fails to make us realise how scarred and tension-ridden these areas can be. *Aranyak* focuses on the socio-political and economic aspects which transform the otherwise idyllic rural areas of Phulkia- baihar. The author deftly portrays the struggle between tradition and modernity through the protagonist Satyacharan's dilemma. Satyacharan's duty demanded of him to clear the lands to lease it out for settlements and cultivation, but his conscience was affected by the loss of forests. He bridged the urban and the rural lives; he was someone with prior experience of urban life and was now learning about rural life too. As his stay in Phulkia-baihar extends, his attachment to his surroundings grows, but his actions at the same time led to irreversible changes around, which we understand deeply pained him. There was not enough consolation to lessen his grief for the transformation he brought for the sake of development.

Aranyak was composed between 1937 and 1939, first serialised in a monthly magazine called "Pravasi" and then published as a book in 1939. It is believed that the author's vast array of information included in *Aranyak* is a result of his experiences from his stay at the borders of Bihar and Northern Bengal. He travelled widely and sometimes even had the pleasure of staying in forest rest houses in Chotanagpur plateau, Hazaribagh, and Ranchi while visiting his friend who was employed under the service of the Bihar government. Bandyopadhyay's father also liked to travel; he was also fond of writing poetry and taught his son whenever he was at home. Apu's father Horihor in *Pather Panchali* is believed to be modelled on Bandyopadhay's father, a poor Brahmin who travels to different places to offer his religious services. In *Aranyak,* the protagonist's experiences are described along with the beautiful landscapes and lifestyle of the rural hinterland. The author's diary can be treated as one of the closest sources to understanding how he carefully observed human life, especially while travelling. One of his diary entries made on 12 February 1928 is referred to by Rimli Bhattacharya in the novel *Aranyak,* which reads:

> I will write something about life in the jungle— —rigorous and dynamic, radiant with courage— —-images of an outcast life. About riding in this lonely forest losing, one's way in the dark paths, living a solitary life in a little shelter ... the poverty of the people here, their simplicity, this Virile [sic], active life, these dense forests of jhau dark in the evening— —- all of it. (Bhattacharya 2002, p.xii)

In *Aranyak,* we find similar representations of life as mentioned in his diary entry. In Satyacharan's estate, most people lived on a meagre subsistence and survived on what they cultivated on their rented lands. They spent their summers and winters alike with minimal necessities and with very few expectations from their lives.

Satyacharan's Journey to Paradise

The novel begins with Satyacharan completing his studies and searching for a job in Calcutta. The city is shown as a difficult place to survive; he fears that he may have to make alternate arrangements for his meals because he has not paid the rent for the last two months. He saw an opportunity to improve his condition when his old friend offered him a job as an estate manager, for which he travelled to the border of Northern Bengal and Bihar. However, he found his workplace disconnected from civilization, often missed his cosmopolitan life in Calcutta and desired to return. He remained quiet even when poor people in his estate had misconceptions about the city, and he did not usually intervene to change their conventional ideas about the city. Whether it be in the case of Raju Parey, who thought of the city as a place full of swindlers, or in the case of Dhaturia, who very naively dreamt about his Chakkarbaji dance form being appreciated in Calcutta, Satyacharan did not correct them. They are allowed to live in their dream world; he does not break the bubble in which they have existed for so long. He could neither tell Raju good side of the city nor tell Dhaturia that his rustic dance may not be liked there. He quickly understood that these poor people in his estate were innocent beings whose world was limited to the forests they were living in, unlike those in the cities for whom material possessions mattered.

Despite his complaints and urge to resign, he stayed and continued his job as an estate manager. After his prolonged stay in Phulkia-baihar, his opinions changed, and he fell in love with the natural surroundings. Pastoral is conceived in terms of an idyllic landscape, in Paul Alpers' words, "locus amoenus"(Alpers 1982, p.449) and Satyacharan's workplace described by the author is no less than one. His prejudices regarding the rural areas changed, he stopped seeing its people as uncivilized, and his initial reservations against staying in a rural area were removed gradually. His desperate desire to return to his city life is replaced by his love for the natural surroundings of Phulkia-baihar, which helped him to understand the natural beauty present in rural life. On his arrival, Satyacharan scoffed off when his accountant informed him about such attraction one would feel for the forests after a prolonged stay. Phulkia-baihar and its natural surroundings slowly start growing inside him, true to his accountant's words. His perspective about life altered; he changed too, from someone who had always been so fond of cosmopolitan life to someone who appreciated rural folks and their lifestyle. The thought of staying elsewhere made him uncomfortable, even when his job sometimes required him to travel to the city. He felt that he—"would not be able to return to the hurly-burly of Calcutta forsaking the vast tracts of forestland, the fresh fragrance of the sun-scorched earth and the freedom and liberation they represent." (Bandyopadhyay 2002, p.22) *Aranyak* also explores the quest of Satyacharan, to understand and value other than just materialistic possessions. His stay in the forests of Phulkia-baihar makes him appreciate the natural beauty around him and perceive the world beyond the city's borders. The city and the countryside are contrasted, the rural is shown as accommodating and friendly, and people in Phulkia-baihar shared a few resources they had, unlike those in the cities who could evict people or not provide food for not being able to pay rent.

Gradually, Satyacharan starts realising the worth of natural surroundings and the simplicity of people there. His contact with different kinds of people in the estate reminded him of their humility and kindness. One such exceptional character is Dhautal Sahu, whom he believes is a wonder to even exist in the twentieth century. Sahu is a moneylender with a kind heart, a rare sight, thinks Satyacharan. One day, when he came to him with almost thousands of defunct deeds, he advised Sahu that he should not lend money anymore. Sahu replied that he did not regret his losses as it formed an integral part of the business. Satyacharan was surprised to hear this because seeing someone not bothered about his loss was contrary to what he had seen growing up in the city. In Phulkia-baihar, people like Dhautal Sahu managed to win over the heart of Satyacharan through their innocence and humility. Raju Parey, Moktunath, Kunta, Ganauri Teowari, and Princess Bhanmati, who all did not desire much from life, made him think of a possibility of life beyond material comfort. Few cattle, shelter and necessities formed their idea of material prosperity. Princess Bhanmati had not even heard of Bharatvarsha, and when asked the name of her country, she replied that it was Gaya district. Despite losing all her previous power and glory, her territory meant the world to her. All of Satyacharan's complaints appeared redundant in front of the challenges these people faced. He felt that these people's proximity to Nature may have induced love and compassion in them- "The forests and the hills had liberated their minds, expanded their vision with generosity; in like manner, their love was deep, generous and liberating." (Bandyopadhyay 2002, p.181) He found them kind and humble and preferred their food and company over the company of rich moneylenders around.

Hardships of Rural Areas

Despite describing the beauty of the rural scape in *Aranyak*, the author unfailingly shows the real struggles of rural areas. The challenges people in Phulkia-baihar lived with defined their identities and made their pastoral existence worthwhile. The hardships of rural areas were unknown to Satyacharan, but his gradual awareness of their problems turned him into a sympathiser. He even cleared lands for poor people and gave them subsidies; a few people in his estate, like Raju Parey were given lands to cultivate and asked only to pay in crops in return after two years. People in these places did not expect much from their lives; to procure necessities was equally difficult for them, but they remained unbothered. Many incidents in the text reflect the misery of those poor people; rice, the country's staple food, is a luxury to them. Their survival on cheena grains and bathua greens, travelling long distances to sell their produce, and creating performances for a meagre sum of money indicates their impoverished state. On knowing about a new manager's arrival in the estate, many of them went to see him and to eat the treat, which consisted of a humble meal of rice and vegetables. Satyacharan was surprised to learn that people travelled long distances to his place to eat rice. When asked, they told him that the last time they had eaten rice was many months ago, so they did not mind walking long distances for a rice meal. This was far from Satyacharan's imagination because the place from where he had come would see even the poorest of the poor eating rice as a staple diet.

Phulkia-baihar and its surroundings were deprived of basic comforts; the nearest railway station was miles away from human habitation. These areas were not visited by people frequently; only those who wanted to rent lands for cultivation or those searching for means of survival came there. The geographical conditions around Phulkia-baihar were also harsh; during summers, no good drinking water could be found, and the heat from Satyacharan's description was terrible. All plants and vegetation would dry up, and even the birds were not visible in the skies due to the extreme heat. Sometimes, people lost directions too because the forests were dense; danger from wildfire and the threat from wild animals made the surroundings difficult for inhabitation. Despite these harsh circumstances, people rented lands for cultivation and stayed back due to extreme poverty. People like Ganu Mahato were living alone in the forests for many years. Another person called Jaipal Kumar spent life alone; he had lost his family a long time ago and yet had no complaints. Satyacharan could not imagine living in that hovel of Ganu alone on meagre subsistence, fighting the wild animals or living a monotonous life like Jaipal's. Until now, he was only acquainted with city life and had been surrounded by his friends and family, so even the thought of staying without human company seemed impossible. He thought to himself- "I could never understand the sentiment of Jaipal's. I had been a college student in Calcutta. I did not have a clue as to what a person might do if he was not working or chatting with friends, or if he was not absorbed in books, films, outings, and the like." (Bandyopadhyay 2002, p.46) Episodes like these further portray contrasting pictures of city and village life in *Aranyak*.

Other than extreme poverty, wild animals and harsh climate, stiff challenges from moneylenders and upper caste people were everyday problems for people around. Men like Nandalal Ojha and Rashbehari Singh were cunning and witty and would take advantage of their position to suppress the villagers. Contrary to the lifestyle led by other people, theirs was a very successful life but devoid of love and compassion. Nandalal Ojha is shown bribing

Satyacharan for his son's job, and Rashbehari Singh had his empire built on the high interests taken for the money lent to poor people. On the occasion of Holi, Satyacharan accepted the invitation of Rashbehari despite initial hesitation. He was given a grand welcome followed by firing gunshots and was offered delicacies to eat. Rashbehari was very rich, and his wealth is described in this manner:

> There were about sixty to sixty-five heads of cattle in his cowshed ...They had got about nine mounds of wheat from the land; more than eighty people had meals twice a day, and he breakfasted on one and a half seer of milk and seer of bichri from Bikaner after his daily bath. (Bandyopadhyay 2002, p.90)

The author has deftly portrayed the contrasting images of the rural scape, where on the one hand, people like Rashbehari and Nandlal are filthy rich and, on the other hand, poor people are not even capable of providing two meals a day for themselves. When the estate next to Phulkia-baihar is hit by an epidemic, we see the poor living conditions of the affected poor in shanties and surviving on leftovers with no access to clean drinking water. *Aranyak* not only portrays the contrast between the rural and urban but also shows the disparity in living standards of people from rural areas.

The estate and its surroundings, like the rest of Indian society, are ridden with problems related to caste. The lower castes faced inhuman treatment, Phulkia-baihar had a large population of lower caste people called gangotas, who were usually deprived of their rights. In *Aranyak,* many references are made to the caste system and its evils; people like doshads and gangotas from the lower castes were treated differently. They were not welcomed, and no one even preferred to sit next to them; despite receiving inhuman treatment, they were very kind. Satyacharan also learnt very early on that people from the lower castes were meek and humble. He was immensely moved to see Giridharilal, a gangota by caste, sincerely performing his duties during the fair. In the novel, the story of Kunta, the daughter of a baiji and widow of a Rajput, provides the readers with an example of caste politics. Debi Singh, a wealthy Rajput moneylender, had married Kunta and fought his people to accept her legally. After Debi Singh's death, Kunta was neither accepted by the Rajputs nor by the members of her caste. She had no caste, and no one showed her any mercy except to take advantage of her. An incident reported by a young woman named Manchi also is an example of the indifference of the upper castes towards others. She was the young wife of Nakchhedi, who was dragged and beaten only because she wanted to take a dip in Suraj-Kund, which the Brahmins considered sacred. It was just a mountain spring, she told Satyacharan and asked him to write it down so that the world would know about such cruelties. The beauty of the natural surroundings of rural areas is described along with the harsh realities. The good and the evil side of human nature pervaded equally in this place.

Several entries in Bibhutibhushan Bandyopadhyay's diary show his concern for nature and humanity. He felt that Nature never differentiated one from the other and was always giving; therefore, humans also should be equally grateful for what they receive from her. Bandyopadhyay's *Smritir Rekha* mentions- "We come to this world for few days— —from this world, we take fruits, water, love, compassion, so being human beings cannot we think of doing something for this world?" (My Translation) (Bandyopadhyay Mahalaya 1362, p.18) This same idea is reproduced in Satyacharan's efforts to help Jugal Prasad to plant trees around Saraswati Kundi. As an estate manager, Satyacharan would have done much better if he had rented the fertile grounds of Saraswati Kundi to tenants. Instead of doing so, he encouraged Jugalprasad to plant trees there, who prioritized planting trees over spending time with humans. He even procured seeds and tried his best to keep the area around kundi safe from being cleared, and his heart would hurt thinking about the forests being destroyed for settlements and cultivation. Despite several attempts by the estate manager and people like Prasad to protect Phulkia-baihar, corrupt and modern practices infiltrate its peaceful surroundings. Rich people like Chhotu Singh tried to dominate poor people by using unfair means; he had his eyes on the harvest of the poor gangotas during the harvest time, and had it not been for Satyacharan's timely intervention, they would have suffered. He requested the gangotas to leave their harvest unguarded; his presence there as a guardian of the oppressed signalled a threat to the upper caste Rajputs, and hence they could not budge an inch after that. During the fairs, he stayed alert to stop the malpractices of the traders and moneylenders because he knew that people around were gullible and could be easily cheated. Satyacharan was more than just an estate manager for the people in his estate but was also their guardian, educator and protector.

Another threat to these rural folks came from the glamour of the cities, and in a few cases, proved to be the cause for their downfall too. Most of them were fascinated by the fancy objects found or sold in the city, which they may have seen in the traditional annual fairs. Of course, there were people like Raju Parey who had heard terrifying stories about cities like Calcutta and were scared to go there even on Satyacharan's invitation and people like Dhaturia, the dancer on the other hand, wanted to show his Chakkarbaji dance to the folks in the city. Dhaturia felt that his dance form was more likely to be appreciated by the city people and had requested Satyacharan to take him to Calcutta. And few other people held the opinion of Satyacharan very high only because he had received his education in the city. Venkateshwar Prasad the poet, on learning about Satyacharan's arrival, went to see him to recite his poetry. He had no regrets that his people called him mad because he felt that rural people like them did not understand art. Satyacharan's opinions were valued because he was an educated fellow from the city who was intelligent, with refined taste in art and poetry. Another story of a young woman like Manchi showed women's fascination for pieces of jewellery and decorative items and how they harboured a desire to see Calcutta. Manchi would still feel proud of her bargaining skills, not knowing that she also has been cheated like the rest of the village folks by the traders in the fair. One day, she disappeared; her disappearance is one of the examples of how young girls and women from rural areas are lured away to the cities. She was not found anywhere nearby; she may have become one among many wage labourers in the cities or the tea gardens in Assam, thought Satyacharan. The cities attracted these naive people mainly for work, but little did they know that their hardships would continue.

Custodians of Nature Loses Paradise

The vastness of the forests and their age-old existence overwhelmed Satyacharan. He would receive several warnings for wandering alone in the forest areas occasionally. He considered those forests sacred and sometimes saw humans as intruders, settlers who settled on lands which did not belong to them. Through two episodes in the novel, the author maybe trying to make us think that the custodians of Nature are protecting their areas from trespassers. One day, Satyacharan was reported by Ashrafi Tindale the news of a woman being found in Amin Ramachandra's tent. Ramachandra would wake up at night and complain about the presence of a white dog inside his room, but Tindale swore that it was a woman instead. Gradually, Ramachandra's health deteriorated as if he was cursed for his presence in the forest. Later on, he turned insane and was taken home by his brother. A few months later, a similar incident occurred when the same area was rented to a man and his son; the new tenant also reported a mysterious woman under his son's bed, and a few days later, his son was dead. These incidents made Satyacharan feel that humans may be cursed for trespassing into sacred territories, and his immediate instinct told him to flee the place. Then there is the other story of Tarbaro, the God of wild buffalo herds, who was revered by people living in those areas. Dasrath Jhandawala, who had accompanied Chhotu Singh to capture wild buffaloes, told everyone present there that Tarbaro prevented buffaloes from falling into the trap and rendered them unable to capture any. Dasrath described seeing a huge black figure in front of their baited traps guiding the buffaloes away from it. These stories make us understand that there are good forces or spirits in Nature who protect their areas from trespassers. Nevertheless, the corrupt practices of humans continued and ruined the beauty of natural repositories around Phulkia-baihar.

The author of *Aranyak* was ahead of his time in raising concerns regarding the effective use of natural resources. In his diary, he wrote about his empathy for both Humans and Nature, where he also mentioned *Aranyak* as a novel which spoke of Nature and the World alongside Man and Time. Suniti Kumar Chatterjee's essay "Banga Bharati—Sangiti-Banasri-Raag O Bibhuti Bandya" in *Bibhutirachnabali* relates how Bandyopadhyay had immense empathy for man but was in no position to differentiate Man from Nature. He held an equal amount of compassion for both Man and Nature and felt that the world would have been a much better place to live in if there was mutual co-existence between the two. In *Aranyak*, the protagonist was pained to see the forest areas being destroyed and noted: "I experienced a curious sense of pain; I could not bear to go in the direction of the fire. A national resource that might forever have given peace and joy to people was being destroyed for a mere handful of grain." (Bandyopadhyay 2002, p.121) Inroads inside rural areas and forestlands were being made to counter the demands raised by the growing population and cities. His wish was to let people in the future also witness "pristine, undisturbed" (Bandyopadhyay 2002, p.248) forests. Dobru Panna was a tribal ruler on the Dhannjari Range whose territory was still not exploited because of its rocky surface. Satyacharan feared that if mining started there, even the untouched lands of Dobru Panna may go through extensive changes. He shared a long and unpleasant picture of the ruler's territory in case mining for copper ore started there:

> Chimneys of the copper factories, trolley lines, rows of bustees for the coolies, drains overflowing with dirty water, discarded heaps of ash spewed from engines, clusters of shops, tea-joints, cheap films ... Country liquor shacks, tailors' shops... The three-o clock whistle sounds from the factory. (Bandyopadhyay 2002, p.244)

For Satyacharan, this would have been a heartbreaking sight because the beautiful pristine forests of Phulkia-baihar would not remain the same paradise anymore for which Satyacharan had deep reverence. It is already altered and prone to attacks from corruption. Not only did the natural surroundings change because of its lands being cleared for settlements and cultivation, but the gradual influx of modern ideologies also brought the changes. He returned to Calcutta, maybe because he wanted to avoid further accountability for bringing the destruction of the pristine forests of Phulkia-baihar. He was guilty of inadvertently damaging the natural resources, and even fifteen years later, all he could do was seek forgiveness from the Gods of the forest.

Guilt and Apology

Satyacharan's sense of awareness culminated in an apology that he sought from the forests. He was responsible for clearing and leasing out lands for settlements and cultivation, despite the unwillingness of his conscience to do so. Although his unconditional support for a few needy people in his estate could also be provided only because of his position as an estate manager, his pain continued. He mentioned the pain which he derived from destroying the forests of Narha-baihar, which he had started to admire "... I grieved, knowing that the forests of Narha-baihar would not stand for long. I loved the place so greatly, but my own hands had destroyed it ... Forests, primaeval and ancient, forgive me." (Bandyopadhyay 2002, p.196) Seeking forgiveness from the forests only confirms the intense guilt he must have felt for his actions. The perpetual reminder of humans' callousness towards Nature's riches reverberated throughout the text. The lackadaisical attitude of people living in the cities worsened the situation when they saw rural spaces as just some sort of escape. Bandyopadhyay deftly portrayed the city folks prioritising their pleasure over anyone else's and their lack of awareness regarding the rural lifestyle. In the novel, a Bengali family was shown coming to the forests of Phulkia-baihar for a picnic from the city; they were least interested in the beauty of forests and wildlife, and unwilling to stay back even after Satyacharan's hospitality. They had come there only to hunt, seek some pleasure and return home. They resemble a large section of city folks who remain unaffected by the change occurring in rural areas and are least bothered by the sad plight of people living there. Satyacharan regrets that forests in his country, if located elsewhere in any part of the world, would have been preserved and turned into National parks and sanctuaries.

The author's message to adopt measures to safeguard natural surroundings and seek alternatives to make the world a better place stays predominantly in the novel. These lines taken from his diary stand as a yardstick to measure the author's love for nature and natural surroundings:

> Who cares for the abundant incomparable gifts of Nature? None. Everybody is busy with wealth, fame, and honour. Who has time to appreciate the intoxicating beauty of this night flooded with moonlight? I am grateful to God that he has given me eyes that can appreciate beauty." (Chattopadhyay 1994, p.61)

In an age when people pursue wealth and material prosperity, the author hankers for natural beauty and its sustenance. The protagonist of *Aranyak* left Phulkia-baihar perhaps because he could no longer see its devastation. It was no longer the Paradise that the protagonist was so fond of, it underwent several changes, and shortly he feared there might be no Phulkia-baihar too. It is said that sometimes it is better to die with beautiful memories than to see those memories changing into bitter truths. Maybe, the protagonist also preferred to take away with him those beautiful memories and live with them forever. The Paradise-like Phulkia-baihar may be losing its beauty, but it will remain alive in the heart of Satyacharan forever.

Works Cited

Alpers, P. (1982) 'What is Pastoral', *Critical Inquiry,*The University of Chicago Press, vol. 8, no.3, p. 437-460.

Bandyopadhyay, B. (Mahalaya 1362) *Smritir Rekha,* 2nd ed., Calcutta Publishers, Calcutta.

-(1994) *Bibhuti Rachnabali.* Mitra, Gajendra Kumar, et al., (eds). vol.1, Mitro O Ghosh, Calcutta.

-(2002) *Aranyak.*Translated by R. Bhattacharya. Seagull Books, New Delhi.

Chattopadhyay, S. K. (1994) *Bibhutibhushan Bandopadhyay.* Translated by A. D. Choudhuri. Sahitya Akademi, New Delhi.

Ghosh, A. (2016) *The Great Derangement: Climate Change and the Unthinkable,* Penguin Books, Gurgaon.

Hardin, R. F. (1979) *Survivals of Pastoral,* University of Kansas Publications, Lawrence Kansas.

Hiltner, K. (2011) *What else is Pastoral? Renaissance Literature and the Environment,* Cornell University Press, Ithaca.

Mishra, N. (2015) *Coal Mining, Displacement and Rural Livelihoods: A Study in Mahanadi Coalfield Odisha,* National Institute of Technology (NIT), Rourkela.

P(i)e(a)ce in Pastoral

This chapter discusses that the pastoral is used in contemporary Indian writing to denote and replicate environmental concerns and that in the process, changes are made to instill the conventions of the mode. Analysing the use of pastoral, this chapter maintains that the mode itself is found in new forms in this case. The objective of this chapter is to analyse the pastoral devices in Anukrti's *Bhaunri, and* perceive the text as a modern pastoral novel. By this analysis, the chapter establishes that new modes of experimentation with the pastoral notion can be found in contemporary nature writings that discuss the idea of escape, return, and a retreat from the bustle of city life. It also observes the implementation of pastoral modes of writing with the emergence of environmental instability using the themes and modes of alienation, estrangement and probing for the solution.

To acquaint with the pastoral, this section will offer an overview of the terminology and development of pastoral. Pastoral genre is a much-debated term since its inception of origin, form and definition. Some critics argue that it is not a literary genre rather it encompasses many genres. To a certain extent, it is true, as we have pastoral drama, pastoral elegies, pastoral poetry and so forth. According to Greg, it is "a vehicle to expound their philosophies relating to nature and city, to discuss the aspects of love in terms of the usually contented life of the shepherd and to comment tangentially on politics and religion" (Greg, 1959, p.1). As an adjective, "pastoral" is synonymous with "idyllic." It is fascinating to know that "Pastor" is the Latin word for "Shepherd."

With time, this term has undergone many changes. It means to be about the environment, yet allegorically it represents something else. The term 'pastoral' suggests characteristics such as simplicity, nostalgia, innocence, Nature, uprightness, directness, sincerity, faithfulness, honesty, trustfulness, politeness, compassion, tranquility, the myth of the Golden Age and the garden of Eden, happiness, contemplative life, refuge and retreat, peace, serenity, courteousness and humility. The term 'anti-pastoral' implies qualities contrary to pastoral. Some literary devices are used to present the traits of pastoral such as contrast, satire, nature binary, pathetic fallacy, and hyperbole.

From the earlier writers of pastoral, the garden of Eden is considered the Golden Age of pastoral. The origin of the pastoral text can be traced back to the earlier texts with environmental concerns, not in Theocritus but maybe in the *Epic of Gilgamesh*. Philips acknowledges the early masters in this genre, "Theocritus, Virgil, and Spenser are the only writers that seem to have hit upon the true Nature of Pastoral Poems" (1937, p. 3). There is a nostalgia for the lost past and a desire to revive the environment through writing. There has been a concern for the developing environmental consciousness. However, before embarking on the works of various writers and those that elucidate the idea of pastoral. It is better to have an understanding of what pastoral is by navigating through different definitions postulated by various critics.

Charles Batteux (1761) opines that "Pastoral poetry may be defined as an imitation of rural life represented with every possible attraction" (Congleton, 147). William Empson considers the pastoral process as "putting the complex into the simple" (2020, 37). Alexander Pope in the neoclassical age defined pastoral in his *A Discourse on Pastoral Poetry* as "an imitation of the action of a shepherd, or one under that." (in Butt, 1965, p. 119). Terry Gifford (1999) defines pastoral in three ways in his critical book *Pastoral*. He also emphasises depicting the country and its life. W. W. Greg states that "the pastoral, whatever its form, always needed and assumed some external circumstance to give point to its actual content. The interest seldom arises directly from the narrative itself" (1937, p. 67). According to Sukanta Chaudhuri:

> It selects details from that [pastoral] life, adds to them and reorders them to create a world of, the imagination, invested with urban longing for an ideally simple life in nature. In other words, it is subtle and sophisticated, exploring the gap between the complex existence of the poet and reader and the designedly naive dream of rural simplicity. All pastoral implies this duality, this awareness of two opposed worlds: country and city, simple and complex, imaginary and real (1989, p.1).

It has its root in antiquity, in Rome, in the works of Homer, Theocritus's *Idyll,* Virgil's *Ecologues,* Ovid's *Metamorphosis,* Cicero's *De Senectute,* Chaucer's *The Canterbury Tales* and others. Since then, it sparked and ignited the minds of English writers and the age of renaissance can be considered to be a flowering age for it. They provided the fertile soil required for its development. We find its elements in the works of Sidney's *Arcadia,* Spenser's *The Shepheard's Calender,* and Thomas Lodge's *Rosalynde.* Shakespeare has masterfully used this genre in his plays, *As You Like It, Twelfth Night, Much Ado About Nothing, Midsummer Night's Dream, The Winter's Tale, Macbeth, King Lear, Henry VI, Othello* and *The Tempest.* Milton's *Lycidas* and Thompson's *Seasons* are pastoral works. In the age of the eighteenth century, the works of Alexender Pope's *Windsor Forest* and Gray's *Elegy Written in a Country Churchyard* are pastoral compositions. Romantic writers couldn't remain aloof from the fragrance of pastoral they too caught the contagion most prominently in the works of Shelly, Keats, Byron and Wordsworth poetry. In the Victorian age, we find its impact in the works of George Eliot, Browning, Hardy, Tennyson, Arnold and other writers. In the twentieth century, writers were greatly influenced by pastoral trends such as Thoreau, Emerson, Whitman, Faulkner, Hemingway, and so on. From the above discussion, we have developed an overview of the pastoral genre. By taking the clues from the aforesaid discussion, an analysis of the text will be done.

Poetry and drama are considered to be the genres that depict pastoral strains. However, novels which have become a popular genre in the twentieth century are not aloof from it. There are many writers and their works depict pastoral tendencies. Monica Ali in her acclaimed novel *Brick Lane* talks about the attitude of the migrants living in London. "They don't ever really leave home. Their bodies are here but their hearts are back there. And anyway, look how they live: just recreating the villages here" (2003, p. 45). And further adds, "Working like a donkey here, but never made a go. In his heart, he never left the village" (2003, p. 193).

Bhaunri

Writers across the world are enamoured by this fascinating genre of pastoral. They imbibe the elements of pastoral in their writings to suit their purpose. Indian writing in English has also been enriched with the pastoral tradition. Writers from R K Narayan, Raja Rao, Mulk Raj Anand, Sarojini Naidu, Nissim Ezekiel, A K Ramanujan, Amitav Ghosh, and Anita Desai to contemporary writers have embedded and intertwined the elements of pastoral in their works.

For the present analysis, I have taken *Bhaunri* as the subject of this study. Anukrti's *Bhaunri* is a pastoral novella that provides the audience with a complete catalogue of pastoral life and tradition. The novella has close associations with the notion of the pastoral in alliance with setting, recollection, and execution. It is a sort of post-pastoral novella Anukrti employs versions of pastoral as an environmental correlative in the initial and the final stages in the development of her character. The materials that Anukrti uses in fashioning her pastoral are drawn from her surroundings in Rajasthan. She portrays the life of the tribes as being ideal in that all social and economic classes work and rejoice together as a whole society.

The chapter locates the modes, motifs and methods of the pastoral conventions within the text and understands how it is embedded in the narrative devices, that enhance the development of *Bhaunri's* narrative in particular. The characters of the novel are not shepherds. They are farm labourers, *lohars,* and tribal people who by living in the vicinity of the land, value work and duty. It is a sort of inverted pastoral. The pastoral writers do not write about nature; they use nature as the scene.

Despite the growing menace of industrialization, or possibly because of it, Anukrti considers that it is better to adhere to the value of rural setting and rural life, as in the Wordsworthian notion that these people are close to nature, they converse in its language and bask in its ambience. Anukrti's novel appropriates the concept of the pastoral genre. Her novel finds a fresh avenue of various strata for meaningful and insightful discourse by interacting, conversing and exchanging ideas with the pastoral genre. It shows that this interaction and discourse provide ample scope for Anukrti to question and criticize the social ideology and environmental discourses of her time. Her work is in line with Terry Gifford's remarks "The two other uses of the pastoral: one concerns the focus of the work on the country as opposed to the city, whereas the other is already a revised reference as it acknowledges the false idealisation of the rural world involved in the other two uses of the term" (1999, pp.1-2).

Pastoral features, as one would expect, are not noticeable in the novel, but even their anti-pastoral ones have not received any significant consideration. In this paper, I explore that both pastoral and anti-pastoral elements may be found in the novel. With the elements of philosophies of life, the pastoral mode is more attuned to a novel than any other genre. Pastoral aspects can be traced from the beginning with Bhaunri's characterisation as a pastoral girl and use of animals, birds, trees and landscape. The attributes of pastoral such as nostalgia, contentment and trust are found in the narrative of the text, anti-pastoral elements interfere where there is harmony and bliss, creating a vicious disturbance of tranquility and peacefulness.

Bhaunri is the very embodiment of the pastoral aspects of the countryside. "Bhaunri belonged to the desert clan of Gadoliya Lohars. Her father, a nomadic blacksmith, used to traverse the desert in his ox cart, making and repairing pots and pans, hoes and scythes" (*B*, 2019, p.1). "She was from the tribe of Gujjars who kept cattle and farmed" (*B*, 2019, p. 2). "She dreamt alone, flowing inward like a subterranean river in the desert, occasionally flashing in the sun, nourishing herself from unseen sources" ((*B*, 2019, p. 2). "Her smell, like that of the dunes and desert breeze" (*B*, 2019, p. 6). "She is, tall and shadowy like this mango tree" (*B*, 2019, p. 81). "She is as tall as a doorpost and lovelier than a date palm more curved than the Ghaggar river herself" (*B*, 2019, p. 29). "Her eyes, the colour of winter sunlight," (*B*, 2019, p. 41).

W. W. Greg states that a consistent element in the pastoral is "a contrast, implied or expressed, between pastoral life and some more complex type of civilization" (1937, p.7). This can be seen in the marriage of Bhaunri and Bheema too. Bhaunri's marriage to

Bheema is antithetical to the surroundings of her parents. She moves from the pastoral set-up to an anti-pastoral one. Her husband typifies many anti-pastoral traits as "He is crafty and wise like the upper-caste folk" (B, 2019, p.11). "Tall, like a camel and dark like the cloud of Ashadh" (B 9). The setting of the house is remarkably different from hers, "the roof of our house is made of stone and cement, not thatch" (B, 2019, p.17), "The house was large, larger than her father's and made of bricks and cement" (B, 2019, p. 21).

Bheema has anti-pastoral attributes, as he is harsh, violent, disloyal, urban and discourteous. And in a fit of rage, Bheema hurt and beat Bhaunri, "His wooden club hit Bhaunri's left shoulder with a thump" (B, 2019, p. 86). He said, "I will snap your neck like a lotus stem" (B, 2019, p.112). The violence against a woman can be related to the violence of men towards nature and its destruction. "Though her mother-in-law is like a cow, loving and simple" (B, 2019, p. 9).

However, he is not a city man. Bheema's simplicity links him to the shepherd figures of the conventional pastoral genre which luckily spares them any encounter with subtle and malevolent schemers. Bhaunri's husband, Bheema has a mistress to whom he often visits, spending his days over at her house when Bhaunri comes to know about it she is infuriated, and an eternal fire rages inside her heart. Bheema's indifference towards her further accentuates it. She tried her best to bring him back, but he was adamant and headstrong in his attitude. He was not ready to budge to the demands of Bhaunri. He turned more and more violent, "effectively breaking with the possibility of the pastoral" (Gifford,1999, p.119). It didn't bring his senses. Men have become violent reflecting the outer destruction of Nature which in turn becomes part of their inner nature, "the recognition that the inner is also the workings of the outer, that our inner human nature can be understood in relation to external nature" (Gifford, 1999, p.157).

As long as Bhaunri's faith and trust in Bheema remain unshaken, their relationship exhibits a genuinely pastoral complexion. Their union demonstrates the pastoral quality of happy harmony. From this stature, Bhaunri is tossed into the depths of despair, bitterness, sexual jealousy, rage and hatred as a result of the knowledge about Khateek's daughter. Interestingly, though, there are moments when she still glimpses Bheema through a pastoral lens, despite her hostility to him.

Her efforts, perhaps over-enthusiastic, to reconcile her father-in-law and her husband, likewise bespeak a nature bent upon healing strife and spreading concord. And rather than inflame Bheema, after he has unjustly hurt her by striking her badly, she pins her hopes on a reconciliation. Nor does further beating change her attitude, her willingness to confront or cross Bheema springs not just from her love for him but also from the hope of restoring concord between them. Finally, her innate gentleness, natural refinement and dignity carry a pastoral reminiscence.

We have already witnessed how Bheema's brutal behaviour towards Bhaunri in his striking and insulting her for Khateek's daughter — the desertion of the pastoral-like ethos he once endorsed and, in its place, of an anti-pastoral one. In behaving as he does, Bheema turns himself into an anti-pastoral caricature of the man he once was. The handsome caring husband who once loved his wife has fallen into the physical and verbal abuse of his wife. But it is not only through his actions that Bheema's decline is seen. What happens to his diction tells the same story. When we first meet Bheema, his mode of speech is normal but it changes dramatically. His treatment can be viewed under the term, ecofeminists which according to Gifford is a "realisation that the exploitation of the planet is of the same mindset as the exploitation of women and minorities" (2000, p.221).

The protagonist is seen as a rather simple pastoral-like character and Bhaunri as an innocent pastoral-like heroine. Parallels are drawn between what occurs in Bhaunri and what happened in the Garden of Eden to highlight pastoral and anti-pastoral elements in the novel. The primarily blissful world of Bhaunri and Bheema is infiltrated and then devastated by an evil force in the person of Khateek's daughter, even as the blissfulness of Adam and Eve was shattered by the wiles of Satan.

The story of Bhaunri confirms that the pastoral-like qualities and personages that make its appearance in the early scenes of the novel are easily overwhelmed and crushed by anti-pastoral forces, such as human or natural and that those forces, after enjoying a temporary success, themselves come to grief at the end of the action, leaving the slate clean for the possibility of a new beginning. Bhaunri and Bheema's marriage, unclouded and happy to begin with, has much in common with the untroubled contentment of the pastoral dispensation. Bhaunri, moreover, has a simplicity, openness, and sense of honour that link her to the traditional pastoral country-dweller. Bhaunri's innocence, trustfulness, kind nature and fidelity similarly suggest links with the pastoral world.

Plot

When Bhaunri married Bheema, her life underwent a great transformation and paradigm shift. She falls in love with her husband. She thought that her husband would remain honest and faithful to her. However, he was a philanderer and lived a flippant life. With time, she discovers many facts and dark secrets of the households such as: on the arrival of her mother-in-law's sister, the placid surroundings of the house become turbulent and ruffled the lives of others. Bhaunri's father-in-law set his eyes on her and troubled her life. However, Bhaunri later learned from her father-in-law that she too loved him and wanted to be with him. But she couldn't bear the pangs of the misery it would cause her sister and committed suicide. After this Mangla went mad. And there is a rift between Bheema and his father.

Pastoral

Since its inception, the pastoral genre has been fraught with irony. Its ideas of the ideal of innocence and perfection are questioned and critiqued. It is found that it belies with experience and observations of life. Anukrti uses these conflicts and adds to them in her novel in a way that encompasses more modern concerns about work, play, class, and gender in the context of modern contemporary culture. This tension, conflict and turbulence are at the heart of the pastoral genre. Learning a lesson of life through nature, living in its lap, and working in the field, there exists harmony between man and the soil when they work in tune with nature. Anukrti values and respects the common man and the deeds that he performs by toiling the soil because they make direct communication with nature, spending their time and toiling in natural surroundings. Gifford puts it "the concern for the exploitation of people (in terms of gender, class and race) must accompany concern for the environment (in terms of species, elements and atmosphere) and vice versa" (1999, p.166).

Nature plays an important role in the novel. It is nature that validates the pastoral ideology the novel has referred to. Nonetheless, Anukrti also tests the limits of pastoral representation by deliberately integrating problematic elements. In his introductory discourse on pastoral poetry, Sukanta Chaudhuri (1989) states that it is a sort of mixture of elements of pastoral life with a desire for the comfort of urban life in simple dwellings in nature. The powerful yearning to take shelter and recourse in the paradise age is the outcome of an unattainable desire for a state when a man was "as free as nature first made man" (Cuddon, 1991, p.743).

The pastoral is primarily and emphatically concerned with nature, innocence and tranquility. The countryside is unpolluted and unspoiled in distinction to the city spoiled and degraded by man. Kermode reflects on this contrast between country and city "as the seed of the pastoral" and "the social aspect of the great Art-Nature antithesis which is the philosophical basis of pastoral literature" (1952, p.37). He exemplifies nature as "the uncultivated, the pure, the untamed, uncorrupted fields and the world of Art, the civilized, the cultivated, the sphere in which men had meddled with nature" (1952, p.37). To put it in other words, the pastoral is a return to the essentials of life in a natural habitat.

The setting and the atmosphere are reminiscent of the pastoral pleasantness. The mood, as in the rest of the images, suggests harmony, gesturing towards the richness of life, human warmth and loyalty. The people from rural hinterland and tribes enjoy things provided by nature with relish as eating food or singing songs: "They eat fresh goat meat, and there is milk to soak your tikkad morning, noon and night" (B, 2019, p. 9), "rotis, onions and chillies in a piece of cloth". (B, 2019, p. 72), "Milking cow, Rotis of gram flour and millet mixed with jaggery and cooked bitter methi leaves" (B, 2019, p. 96). "Your carefully nurtured bird, fed on rice and sweet milk, is leaving her father's home" (*B*, 2019, p. 19). Even the day-to-day ritual has the importance of nature, nature is at the centre, "Mai said we should pray at the tree outside our door" (*B*, 2019, p. 34), "Sprinkling water around his platter" (*B*, 2019, p. 25). Furthermore, the similes are also attuned to the pastoral ideas, "Like a bajra stalk in the wind" (*B*, 2019, p. 46), "The blossom on the mango tree began dropping like tiny, pale butterflies" (*B*, 2019, p. 47), "I will crush him like a camel crushes an aak bush" (2019, p.69). These instances of primal descriptions are manifestations of the first and foremost element in any post-pastoral work, namely nature. Nevertheless, these descriptions and representations of natural surroundings are exploited to initiate a subversive discourse with the pastoral genre in terms of benefiting from the post-pastoral codes and then undermining them.

The text has a rich fragrance of pastoral proverbs that are strewn and permeate the narrative of the text such as: "Don't imagine snakes under every shade tree". (*B*, 2019, p. 11), "Why plant a tree if you can have fruit from another's?" (*B*, 2019, p.35), "Hearing the truth hurts worse than a scorpion's sting" (*B*, 2019, p. 51), "Even sandalwood catches fire if rubbed too long" (*B*, 2019, p. 111), "The older the banyan tree, the stronger it is" (*B*, 2019, p. 131). The animals and plants motifs are repeated signaling the pastoral presence in the novel.

Contentment, and peace of mind, are key constituents of the pastoral ethos. Consequently, whatever seeks to undo contentment and peace of mind is anti-pastoral in its impulse. In *Bhaunri*, the anti-pastoral agent whose mission is to destroy others' contentment is as we have noted, Khateek's daughter. Khateek's daughter may be regarded as an anti-pastoral figure as she goes against everything innocent, pure and virtuous. She is driven to destroy anything that brings harmony and joy to people's lives. As an anti-pastoral force, Khateek's daughter takes delight, and is even flippant, in her remarks about all that is good. The pastoral values of love, harmony, integrity and innocence are an affront to her.

Bhaunri's father-in-law went to the city for long time ago. "He has broken away completely from the clan's traditional iron craft and has set up a shop in the village selling all kinds of dry goods,"

(2019, p.13). He left his village for some comfort. A kind of longing to explore the newer aspects of life, attracted by the city life. However, he returns to his village. It's a kind of pointer that the temptation of city life can't be resisted but can't be endured for long. There is a desire for retreat and return. His nature also has changed, from a violent crazy bull to a comforting and understanding father-in-law. However, it does not rescue him from the scuffle and his return to the countryside does not make him learn and acquire new experiences. His consciousness does not make him conscientious of others and also does not enable him for any reconciliation with his fellow human beings.

In this very context, the discourse of retreat and return becomes of utmost importance. Terry Gifford has acknowledged this "essential paradox of the pastoral" that the retreat "delivers insights into the culture from which it originates" (Gifford, 1999, p. 82). We find that the retreat and return take place in the novel. However, it does not give and offer the characters any respite, comfort or relief. Lastly, consciousness does not promote and enhance conscience and a sense of responsibility towards others. Despite the presence of these pastoral codes strewn across the text; the fertility, peace, order, conscience and responsibility demanded of this genre remain unfulfilled. So, the differing treatments of the pastoral in each epoch, milieu, time and space originated. It demands and depends on the temporal and special matrices, culture and social ideology of that time and space.

Conclusion

Thus, Anukrti, like other pastoral writers, yearns for an earlier time when the pace of life was slow, calm, and composed and man was more submissive to nature. She underscores the significance of the lush, peaceful, healing power of the natural setting. However, she is not blind to the indifferent, even cruel, display of this powerful force when man forgets or chooses not to be in harmony with Nature. As we witness in the episode of the attack of locusts in the field.

The turn of budding Indian writers towards nature is the resurgence of pastoral tradition. It is 'art itself is nature', post-pastoral literature might appear as nature's way of offering us new avenues of imaginative hindsight to ideas that point to the cause of our extinction. A pastoral text and its reading develop and instill a sense of humility. It questions the emergence of the crisis of environmental degradation, deliberating the problem of nature and culture and vice-versa, and conveys an eco-consciousness. In a way, it offers hope for a better future for us. Through the arguments presented the chapter has posited those new trends of pastoral emerged during the past couple of years and hence it demands new themes and conventions associated with it.

As Horace declares, literature's ultimate aim is to be sweet and useful and the best writing is to teach and delight, Anukrti attempts her best in her *Bhaunri*. It is by the reconciliation of the duet of her pastoral ideal with the usual ethical order. The analysis shows that elements of both pastoral and anti-pastoral are embedded in *Bhaunri*. Characters, setting and elements of the landscape accord with many of the conditions of literary pastoral and anti-pastoral. The character of Khateek's daughter shows how a world that could become a haven of pastoral-like contentment is changed, through her own base choices and conduct, into the very opposite. Pastoral is undeniably in danger of descending into anti-pastoral. When that happens, the lost pastoral world becomes, as Bheema and his wife learn the object of nostalgic reverie and futile regrets.

With the growing interest in pastoral, there is remapping and tracing of the environment in contemporary writings. The complex understanding of this subject makes a demand for its representation and reflection upon its relation to humans and nature. Its shift from margin to centre calls for its central position, to acclimatize, enhance and develop to provide unique flexibility. Pastoral has been a varied form that exists and counter-cultural discourses, changes and concerns have emerged in the last two decades. Due to the proliferation and intrusion of cultural changes and the advancement of its principles, it has transformed into a new context affected by new demands of considerations. Despite all these changes, its core remains intact. In contemporary times its concerns are more towards the environment and hence its themes and conventions are being re-orientated.

As a result of this, the pastoral is used to discuss, represent and reflect upon these concerns, emerging in new forms. Not only that its themes and conventions relevant to environmental concerns, but also the change of its forms, principles, definition and theoretical orientations are in tune with it. It enables such adaptations and offers newer possibilities to relate, resolve and respond to these topics as how they are understood shifts, develops and continues. The real achievement of man is in the lap of nature and the real songs are songs of nature. Anukrti acquaints us with this pastoral that can make man in touch with nature. That is basically and perpetually significant, enlarging the soul with a profound understanding of nature and its ennobling power. Thus, it instils greater sympathy for fellow man.

Works Cited

Abrams, Meyer Howard, and Geoffrey, H. (2014) *A Glossary of Literary Terms*. Cengage Learning, The USA.

Ali, Monica. (2003) *Brick Lane*. Black Swan, London.

Alpers, Paul, (1996) *What is Pastoral?* University of Chicago Press, London.

---. (1983) "Convening and Convention in Pastoral Poetry", *New Literary History*, Vol. 14, no. 2, 277-304.

---. (1979) *The Singer of the Eclogues: A Study of Virgilian Pastoral: With a New Translation of The Eclogues*. University of California Press, Berkely Los Angeles.

Anand, Pulkita. (2021) Review of *Bhaunri: A Novel*, by Anukrti Upadhyay, *The Criterion: An International Journal in English*, Vol. 12, no. 1, pp. 457-60.

Barrell, John and Bull, J. (eds.). (1974) *The Penguin Book of English Pastoral Verse*. Penguin Books, London.

Becket, Fiona and Gifford, T. (eds.) (2007) *Culture, Creativity and Environment: New Environmentalist Criticism*, Rodopi, New York.

Butt, John. ed. (1965) *The Poems of Alexander Pope*. Methuen & Co Ltd., London.

Chaudhuri, Sukanta. (1989) *Renaissance Pastoral, and its English Developments*. Clarendon Press, Oxford.

Cooper, Helen, and Helen S. Cooper. (1977) *Pastoral: Mediaeval into Renaissance.*, Rowman & Littlefield, NJ.

Congleton, J E. (1968) *Theories of Pastoral Poetry in England 1684 – 1798*, Haskell House Publishers Ltd., New York.

Cuddon, J A. (1991) *Penguin Dictionary of Literary Terms and Literary Theory*, Third Edition, Penguin Books, England.

Empson, William. (2020) *Some Versions of Pastoral and Related Writings*, ed. by Seamus Perry, OUP, Oxford.

Greenblatt, Stephen, and Abrams, M. H. (2006) *The Norton Anthology of English Literature*. W.W. Norton, The USA.

Greg, W. W., (1959) *Pastoral Poetry and Pastoral Drama*. Russell & Russell, New York.

Gifford, Terry. (2006) "What is Ecocriticism For? Some personal reflections in response to two recent critiques." *Green Letters* Vol. 7. No. 1, pp. 6-13.

---. (2006) "Post-Pastoral as a Tool for Ecocriticism" in *Pastoral and the Humanities: Arcadia Re-Inscribed*, eds. Mathilde Skoie and Sonia Bjørnstad Velázquez, Bristol Phoenix Press, Bristol, pp. 14-24.

---. (2006) *Reconnecting with John Muir: Essays in Post-Pastoral Practice*, University of Georgia Press, Athens.

---. (1999) *Pastoral*. Routledge, London.

Gifford, Terry. (2000) "Pastoral, Ant-Pastoral, Post-Pastoral," in Laurence Coupe (ed.) *The Green Studies Reader: From Romanticism to Ecocriticism*. London: Routledge, pp. 219-222

Hilther, Ken. (2011) *What Else Is Pastoral? Renaissance Literature and the Environment*. Cornell University Press, Ithaca.

Kermode, Frank, ed. (1952) *English Pastoral Poetry*. Norton, New York.

Kermode, Frank (ed.). (1952) *English Pastoral Poetry from the Beginnings to Marvell*, G.G Harrap, London.

Lynen, J.F. (1960) *Nature and Pastoralism*. Yale University Press, The USA.

Marx, Leo. (1992) Does Pastoralism Have a Future? ' in *The Pastoral Landscape*, ed. John

Dixon Hunt, National Gallery of Art, pp. 109-225.

---. (1964) *The Machine in the Garden: Technology and the Pastoral Ideal in America*. Oxford University Press, NY.

Marinelli P. V. (1971) *Pastoral*. Methuen, London.

Philips, Ambrose. (1937) *The Poems of Ambrose Philips*. Ed. M. G. Segar, Basil Blackwell, Oxford.

Sukanta Chaudhuri. (1989) *Renaissance Pastoral and Its English Developments*. Clarendon Press, Oxford.

Smith N. D. (2000) "Changing Landscapes." Rev. Pastoral, by Terry Gifford. *Essays in Criticism* Vol. 50, no. 2, pp. 191-98.

Snyder, Gary. (1992) *No Nature: New and Selected Poems*. Pantheon, NY.

Upadhyay, Anukrti. (2019) *Bhaunri*. Fourth State, New Delhi.

William A. McClung. (1977) *The Country House in English Renaissance Poetry*. University of California Press, The USA.

Williams, Raymond. (1973) *The Country and the City*. Chatto and Windus, The USA.

Pastoral Paradoxes: A Study of Ankush Saikia's *The Forest Beneath the Mountains*

> In the beginning were the hills and the mountains, with rivers running down from them to the forests and the plains. Wild animals roamed the land and man was nowhere to be found. (Saikia 2021:17)
>
> And now that forest has almost disappeared. (Saikia 2021:12)

Since the last 10,000 years when humans started tilling the land and embarked on a journey of 'civilization and progress', we are supposedly living in the Holocene Age. However, a popular theory is that with the advent of the Industrial Revolution in the 1800s, the human impact on the earth has increased manifold in the form of carbon dioxide concentration in polar ice or the ocean waters, or increased methane in the atmosphere, or non-biodegradable litter everywhere. Moreover, since the mid-twentieth century, humans are leaving negative footprints on the planet in unprecedented ways. Thus, it has been variously argued that the Holocene must give way to an era marked by heightened human impact. In 2000, Nobel Prize-winning atmospheric chemist Paul Crutzen claimed that currently, we are in the 'Anthropocene age'.

The growing 'ecological imperialism' has placed the environs of the pastoral under unparalleled threat. Early on, Goethe, in "Hermann and Dorothea" (1797) offers a key to understanding how the epic pastoral, with its plentiful materiality, points toward the impending modernity of capitalism. He offers a picture of the naturescape contained within gated (confined) agricultural spaces of the 'landed nobility', a class that ascends with forceful capitalism. Needless to say, the pastoral landscape, with its 'abundance', and 'mankind' with its power-based relationship with nature, perceives the former as being 'out there' to be exploited and satisfy its insatiable capitalist agenda:

> The pastoral potentially connotes colonial exploitation and genocide as well as the exploitation of natural resources both locally and globally with the corresponding extremes of social injustices. (Sullivan "Dark Pastoral": 3)

In doing so, the anthropogenic re-shaping of the planet darkens the pastoral dream and ironizes its prospects with the complicity of our actions in the sixth mass extinction episode.

Goethe's "Hermann and Dorothea", unlike traditional pastoral narratives longing for a lost 'golden age', modifies this orientation into an ironic shift, one that paints the future in a dark, skeptical light — heightened power play, traffic and commodities. And thus, one ominously enters the Anthropocene era or the 'dark pastoral' in literary terms.

This being the prime concern of environmental and nature researchers for a long has, of late, crossed disciplines, and theorists have come to a consensus that humans have become an unparalleled geological force. In literature, it is argued that along with de-centering humans, writers in the Anthropocene era must find fresh perspectives to write with, new vocabulary to deliver the unimaginable, rigorous willingness to register that natural calamities are not simply natural anymore, but can be human-induced too. A figurative challenge in this respect is to find ways for the comprehensive manifestation of extinction in literature. Adam Trexler (2015) contends that the novel has become a vital apparatus to create meaning in an age of climate change. Trexler contends that Anthropocene fiction not merely shows global climate change, but also throws light on the fact that "climate change and all its things have changed the capacities of recent literature" (2015:13). The novel has adapted to new frontiers merging truth and fiction, economies and nature, and individual actions and grander natural phenomena. One must recuperate a sense of collectivism in narratives and not just allow the literary pieces to be simply an "individual moral adventure" (Updike "The New Yorker":1988). The stories being told must exhibit how the "lush foliage...hides threatening cultural change" (Sullivan "The Dark Pastoral": 2), for "stories...readily incorporate themselves into our felt experience" (Abram *Spell*: 120).

A dark pastoral framework points out how, in the Anthropocene, ecological and economic cycles are not to be considered functioning independently. Hence narrative approaches that illustrate an assimilation of human industrial/economic sequences with ecological cycles, and thus of natural and human history together, are of supreme importance. In *The Forest Beneath the Mountains* (henceforth *The Forest*), the narrator carries the burden of memories from his childhood of the "complacent and comforting representations of nature" (Gifford 2012: 8) similar to Theocritus's longing for his childhood in Sicily in *The Idylls* (3^{rd}c. BCE). However, on his subsequent visit to his childhood idyll twenty-five years later, he finds the forests surrounding his native town, Tezpur (Assam), turned into a decapitated landscape due to mindless human encroachment into the terrain of trees and wild animals. His painful predicament in witnessing the wildlife crimes reflects Leo Marx's (1960) idea in *The Machine in the Garden*, in which the machine serves as a symbol of the technological 'progress' of humankind that transcends the rural-urban relationship and thereby, threatening the 'arcadia' in the New World. Ortega Y. Jose (1930:89) sums this up aptly in *The Revolt of the Masses*:

> The world is a civilised one, its inhabitant is not: he does not see the civilisation of the world around him, but he uses it as if it were a natural force. The new man wants *his* motor car and enjoys it, but he believes that it is the spontaneous fruit of an Edenic tree.

Writers with such a stance, do not necessarily intend to frighten and threaten, "but to engage with the complex questions for our species, might better be described as 'post-pastoral'" (Gifford 2012: 20). Therefore, Post-Pastoral narratives could claim to offer a holistic understanding of our 'notions of humanity' by merging the exigencies of 'progress', cultural geography and environmental ethics.

The Pastoral Abundance

> Lead us on to emancipation and give us this feeling of higher harmony which compensates for all his troubles and secures the happiness of the victor!
> (Schiller 1875:318)

Ideally, pastoral literature appeals to both the mind and heart, even though Schiller finds no perfect embodiment of the ideal pastoral. Nevertheless, each narrator has a quintessential portrayal of the (perfect) pastoral recollected and embodied in their writings from their sensory experiences. Coming back to his native place, Tezpur (Assam), after twenty-five years of being in Delhi and in 'big' cities, Abhijit finds the place of his memories to be an altered landscape, but still a breath of fresh air compared to his state of being "trapped in a forest of shoddy concrete buildings" (Saikia 2021:9). The news of his mother's death makes him leave his job in Delhi and return to Assam. Twenty-five years ago, his father, a forest officer in Tezpur, was found shot dead in his jeep. As he tries to make sense of his long sense of displacement and dive into the bottom of his father's mystery, the plot plays out through a topography of unrequited questions suppressed by politics and merciless transformations, and an all too discernible ecocide side-lined by layers of political discord. His stimulating sojourn in Tezpur was about to mediate and negotiate his relationship with the land of his memories upon which depended the forces of nature at work— both 'outer nature' and 'inner nature'.

Historically, The Northeast of India has been termed as one big 'jungle' by people from other parts of the country. Shedding the metaphorical implication of the term, the Northeast has been a green paradise for long:

> When the British took over Assam and Burma in the early part of the 19th century after the Anglo–Burmese wars, there stretched thick forest cover all across what is now northeast India and northern Myanmar, save for the rice fields in the Assam valley and scattered settlements. (Saikia 2021:33)

Abhijit grew up in the '90s around the still-thick Chariduar Reserve Forest at the foothills of Arunachal Pradesh. His father was in the forest service which lent him all the more proximity that one could have grown up in that part of the 'green' country. The instilling of oneself in the lap of nature and getting dissolved into it depends mostly on the availability of an escapist life devoid of the "politics" and limiting conventions of modern city life. If 'rural', in current times, is the major synonym for pastoral, then:

> ...there was still a rural connection to Tezpur; paddy from the family fields arriving at his father's house to be threshed, the cows in the guhali or cowshed, their dung used in the garden as fertilizer and in the pakghor (kitchen) for fuel. (Saikia 2021:21)

It was almost a 'Eutierria' (see Glenn Albrecht) that Abhijit sinks into — love for and a deep sense of connection with nature that pervades the consciousness — at an intersection of the ecosystem and human mind (and health). Viviane Crowley (2014: 14-15), in "Experiencing Eutierria" says:

> As adults, we can still have these intense experiences of oneness with nature through meditative walking, when camping or in any activity that gets us time to just with be trees, birds, and the landscape, and take time to use our senses to kisten, smell, touch and see all that is around us.... We do not have to label ourselves 'spiritual' to experience a sense of oneness with nature.

Abhijit's visit 'home' opens myriad dialogues with nature and people from different rungs of society who belong to and represent an era of the 'once' densely forested Assam. His roots seem to lie so deep in 'Eutierria' that even while being in Delhi and Shillong, he could, in his mind, feel both 'endemophilia' (a love for some specific area from your experience) and 'soliphilia' (a recognition and love for a place, its history and the ancestors) for Tezpur. When in the concrete jungles of the big cities or towns, he just had to close his eyes to get transported to his childhood idyll:

> In his later years in Shillong and Delhi, Abhijit could return to that winter landscape of Assam by just closing his eyes: the morning mist hanging over the yellow paddy stalks in the harvested fields, stands of trees and bamboo groves beside them, ducks in ponds, warm sunshine, the odd village: huts with thatch or tin roofs under betel-nut trees, paths white with dust. (Saikia 2021:21)

As a child, Abhijit made several rounds and overnight halts at forest camps with his father and his friends Khagen Sakia and Pradip

Deka. Those were days of 'abundance' and people still went occasionally hunting in those "thick, dense forests, with towering trees and creepers draped over the undergrowth" (Saikia 2021:22). Without any intent at justifying the acts of sporadic hunting, Abhijit does put across a point that there was still a pattern of rejuvenation and balance in nature left behind by people like his father or his friends; what followed that era has wreathed havoc on that delicate human-nature balance and resulted in gruesome ecocide. Their jungle trips were mostly at night; those areas were still safe even amidst all the 'wild' animals and ironically misfortune had befallen his father at the hands of a (gunned) human. Meanwhile, Abhijit was getting to 'know' wildlife and meeting it 'in person':

> He knew animals generally avoided the road during the day, but he had seen wild buffaloes and elephants crossing it. The trumpeting of elephants could be heard from within the forest, and sometimes the heavy flapping of a hornbill taking off from a tree at the approach of the vehicle. (Saikia 2021:22)

He learnt several minute details about the incessant dialogues between humans and nature. The Arunachal foothills are known for around four species of Hornbills. He learns how "in the old days people used the oil from a gland below the hornbill's head for their aches and pains" (Saikia 2021:31). The Northeast of the 90s had still the generation that kept touch with the ancient world thriving, and "years later, he regrets "not being born forty or fifty years earlier" (Saikia 2021:11). It is only when he is estranged from this pastoral-academia that he realizes this deep sense of loss. But through the narrative, he draws on his memory and tries to negotiate between his 'modern' barrenness the past affluence:

> Once, at sunset, Abhijit saw a flock of hornbills, twenty—five to thirty of them, flying from the direction of the forest, alternately beating their wings and then gliding: as they crossed the river, headed for the hills above, the slow, heavy flapping of their large wings going whup whup whup seemed like a link to something ancient and prehistoric, to the time of the dinosaurs, when man hadn't yet appeared on the earth. (Saikia 2021:23)

> Elephants roamed these forests in immense herds; the ground shaking when they passed. Abhijit had read that elephant had a complex society, second only to that of humans; their family and clan structures resembled those of man before the advent of agriculture, at the hunter-gatherer stage. In the Dzukou valley stretching across present-day Nagaland and Manipur, there is a narrow pass known in the language of the local Angami tribe as the 'Elephant Pass', possibly lying on the route by which these giant animals had moved between Myanmar and Assam. (Saikia 2021:34)

Through such episodes of memory and encounters, Abhijit's narrative establishes a productive conversation between humans and the environment. Once in touch with nature, humans are instructed in her way and "this instruction will allow the initiate to live well in his complex world after leaving his pastoral retreat" (Hardin 1979: 2). Years later when Abhijit comes back, literally, to the lap of nature, this retreat could be seen "more consistently a trait of what is called primitivism than pastoralism" (Hardin 1979: 3):

> he had the sense of entering a more primal world—Abhijit would remember that great forest many years later, while studying *Heart of Darkness* in college, feeling, like Marlow, that he had been 'travelling back to the earliest beginnings of the world'. (Saikia 2021:22)

Tezpur (Assam), in those days, seemed to sustain the primitive bond between animals and humans where no man-made establishments disrupted the natural movement of wild animals and very rare cases of man-vs-wild conflicts. There were myriad elephant herds that "came down in the winters from the hills of Arunachal Pradesh to feed on ripe paddy and sugarcane and moved back up into the hills as the Bhoroli river rose" (Saikia 2021:111). Similarly, Abhijit also made his life free-flowing in tune with nature:

> Abhijit liked going down to the river, which receded during winter, exposing the large boulders brought down from the mountains yonder. Sitting by the river he was aware of the clean air, the dust raised from the fine sand, the winter sun, the cold river water, the creeper with flowers known as Germany bon (some said it had been

brought from there during World War II) growing wild, and it all made him feel strangely alive. (Saikia 2021:23)

To sum up, a life that Abhijit lived as a child, and one that he tries to regain as an adult, displays a sense of holding together "against the turbulence and confusion of the present and the future, a pastoral past often provides the image in literature of order, stability and agreed values—a stable 'living' in Wendell Berry's terms" (Gifford 2012:12). Amidst the growing conflicts between man and wild, terrorism in the area, upon his return, Abhijit still made it to the Jungles, or the remnants of the jungles, as if reiterating Thoreau's (1983:135) thoughts: 'I went to the woods because I wished to live deliberately…". Evocative of post-pastoral literature, Forests runs wild on the (imaginative) challenges to notions that are leading to the imminent mass extinction. These narratives also point towards an important perspective that says one must not just think towards nature but think in nature.

Pastoral Paradox

> A landscape altered by human hands. (Saikia 2021: 87)

Goethe suggests how the impending destruction of modern capitalism is ironically hidden in the abundance of nature. Striking a similar note, Sullivan (2015: 27) opines:

> The various scenarios of the human-land relationship in terms of our agency provide an Anthropocenic mosaic in which a deeply felt pastoral love of specifically humanized landscapes combines with devastating disasters of natural-cultural origins and no clear solutions. The dark pastoral functions within such unbridgeable divides and is thus a trope of paradox and contrast, of irony and exposure. Yet it continues to tell stories since stories easily contain irony and are part of the human-world creation where we retain some agency if only in speaking.

In *Forests*, one can see how Assam has been systematically robbed of its green abundance amid a complete system and cultural fiasco. Never before have we seen such unprecedented ecological imperialism in the history of evolution. As Abhijit was growing up in the 90s, he was already in the fading kingdom of the wild. Twenty-five years later he found it difficult to even recognize his state and his native town. The narrative puts into place the fact that "dark ecology puts hesitation, uncertainty, irony, and thoughtfulness back into ecological thinking" (Morton 16-17). The narrator understands the social, political and ecological dynamics at work in tangent. He provides a well-explained picture of what went wrong in that part of the country.

Anthropos

> Animals have limited wants, unlike us humans, whose wants are never-ending. (Saikia 2021:13)

The need and greed of humans, politics and nature have been intertwined since time immemorial. The Brahmaputra Valley has also been a witness to this "murder or suicide" (Saikia 2021: 30). Abhijit looks up at a photo dating back to 1835 when the British had set foot on Tezpur—it was a sepia-tinted photo showing "the banks sprawled down and there stood a jungle above the near bank, giving the photo a touch of wilderness" (Saikia 2021: 30). What Abhijit witnesses now is massive "deforestation and the plight of wildlife" alike at around the same place and far and beyond it. It can only be imagined how green the Assam Valley might have been when the British landed. When Assam was annexed by the British, "six-eighths or seven-eighths of the province was under forest cover. These were considered as wastelands as they earned no revenue for the administration and hence expansion of agricultural land was encouraged by clearing wastelands (forest areas)" ("RE looking at forest policies in Assam" 2009). However, on their arrival, "the British cleared vast tracts of forest in Assam to establish tea plantations, and their fondness for hunting meant that tigers, rhinos, deer and elephants were shot in large numbers as sport" and this lead to a huge crisis when "there were just a handful of rhinos left in what was now the Kaziranga national park in the first decade of the 20th century, and it was only the creation of a wildlife sanctuary that had saved the animal" (Saikia 2021: 34). Even Elephant hunting almost had a British monopoly, as it was one of their favourite animals because of its strategic importance— hauling, transportation, help in hunting and administrative purposes. The British administration left an indelible mark on the sociological fabric of the state as well, which in turn harmed the ecological canvas of the region at large.

In more recent times, the Bodoland Movement has been unleashing adverse effects on the forests surrounding Tezpur. The struggle for a Bodo homeland, or 'Bodoland' started in the late 1980s, and continued well into the 1990s until 2003…. The Bodos demanded separate recognition of their cultural and linguistic heritage. (The Action Northeast Trust 2017)

Marred by a lack of depth of and farsighted perspective, the upper hand of the politicians who look into their benefits while claiming mass benefit, and the "effects of change upon tribal societies" (Saikia 2021: 20) in the Northeast, the Bodos have been hardly hit as they have hit the ecology in the foothills of Arunachal surrounding Tezpur. This is a tribe "caught as they were between the British–ruled society of their parents and the mutations of democracy in a distant corner of a newly—independent country" (Saikia 2021: 20). By the 90s, the "Bodos had taken over the Chariduar Reserve Forest" (Saikia 2021: 45) while also issuing demand notices in the villages:

> …they spread all over. 'Most of the Chariduar reserve forest, 460 square kilometres, is gone. The government carved the Sonai Rupai sanctuary out of it, 220 square kilometres…that's why a small portion of the reserve forest was saved…but even there, half of that is gone. There are only about 80-90 square kilometres of the sanctuary left. (Saikia 2021: 48)

Abhijit meets an old man from Arunachal, Nana, and asks him to describe the process that led to the disappearance of the reserve forest as he remembers from his childhood. He draws a disturbing picture:

> They (Bodos) cut everything and sold it, all the trees, in just four or five years. We used to hear it from up here at night, dham dham dham, the big trees falling one by one.' the less valuable trees were set alight, and covered with earth, to be turned into charcoal. (Saikia 2021: 45)

These people then put up in "plastic-sheet covered dwellings" (Saikia 2021: 77) all over the cleared and burned patches. During the daytime there would be groups of young boys "with catapults in their hands" (Saikia 2021: 41) and girls following them to collect the fallen birds back home. After the massive relocation of this tribe and deforestation that followed, what Abhijit beholds twenty-five years later is village after village of extreme poverty and terrorism. His research into the matter of human-elephant conflict offered him "links to the issue of deforestation, and to the groups involved in the struggle for a separate Bodo state" (Saikia 2021: 181). He wonders, "who would have benefitted from clearing the forest, from chopping down those massive trees. It didn't appear to be the people he had just seen" (Saikia 2021: 43). In fact, Abhijit's probe into the matter furthers takes him to crossroads of politics, Army, AR and terrorism alike on the point of illegal money-making. Jagat Kumar, a Junior Engineer with the BSO, along with a faction of insurgents, "made lakhs of rupees from the sand and stone business" (Saikia 2021: 75). The BSO, buildings and store officer, a guy from UP, "would comfortably clear about 50 lakhs rupees from a three-year posting, over and above his salary" (Saikia 2021: 73). Pegu, the police officer from Tezpur, tells Abhijit about the arrangements in the village centres where "they sold it off cheap, just 100 to 150 rupees per cubic foot. Titasopa, bonsum, sal, segun, mekuridima: such fine wood. The insurgents took about 20 to 25 rupees a CFT as their cut. Gulai Centre was the main place for all of this (Saikia 2021: 82).

Pegu also talks about the multiple unsuccessful eviction drives undertaken. However, each time they would retaliate and resurface:

> 'We tried evicting them many times. They would surround us, and threaten us with days (machete).... There are no good trees left in

Assam…all cut and finished, and now the hills of Arunachal are slowly turning bald as well.' (Saikia 2021: 79)

Dulu da, a character from yesteryears, put it more blatantly to Abhijit, "'There isn't a more destructive group than the Bodos, I'll tell you that. They cut and burn and kill everything they can. Look at what happened to the Manas sanctuary'" (Saikia 2021: 72). What started as a call for a separate land for themselves, seems to have transgressed into the usual politico-terrorism vendetta. The rich got richer, and the poor poorer. The resultant desperation also took the form of an anti-India stance where "India was the villain" and "they would have to use force to liberate their land from India" (Saikia 2021: 182). The matter of the centre exploiting the NE states remains a matter of political, social and cultural unsettling, but the point that cannot be ignored is that the wilderness got entrenched in between losing major grounds.

The social fabric of Tezpur is also majorly taken over by the 'Miyas' and this doesn't fail to find a place in the narrative. They are Muslims of Bengali descent from the state of Bangladesh, and a large group of illegal immigrants into the region. They mostly put up in the *sor-sapori* (riverside). Abhijit goes to meet Rafiqul Ali, a retired forest guard, an acquaintance from old times, who lived near *Bhumuraguri,* riverside. There were "posters on the plaster walls, including one of a bridge with 'Bangladesh' printed below" (Saikia 2021: 173). He tells Abhijit about how like Bodos, they spread under a dewani system: "One person goes ahead looking for new land, and then comes back and informs the others" (Saikia 2021: 179). However, all that comes down to is politics on the higher level and pitiable living in the lower rungs, as Ali says, "our political leaders do all these things" (Saikia 2021: 180). Even though they might not invade the forest areas directly, as Ali claims, the population pressure on the geography nonetheless persists and is ever-increasing. In recent times, Miyas, Abhijit notices, have invaded the local markets with "their fertilizer-enhanced vegetables" (Saikia 2021: 64).

Ecosystem & Animals: The Plight

> Wild elephants—how they were being squeezed into ever-shrinking areas in Assam by the spread of human activity and the loss of forests. (Saikia 2021: 60)

Wild animals are worst hit by human politics and mindless exploitation and destruction of natural resources. It is not just direct hunting that leads to the extinction of animals, but the natural world is an invisible delicate chain, and tampering with any part of the chain finally results in global deluge. To talk about Elephants, they are "large animals which require vast areas to wander" (Saikia 2021: 119). The giants understandably require larger food availability and the wide wandering zones "allow areas they feed in to regenerate" (Saikia 2021: 119). To this, Abhijit observes:

> When the herds are confined to smaller patches of forest, regeneration isn't complete, and over time the nature of the forest itself changes, and not for the better. (Saikia 2021: 119)

This inevitably results in Elephants heading towards human settlements (that have encroached into the formers' territory in the first place) in search of food. This has indeed become a commonplace occurrence in Assam. The man-elephant conflict has risen manifold since the 1990s. Pegu puts it palpably:

> The forest disappeared...and what are the animals going to eat now...they've started straying out of the forest looking for grain in the villages, tearing down people's houses and granaries.... Last night I had two forest guards to chase out a male elephant from the army base. .... A week back ...a herd from Rangapara from Sonai Rupai trampled a family of four to death. During your father's time, there were hardly any elephants coming out of the forest.' (Saikia 2021: 52)

Not content with encroaching into Elephants' space, humans have also devised electric "'wires strung across poles'" around human settlements "beyond which was a vast emptiness where the forest had once stood'" (Saikia 2021: 81). These are called *Jhatka* fencing which mostly runs on "12-volt direct current from solar panels" (Saikia 2021: 81).

In earlier times, right from the British presence to well past independence, "*hati mahals* existed all over the state of Assam, where businessmen hired *mahouts* and *phandis* to capture wild elephants…then tamed and sold to people, mostly for hauling logs" (Saikia 2021: 33). Plight of wild animals from being broken down to domesticate, gaming and illegal hunting to annual floods have never ceased to exist. With "growth and development" in human society, the plight of animals has only risen manifold. Tigers, deer, rhinos, aves, etc. have all faced dwindling populations in the last few decades in the region.

A lost landscape

> End of an era: larger forces were sweeping the region, and a small place like Foothills couldn't stay isolated. (Saikia 2021: 19)

Diving into his memories from his childhood and the myriad stories of the past that he gathers from various sources on his return to his native place, makes Abhijit feel the past to be a "*xadhukotha*" (fairy tale) (71). With much of the green splendour lost, Abhijit deduces that "in another ten years", his sleepy little hometown "will become like Chandigarh" (Saikia 2021: 38). He visits the Kolamati forest gate from his childhood, "now a range office, with larger buildings painted orange-brown…with a single gigantic tree before the buildings" (Saikia 2021: 38). To him, the memory from yesteryears was so strong replete with forest "looming large" around the area that "what he saw now made him feel disoriented and slightly dizzy" (Saikia 2021: 38). At a place where "he and his father had seen the tiger that evening long ago" was left with "no forest …just huts with thatch or tin roofs… a solar panel on a roof and in front by the road two or three wires strung across wooden posts like the earlier fence" (Saikia 2021: 40). The narrative pens down his dismay poignantly:

> Sadness, anger, wonder—he had felt all of that, and something more: a feeling of awe at what he had seen, which was nothing less

than the story of how man had spread upon the face of the earth. (Saikia 2021: 52)

Abhijit visited the home of one called Dhananjoy at a place called 12 Mile Centre. If not told or seen firsthand, "there was no way one would realize, unless one already knew about it, that there had been another vast reserve forest, the Balipara Reserve Forest, from more than a century ago" (Saikia 2021: 105). Beside Dhananjoy's home, there was another Bodo family, the Swargiary's. The elderly father of the family informs him of his arrival in 1995:

> '*Forest-or mati dokhol koribo ahisilu*,' he said: 'we had come to lay claim to Forest Department land.' It was only much later that the enormity of that simple sentence would sink in. (Saikia 2021: 105-06).

Deforestation has not only shrunk animal kingdoms but also resulted in increased floods in the last decade. Also, the increase in the illegal sand and stone business from the rivers results in less protection from floods downstream during the monsoons. The increased influx of the Miya population has made irreversible changes:

> Earlier, people had avoided living in flood-prone areas, especially by the Brahmaputra river, but those areas had been slowly occupied too. Living in Tezpur, with its natural protection against the rising waters of the great river in the form of a rocky bank, wasn't something Abhijit had paid much attention to. On the bus to Guwahati, he saw some places that were still underwater. (Saikia 2021: 164)

Even the incidence of "malaria in the Chariduar reserve forest area had risen as more and more settlers had come in and the trees were cut down" (Saikia 2021: 95). Despite such changes, humans fail to acknowledge the delicate nature's chain that must be maintained at any cost. Off late, using power saws has become a trend (illegal though) even in the hitherto pristine Arunachal Pradesh. The narrative establishes both Assam and Arunachal foothills as "landscapes altered by human hands" that were replete with green in all directions" (Saikia 2021: 87) in Abhijit's childhood, just twenty-five years back.

Conclusion

We live in an age of "uncertainty" where values seem to have eroded, if not fully annihilated. Pastoral narratives serve not just as literary but also as cultural discourses, displaying strains and inherent contradictions as rich sources of environmental thought processes. Gifford, resounding Goethe, explains how the 'dark' lies in the abundant green. *Forests* show an ecocide, almost dystopic, in which humans have devastated the environment in which they reside and have chosen to remain oblivious to the fact that it heralds their extinction. Gerard Manley Hopkins, in his poem 'God's Grandeur', led us to the important lesson of humility. This is obligatory in doing away with the hubris that our species demonstrates in treating its environment.

Abhijit narrates an incident that he gathers from a tea garden about an adult male elephant striking a man down and stamping on his right leg, breaking the thigh bone— "As he lay in agony on the ground, thinking he would surely be trampled to death, a few more wild elephants appeared. A female elephant charged and butted the male elephant away from the fallen man. The man said she tapped him on his back as if warning him to stay down, even as she fought off the male elephant, which then backed away. 'Maybe a human being had been kind to her earlier, given her food or rescued her,' the man said" (Saikia 2021: 188-89). This is a strong portrayal of other species' recognition of their fellow beings in nature and the need to co-exist and acknowledge the relationship. The narrative rings in Sullivan's idea of:

> "dark pastoral" and a literary framework for acknowledging "human beings' oldest and most powerfully moving strategies for describing our identities, relationships, the connection to our surroundings, and our origins" (Sullivan 2015: 25-26).

The Anthropocene is a mixed bag of pastoral paradoxes, but human beings must harness its potential for a deeper understanding of the ecology around them.

Works Cited

Abram, D. (1996) *Spell of the Sensuous: Perception and Language in a More-Than-Human World*, Random House, New York.

Albrecht, G. (2011) 'Creating a language for our psychoterratic emotions and feelings', *Health Earth*, 8 September. Available at: http://healthearth (Accessed: 30 June 2021)

Crowley, Viviane. (2014) 'Experiencing Eutierria: Oneness with Nature', *Green Spirit*, Vol. XX, No. 1, Pp. 14-15.

Gasset, J.O.y. (1932) *The Revolt of the Masses*. trans. anon. Norton, New York.

Gifford, T. (2012) Pastoral, Anti-Pastoral and Post-Pastoral as Reading Strategies. In Scott S. ed. *Critical Insights: Nature and Environment*, New York: Salam Press, pp. 42-61.

Gifford, T. (1999) *Pastoral*. Routledge, London.

Goethe, J. W. von. (1797) *Hermann and Dorothea*, London, Dodo Press.

Hardin, R. (ed.) (1979) *Survivals of Pastoral*, Kansas, University of Kansas Publication.

Marx, L. (1964) *The Machine in the Garden: Technology and the Pastoral Ideal in America*, London, Oxford University Press.

Morton, T. (2010) *The Ecological Thought*, London, Harvard University Press.

Saikia, Ankush. (2021) *The Forests Beneath the Mountains*, New Delhi, Speaking Tiger,

Sarma, M., Jennifer L, Balawansuk L., & Jauga M. (2017) 'Health Inequities in A Conflict Area—An In-Depth Qualitative Study in Assam' *The Action Northeast Trust* (Chirang District, Assam, India). Available at: https://idl-bnc-idrc.dspacedirect.org/handle/10625/59410

Schiller, Friedrich. (1875) *Essays Aesthetkal and Philosophical* [Project Gutenberg], Translated by Anonymous, London, George Bell and Sons.

Sullivan, H. I. (2015) 'The Dark Pastoral: Goethe and Atwood', *Green Letters* Vol. XX, No. 1, pp. 1-13. DOI: 10.1080/14688417.2015.1116403

Tamuli, Jitu and Choudhury, Saswati. (2009) 'RE looking at forest policies in Assam: facilitating reserved forests as de facto open access'. MPRA.

Theocritus. (1908) *The Idylls of Theocritus and the Eclogues of Virgil* [online]. London, George Bell and Sons.

Thoreau, H. D. (1983). *Walden and Civil Disobedience*. New York, Penguin Books. 1983.

Trexler, Adam. (2015) *Anthropocene Fictions: The Novel in a Time of Climate Change*. Virginia, University of Virginia Press.

Updike, J. (1988) 'Review of City of Salt' *The New Yorker*, 17 October, p.117.

Dystopian Landscapes, Urban and Rural, of the Spanish Generation of 1898

The nineteenth century saw an explosion of scientific discovery, which snowballed into the Industrial Revolution that first swept Europe, then North America, and finally, the rest of the world Heralding a new way of life that promised less work, more leisure, higher standards of living, and relief from drudgery, disease, and poverty, industrialization and the movement to cities proved to worsen the condition of most, bringing instead longer working hours, the exploitation of men, women, and children in factories, horrific bodily injury from machinery, pollution, overcrowding in cramped living spaces, unsanitary conditions, disease, crime, political violence, and the loss of identity (More, 2014, pp. 138-157). Conditions in rural areas were almost as bad, where poverty, unsanitary hygiene, disease, ignorance, crime, and class violence were equally rampant. Presented with these two realities, how was the Spanish nation to advance? This was just one of the questions raised by the celebrated Spanish writers of the Generation of 1898, including Miguel de Unamuno (1864-1936), Ramón del Valle-Inclán (1866-1936), Pío Baroja (1872-1956), José Martínez Ruiz ["Azorín"] (1873-1967), Ramiro de Maeztu (1875-1936), and Antonio Machado (1875-1939), who attempted to shock the Spanish government and the Spanish people into reforming the nation after the catastrophic Spanish-American War of 1898 in which Spain lost the last of her colonies. Now that Cuba, Puerto Rico, the Mariana Islands, and the Philippines were lost, heralding the demise of the imperial Spanish dream, what did it mean to be Spanish? Although these writers did not "create" the Generation of 1898 (hereafter, "Generation of '98") by mutual agreement or manifesto, it is remarkable to note that they all perceived the same fatal ills in Spain, and proceeded to expose them in newspaper articles, poetry, drama, and especially, in prose.

Having been educated in large cities and often in other European nations, the writers of the Generation of '98 were greatly influenced by the thought of German philosophers such as Karl

Christian Friedrich Krause (1787-1832), Arthur Schopenhauer (1788-1860), and Friedrich Nietzsche (1844-1900), who espoused new ideas that were often in conflict with the traditional ideas of the Roman Catholic Church and the monarchy. To the Generation of '98, Spain's decay was rooted in what they believed to be the false glories of the past. No longer ought Spain to dream of the supposed magnificence of its colonial domination, nor of its brilliant religious struggle as the "Defender of the Catholic Faith" during the Reconquest, the only Christian Crusade to be conducted on Western soil (Gaztambide, 1958, pp. 45-62). The writers of the Generation of '98 urged Spain to heal itself of its spiritual and material malaise, which, in their opinion, was suffered in every corner of the country. Whereas European nations like the United Kingdom, France, and especially Germany enjoyed the benefits of modern science, such as material progress, improved standards of life, and an intellectual renewal that offered a sense of freedom, creativity, and growth, Spain appeared to be trapped in the minutiae of Roman Catholic theology and Scholastic philosophy and was enslaved in a social system that was rife with backwardness, feudal structures, and class struggle. Whereas modern European cities like London, Paris, and Berlin were celebrated as centres of intellectual inquiry, culture, and improved standards of living, Spain preferred to dwell in the fantasy world of its most famous son, Don Quixote. As it attacked the ghosts of the Spanish past, the Generation of '98 recognized that it would need to address the reality of two Spains, the traditional Spain of the countryside and the modern Spain of the cities.

Although it had enjoyed over a century of imperial magnificence from the Columbian discoveries at the end of the fifteenth century through the rapid expansion of the sixteenth, Spain had nonetheless been in a slow but steady decline that began to accelerate precipitously as early as the seventeenth century, and which culminated in the "Disaster of 1898." Even during the heady days of glory, when Spain was, as Fray Francisco de Ugualde asserted, *"El imperio en el que nunca se pone el sol"* ["The empire over which the sun never sets"], the seeds of internal dissolution had unwittingly been sown (Kamen, 2008, p. 99). The burst of expansionist glory had come with a heavy price, both literally and figuratively. As early as 1557 the Spanish government had already gone into bankruptcy and, as both Charles V and his son Philip II struggled against their traditional rivals -- England, France, and Portugal --, as well as the tide of Protestantism in Europe and Islam in the East, the crown increasingly relied on Spain and the Spanish colonies to finance its exploits (Elliott, 2002, p. 199). So desperate was the situation that then Prince Philip wrote to Charles that the Spanish people in every social class had reached their breaking point:

> With what they pay in ordinary and extraordinary dues, the common people, who have to pay these *servicios*, are reduced to such utter misery that many of them walk naked. And the misery is so universal that it is even greater among the vassals of nobles than it is among Your Majesty's vassals, for they are unable to pay their rents, lacking the wherewithal, and the prisons are full. (Elliott, 2002, p. 210)

Extending throughout the sixteenth and seventeenth centuries, royal bankruptcies occurred regularly, almost in perfect intervals of twenty years: 1557, 1575, 1596, 1607, 1627, and 1647 (Vicens Vives, 1969, pp. 383-384). This forced the crown to rely more and more on foreign creditors who demanded exorbitant rates of interest, practically turning intermittent declarations of bankruptcy into instruments of royal economic policy.

The "glorious" days of Spain, as it was becoming a rising empire, had also been devastating to the interior of the nation, as Generation of '98 author Azorín starkly notes:

> By the end of the 16th century, the flight of the inhabitants of the countryside has already
> begun. The cities entrance the villagers. The cities in the 16th century were splendid. New monuments appear. In the broad squares -- many of them surrounded by arcades — those beautiful buildings are erected. The labourer moves to the city. The wars and the conquest of America tempt him. Workhands are missing in the countryside.
> [Translations throughout are mine, unless indicated otherwise.]
> [A fines del siglo XVI ya la fuga de los moradores de los campos se ha iniciado. Las ciudades hechizan a los villanos. Las ciudades

son espléndidas en el siglo XVI. Los monumentos aparecen nuevos. En las anchas plazas—muchas de ellas rodeadas de soportales—se yerguen esos hermosos edificios. El labriego marcha hacia la ciudad.

Le tientan las guerras y la conquista de América. Van faltando operarios en la campiña.]

(Azorín, 1967, p. 126).

As Azorín observes, the dream of finding freedom from social control, gold and silver, and a life of adventure increasingly led to the depopulation of the countryside and a slow but progressive rotting from within (Vicens Vives, 1969, pp. 315-316). Although the Castilian economy was growing rapidly towards the end of the fifteenth century, as we have seen, the sixteenth century showed signs of long-term economic decay. This was particularly noticeable in the raising of livestock and farming.

Established in 1273 by royal privilege of the king of Castile, the *Mesta* or the "Honorable Assembly of the Mesta" [*El Honrado Consejo de la Mesta*], a syndicate of sheepherders, was given a free hand in the raising of "roaming" livestock [*los trashumantes*] that indiscriminately wandered through the fields of farmers (Payne, 1973, v. 2, p. 76; Davies, 1964, p. 18). Because of the vast revenue that the sale of wool brought to the crown, the actions of the *Mesta* were limited by law yet, in practice, were virtually unopposed (Vicens Vives, 1969, pp. 301-302). This led to a decline in agricultural production, a scarcity of food such that grain had to be imported from abroad, and, what was most damaging, a serious rift between herders and farmers that weakened national harmony. Azorín laments the destruction and hatred wrought by the *Mesta*'s wanton activities as well as by others who abused the farmer in every way:

> The Mesta is given all of the privileges. All of the burdens fall upon the farmer. He cannot close off his lands; livestock enter to graze on them; they eat the stubble and destroy the vines; the travelers steal the fruit from the edges of the fields; troops trample down the crops; warriors enter houses to plunder them; they steal the hams that are hanging in the smokehouses; they carry off the hens that are hidden in the thick brush; they tend to force themselves upon the young women.

[La Mesta se lleva todos los privilegios. Sobre el labrador pesan todas las cargas. Sus tierras no puede cerrarlas; los ganados entran a pastar en ellas; se comen los rastrojos y
  destruyen las viñas; los viandantes hurtan la fruta de los linderos; las tropas huellan las cosechas; gentes de guerra entran a saco en las casas; roban los perniles que están colgados en el humero; se llevan las gallinas escondidas en los anchos follados; suelen forzar las mozas.] (Azorín, 1967, 126-127)

Because of immorality, greed, and a disregard for others, the Spanish countryside had been turned into a living hell, where simple existence was a daily struggle, and were suffering abounded.

How had Spain reached this nadir, asked the writers of the Generation of '98, and what was to be done to regenerate the nation? As they saw it, the first step in the process of healing was to confront the ghosts of the Spanish past and to assess the current national reality; this was the daunting "Problema de España" [the "Problem of Spain"]. Intellectuals all, the writers of the Generation of '98 embarked upon a desperate search for the meaning of hispanidad—"Spanishness"—and sought to return to the roots of Spanish identity, the "Ser de España" ["The Being of Spain"], the essence of what it meant to be Spanish. This, of necessity, implied a deeper search for the moral essence of the Spanish people.

Classical scholar, essayist, journalist, poet, novelist, and rector of Spain's preeminent institution of higher education, the University of Salamanca, Miguel de Unamuno was a cultural icon in Spain. Appalled and angered by the war with the United States, Unamuno published his article "*¡Muera Don Quijote!*" ["Let Don Quixote Die!"] in June of 1898, just two months into the conflict. Establishing a parallel, Unamuno argued that the Spanish nation (i.e., the government) and Don Quixote both lived by illusions of greatness; in his opinion, both had to die to return to their true identities: in reality, the "nation" was the Spanish "*pueblo*" ["people"], and Don Quixote was Alonso Quijano "the Good," the humble yet honourable *hidalgo* who represented the downtrodden lower nobility, which, although often poor, defended their greatest treasure, their honour, with the utmost care (Defourneaux, 1970, p. 40). Unamuno asserts that illusory glories must be abandoned:

> We must forget about the life of adventures, of imposing on others what we believed was good for them and looking for a deceptive empire outside. We must
> meditate, above all, on the anti-Christian nature of the chivalric ideal. If the task of the nation, an essentially bourgeois product, has been to assure inequality with war, the mission of a people is to bring to fruition within itself, *ad intra*, justice, and to Christianize itself. A truly Christian person would conquer the world by love.
> [Hay que olvidar la vida de aventuras, aquel ir á imponer á los demás lo que creíamos les convenía y aquel buscar fuera un engañoso imperio. Hay que meditar, sobre todo,
> en lo profundamente anti-cristiano del ideal caballeresco. Si la tarea de la nación, producto esencialmente burgués, ha sido asegurar la desigualdad con la guerra, la misión de un pueblo es realizar en sí mismo, *ad intra*, la justicia, y cristianizarse. Un pueblo de verdad cristiano conquistaría por el amor al mundo.]
> (Unamuno, 1898)

Devout Roman Catholic that he was, Unamuno urges Spaniards to seek that day when Christian love will replace vain pagan desires to dominate others in every realm. Unamuno had observed, just as Machado was to announce, that internecine hatreds were among the numerous and grave underlying causes that contributed to the collapse of the Spanish ideal of greatness.

Deeply influenced by Unamuno, Antonio Machado, the author of the celebrated poetic collection *Fields of Castile* [*Campos de Castilla*], echoes Azorín's despair over the flight from the countryside and its devastating effects. In his poem *"Through Spanish Lands"* ["Por tierras de España"], Machado remarks that:

> Today we see its (Spain's) poor sons fleeing from their hearths;
> storms carry off the silt of the land
> to the sacred rivers towards the broad seas;
> and he (the poor country labourer) works, suffers and wanders in accursèd badlands.
>
> [Hoy se ve sus pobres hijos huyendo de sus lares;
> la tempestad llevarse los limos de la tierra
> por los sagrados ríos hacia los anchos mares;
> y en páramos malditos trabaja, sufre y yerra.]
> (Machado, 1997, poema 3)

Yet even worse than the depopulation of the land is the terrible vice that is found in the countryside and in country villages, which takes many forms:

> The evil man of the countryside and town abounds,
> capable of insane vices and bestial crimes,
> who beneath a brown tunic hides an ugly soul,
> which is a slave to the seven capital sins.
>
> His eyes are always cloudy or sad,
> he guards his prey and cries over what his neighbour gets;
> neither does his misfortune stop nor does he enjoy his riches;
> fortune and misfortune wound and upset him.
>
> The spirit of these fields is bloodthirsty and wild;
> as the afternoon fades, in the remote Big Dipper,
> you will see becoming larger the form of an archer,
> the form of an immense centaur who shoots an arrow.
>
> You will see warlike flatlands and moorlands of the ascetic
> -- the biblical garden was not in these fields --;
> they are lands for the eagle, the piece of a planet
> where wanders the shadow of Cain.
>
> [Abunda el hombre malo del campo y de la aldea,
> capaz de insanos vicios y crímenes bestiales,
> que bajo el pardo sayo esconde un alma fea,
> esclava de los siete pecados capitales.
>
> Los ojos siempre turbios de envidia o de tristeza,
> guarda su presa y llora la que el vecino alcanza;
> ni para su infortunio ni goza su riqueza;
> le hieren y acongojan fortuna y malandanza.
>
> El numen de estos campos es sanguinario y fiero;
> al declinar la tarde, sobre el remoto alcor,
> veréis agigantarse la forma de un arquero,
> la forma de un inmenso centauro flechador.
>
> Veréis llanuras bélicas y páramos de asceta
> -- no fue por estos campos el bíblico jardín --;
> son tierra para un águila, un trozo de planeta
> por donde cruza errante la sombra de Caín.]
> (Machado, 1997, poema 3)

Sadly, the theme of hatred, bitterness, envy, lust, and murder in Spain was a *topos* among the writers of the Generation of '98, who knew only too well that their mission, much more than being simply political, was to forge a spiritual renewal of Spain. Yet, for most, this did not mean to re-establish ties with the Roman Catholic Church, which had too long allied itself with the power and the corruption of the state. What was lacking was the personal conversion from the deadly vices that were common in both the countryside and the city.

One of the most powerful condemnations of the terrible vices of the countryside is Ramón del Valle-Inclán's play *Divine Words* [*Divinas palabras*] (1919), which takes place in a country town with a medieval church, whose sacristan is Pedro Gailo. Centred on Gailo's family, Valle-Inclán crafts a horrific tale of cruelty, hatred, greed, lust, and depravity of every kind imaginable. As the first scene opens, "Poca Pena" ["Little Pity"], the concubine of an escaped criminal named Lucero, is arguing with him about their illegitimate baby, whom Lucero wants to "dump":

> Poca Pena: If my son disappears or dies through any of your doing, I'll stick this knife between your ribs. Don't take my child, Lucero!
> Lucero: We'll have another.
> Poca Pena: Show some pity, Lucero!
> Lucero: Drop it!
> Poca Pena: Jailbird!
>
> Lucero *swipes her forcefully across the mouth. Whimpering, she wipes her mouth with a corner of her shawl. Seeing the blood on the garment, she begins to cry. The man coughs contemptuously, rhythmically striking sparks from his tinderbox. Pedro Gailo, the sexton, standing between the pillars of the portico, raises his arms to heaven.*
>
> Pedro Gailo: Go on, off with you! Have you no shame, in displaying such disgusting behaviour outside the Lord's house?
> Lucero: God's not watching us. He's turning a blind eye!
> Pedro Gailo: Heathen!
> Lucero: Too true! It's been twenty years since I last set foot in a church!
> Pedro Gailo: Are you a friend of the Devil?
> Lucero: We're soul mates. (Valle-Inclán, 1993, p. 6)

[Poca Pena: Si el hijo me desaparece, o se me muere por tus malas artes, te hundo esta navaja en el costado. Lucero, no me dejes sin hijo!
Lucero: Haremeos otro.
Poca Pena: ¡Ten caridad, Lucero!
Lucero: Cambia la tocata.
Poca Pena: ¡Escapado de un presidio!

Lucero *hace un gesto desdeñoso, y con la mano vuelta pega en la boca de la coima, que, gimoteando, se pasa por los labios una punta del puñado. Mirando la sangre en el hilado, la coima se ahinca a llorar, y el hombre tose con sorna, al compás que saca chispas del yesquero. Pedro Gailo, el sacristán, levanta los brazos entre las columnas del pórtico.*

Pedro Gailo: ¡A otro lugar era el iros con vuestros malos ejemplos, y no venir con ellos a delante de Dios!
Lucero: Dios no mira lo que hacemos: Tiene la cara vuelta.
Pedro Gailo: ¡Descomulgado!
Lucero: ¡A mucha honra! ¡Veinte años llevo sin entrar en la iglesia!
Pedro Gailo: ¿Te titulas amigo del Diablo?
Lucero: Somos compadres.] (Valle-Inclán, 1970, pp. 14-15)

Valle-Inclán depicts the violence and moral degeneration of a typical small town in the Spanish countryside and alerts his readers to the need for personal reform throughout the nation. Criminality, lack of faith, mistreatment, and the disintegration of family life all contribute to the weakening of Spain, which has led to the "Disaster of '98." As we have seen, the crisis is much deeper than a political problem; the spiritual bankruptcy of Spain has eroded the very essence of what it means to be Spanish.

As the story continues, readers are introduced to Pedro Gailo's sister, "Juana la Reina" ["Queen Juana"], the mother of Laureano, her hydrocephalic son. As Pedro Gailo greets her, readers observe Juana's motherly concern for the child, and are given a fuller description of this flower of Spanish youth:

Pedro Gailo: And how is my nephew, sister? Is he not awake yet? It looks to me like he's showing some signs of improvement.
Juana la Reina: Improvement! In this Godforsaken creature! You must be joking!

Pedro Gailo *squints at the dwarf who shakes his head in a totally uncoordinated manner.His mother shoos away the flies that gather around his dribbling swollen mouth. Dragging the cart along behind her, she then crosses the churchyard and disappears into the roadside shadows. Lucero's dog, sitting up on her hind legs, begins a slow dance of death in front of the dark earthy figure.*
(Valle-Inclán, 1993, p. 8)

....

[Pedro Gailo: Y el sobrino, ¿va despertándose? El alumbra algún conocimiento, hermana mía.
La Reina: ¡Malpocado!

Pedro Gailo *pone su ojo bizco sobre el enano, que con expresión lela mueve la enorme cabezota. Y la madre le espanta las moscas que acuden a posarse sobre la boca belfa donde el bozo negrea. Tirando del dornajo cruza la quintana y sale a las sombras de la carretera. La perra del farandul, levantada en dos patas, ensaya un paso de danza ante aquella figura triste y color de tierra. Lentamente el animal se dobla, y agacha la cola aullando con el aullido que reservan los canes para el aire de muerto.* (Valle-Inclán, 1970, p. 17)

Valle-Inclán creates even more horrific dimensions of the tale by focusing the action of the play on the family members' vicious fight for control of the hydrocephalic child because of his great value as the source of alms at local fairs. Laureano eventually dies from an epileptic seizure that has been induced by the patrons of a bar playing him with alcohol. This surreal horror show encapsulates in literary form Valle-Inclán's theory of *Esperanto*, the distortions, deformations, and "grotesque and ridiculous aspects of modern life, especially as these were exhibited in Spain, which the author felt was the embodiment of anti-civilization (Chandler and Schwartz, 1961, p. 237).

Contrary to the modern myth that urban life was the solution to all the ills of the rural past, the "*Problema de España*" could not be ascribed either to the city or to the countryside, but to both. As it turned out, Spanish cities were not gleaming citadels of hope that heralded progress, nor were rural towns repositories of purity, faith, goodness, and hard work. Rather, both of these Spanish landscapes were dystopian wastelands that needed to be cleansed of jealousy, hatred, laziness, *abulia* (abnormal lack of initiative or ability to make decisions), faithlessness, and violence. Goodness might still be found in the hearts of the Spanish people, but finding the essence of *"hispanidad"* first required both the town and the city to awaken from the doldrums of the past, so as to avoid further national destruction. The Spanish literary tradition is rich with warnings against the attractions of the city, the court, fame, and fortune, both from religious writers such as Saint Ignatius Loyola and Saint Teresa de Jesús and from secular authors, the most prominent of whom was Antonio de Guevara (c. 1481-1545). Chapter 7 of his celebrated work *Menosprecio de corte y alabanza de aldea* (1539) [*Contempt for the Court and Praise for the Hamlet*], which is entitled, "Que en la aldea son los hombres más virtuosos y menos vicisiosos que en las cortes de los príncipes" ["For, in the Hamlet People are More Virtuous and Less Wicked than in the Princely Courts"], is a declaration of Guevara's thesis; however, as we have seen, from the point of view of the writers of the Generation of '98, nothing could be further from the truth (Guevara, 1984). The people of the Spanish countryside were afflicted with every one of the basest and most destructive vices imaginable. Was the city a site of hope, where the evils of the countryside would be left behind and new possibilities of economic betterment, improved social conditions, advanced education, and the benefits of employment would contribute to the construction of a new, modern, and more progressive Spain?

In what has been called his "best philosophical novel and his most complete," *El árbol de la ciencia* (1911) [*The Tree of the Knowledge*], Basque author Pío Baroja, a prolific novelist, essayist, and journalist, tells the tale of Andrés Hurtado, a young man who comes from the countryside to Madrid to study medicine (Patt, 1971, p. 112). Filled with the illusion of obtaining an excellent education and experiencing a rich intellectual life in a great urban university, Hurtado excitedly anticipates his first day of classes but quickly learns that the environment he has walked into is less than academic. Baroja, who was a physician himself, describes the academic atmosphere of the nation's capital:

> The Madrid student, especially if he came from the provinces, arrived with the intention to copy Don Juan and amuse himself, to gamble and make love to women as the professor of chemistry said with his usual solemnity, to burn himself out in an atmosphere too full of oxygen. (Baroja, 1974, p. 9)
> [El estudiante madrileño, sobre todo el venido de provincias, llegaba a la corte con un espíritu donjuanesco, con la idea de divertirse, jugar, perseguir a las mujeres; pensando, como decía el professor de Química con su solemnidad habitual, quemarse pronto en un ambiente demasiado oxigenado.] (Baroja, 1968, pp. 15-16)

Madrid, like the rest of Spain, was stuck in the past and was oblivious to the realities of the current situation in which the nation found itself: "The whole of Spain, and especially Madrid, lived in an atmosphere of absurd optimism, and whatever was Spanish was best" ["España entera, y Madrid sobre todo, vivía en un ambiente de optimismo absurdo: todo lo español era lo mejor"] (Baroja, 1968, p. 10; 1974, p. 17).The narrator alerts the reader to a theme that is underscored by all of the writers of the Generation of '98 the illusion of being the best because of its role as the "Defender of the Roman Catholic faith" has led to a "fossilization of thought," which is illustrated by Hurtado's chemistry class, which is anything but scientific:

> During the lecture, they (the students) talked, smoked, and read novels, and no one paid any attention to the lecture; one of them even came with a French horn, and, when the professor was about to empty some potassium into a glass, he blew twice on his horn; another brought in a stray dog and it cost no little trouble to put it out."
> (Baroja, 1974, pp. 11-12)

> [En la clase se hablaba, se fumaba, se leían novelas, nadie seguía la explicación; alguno llegó a presentarse con una corneta, y cuando el profesor se disponía a echar en un vaso de agua un trozo de potasio, dió dos toques de atención; otro metió un perro vagabundo, y fué un problema echarlo.] (Baroja, 1968, p. 18)

Rather than being the site of modernity, progress, intellectual ferment, and creative thinking, the capital was instead a repository of the worst of Spanish society and the most execrable traits of the Spanish character. Critic Pedro Laín Entralgo writes that the experience of living in Madrid would affect—for better or for worse—the lives of all of the members of the Generation of '98 in a decisive way. While at first, the city might have seemed thrilling, with the pulsing activity of people from every corner of Spain and every walk of life, the capital, like the innovations of technology themselves, was also a site of dehumanization (1997, pp. 154; 192).

Baroja continues his savage attack on his countrymen's attitudes in the capital by introducing the character of Don José de Letamendi, a professor who is proclaimed a genius:

> Letamendi was one of those men of universal fame who had begun to appear in Spain during the last twelve years or so, men of universal fame whose very names were unknown on the other side of the Pyrenees. Europe's ignorance of such mighty genius was explained on the absurd hypothesis, openly maintained by no one but accepted by all, that by an international hatred and bad faith, the great things of Spain were made to appear small in other countries while the small things of other countries were made to seem great in Spain. (Baroja, 1974, p. 45)
> [Letamendi era de estos hombres universales que se tenían en la España de hace unos años; hombres universales a quienes no se les conocía ni de nombre pasados los Pirineos. Un desconocimiento tal en Europa de genios tan trascendentales se explicaba por esa hipótesis absurda, que, aunque no la defendía nadie claramente, era aceptada por todos, la hipótesis del odio y la mala fe internacionales que hacían que las cosas grandes de España fueran pequeñas en el extranjero, y viceversa.] (Baroja, 1968, p. 59)

Rather than being truly international, Madrid plays a primary role in propagating the myth that Spanish greatness is ignored by the rest of Europe and that anything foreign is celebrated and cherished. While it cannot be denied that the "Black Legend" has to some extent been a reality, writers of the Generation of '98 assail the ignorance, smugness, and insularism that their fellow Spaniards have adopted, without factual basis, to glorify homegrown mediocrity.

As the capital of Spain, Madrid has always been the site of political unrest, protest, corruption, and power. Ramón del Valle Inclán's *Bohemian Lights* [*Luces de Bohemia*] (1924) tells the story of Max Estrella, an older and blind intellectual, poet, and journalist who lives in Madrid with his wife Madama Collet and his daughter Claudinita. Having lost his newspaper job and his means of supporting his family, Max goes with friends to several local hangouts and winds up drunk and singing loudly in the streets. Other groups of people are heard shouting in the streets in various parts of Madrid, reflecting the workers' strikes of 1917 and the mass political arrests in Madrid in 1919. When the police arrive, Max mocks the captain, leading to his arrest. After further insulting the officials at the police station, he is thrown into jail, and, as we later learn, has been brutally beaten. Soon, another prisoner, Matthew, an anarchist, is thrown into the cell, and he and Max discuss the virtual state of combat on the streets of Madrid and Barcelona:

> Prisoner: It's a long story. I am charged with rebellion ... I refused to abandon my job and go to war, and I even started a riot in the factory! The boss denounced me, I had to serve a sentence, travelled all over the place looking for work: I'm still going from court to court, always summoned back by some judge or other. But I know the fate that's waiting for me: four gunshots, for allegedly attempting to escape. Well and good ... if it's only that and nothing else ...
> Max: Why, what are you afraid of?
> Prisoner: That they might enjoy torturing me.
> Max: Barbarians!
> Prisoner: You've got to know them.
> Max: Vermin! And they're the ones who protest indignantly about the 'Black
> Legend'.
> Prisoner: For some miserly pesetas, in some solitary city corner, I'll be passing and they'll put an end to me ... and they're paid to protect human lives! This is what the rich scum proclaims as justice.
> Max: Rich and poor alike; Iberian savagery is common to them all.
> Prisoner: All of them.
> Max: All of them! Matthew, where is there a bomb to tear the guts out of this cursed Spanish plot of ground?
> Prisoner: You're a poet, Sir, and you can foresee so many things but haven't you noticed a raised hand? (Valle-Inclán, 1976, p. 135)

[El Preso: Es cuento largo. Soy tachado de rebelde ... No quise dejar el telar por ir a la guerra y levanté un motín en la fábrica. Me denunció el patron, cumplí condena, recorrí el mundo buscando trabajo, y ahora voy por tránsitos, reclamado de no sé qué jueces. Conozco la suerte que me espera: Cuatro tiros por intento de fuga. Bueno. Si no es más que eso ...
Max: ¿Pues qué temes?
El Preso: Que se diviertan dándome tormento.
Max: ¡Bárbaros!
El Preso: Hay que conocerlos.
Max: Canallas. ¡Y ésos son los que protestan de la leyenda negra!
El Preso: Por siete pesetas, al cruzar un lugar solitario, me sacarán la vida los que tienen a su cargo la defensa del pueblo. ¡Y a esto llaman justicia los ricos canallas!
Max: Los ricos y los pobres; la barbarie ibérica es unánime.
El Preso: ¡Todos!
Max: ¡Todos! Mateo, ¿dónde está la bomba que destripe el terrón maldito de España?
El Preso: Señor poeta que tanto adivina, ¿no ha visto usted una mano levantada?
(Valle-Inclán, 1976, p. 134)

In Scene 11, Max and his drunkard friend "Don Latino," who have been released, are returning home and encounter a woman who is carrying a dead child, his temple shot-through with a bullet hole, and who is screaming hysterically at the police:

Mother: Hired assassins! Killers of children!
Pawnbroker: She's a little upset and doesn't know what she's saying.
The Policeman: The authorities take all of this into account.
Bar Owner: These are unfortunate accidents in the efforts to re-establish law and order.
Pawnbroker: Those damned anarchist mobs destroyed my shop window.
....
....
Mother: Murderers! To look at you is to look at hangmen!
Retired Officer: The principle of Authority is unrelenting.
Mason: Against the poor. We're getting killed to protect the merchants who keep sucking our blood.

Bar Owner: And who happens to pay their taxes? Take that into account too.
Pawnbroker: Honest merchants don't suck the blood of anyone.
Concierge: We have no cause to complain!
Mason: A worker's life means nothing to the Government.
Max: Latino, get me out of this circle of Hell. (Valle-Inclán, 1976, pp. 177; 179)

[La Madre: ¡Sicarios! ¡Asesinos de criaturas!
El Empeñista: Está con algún trastorno, y no mide palabras.
El Guardia: La Autoridad también se hace el cargo.
El Tabernero: Son desgracias para el restablecimiento del orden.
El Empeñista: Las turbas anárquicas me han destrozado el escaparate.
....
....
La Madre: ¡Asesinos! ¡Veros es ver al verdugo!
El Retirado: El principio de Autoridad es inexorable.
El Albañil: Con los pobres. Se ha matado, por defender al comercio, que nos chupa la sangre.
El Tabernero: Y que paga sus contribuciones, no hay que olvidarlo.
El Empeñista: El comercio honrado no chupa la sangre de nadie.
La Portera: ¡Nos quejamos de vicio!
El Albañil: La vida del proletario no representa nada para el Gobierno.
Max: Latino, sácame de este círculo infernal.] (Valle-Inclán, 1976, pp. 176; 178)

By the first two decades of the twentieth century, the streets of large Spanish cities had become battlegrounds for the desperate struggle between the various political factions of the nation. Socialists, Republicans, anarchists, Communists, monarchists, Carlists, and others had begun to draw the battle lines that would define the events of the Civil War. As Valle-Inclán shows so clearly in *Luces de Bohemia*, the urban landscape, unlike its fame as a beacon of progress, merely exacerbated the hatred that had long been boiling in the wretched Spanish countryside. Nor did anarchism, socialism, or Marxism-Leninism, despite the latter's very recent victory in Russia, promise any relief to the complex crises that had plagued Spain for centuries.

A committed socialist as a youth, Ramiro de Maeztu had railed against the economic backwardness of the nation, just as his fellow intellectuals had done. Shocked by the "Disaster of '98," he joined in with the general outcry against the nation that preferred to hide behind the past, especially in the indigent capital, which offered no progress at all:

> This country of fat bishops, of stupid generals, of usurious, intriguing, and illiterate
> politicians do not want to see themselves in those desolate plains without trees, sandy
> soil, which can barely be made out of mud cabins, where twelve million worms live an animal life, who double their bodies over to till the land with that plough... in those
> Universities with interim professors; in that hungry Madrid; in that press of empty words; it always sees itself in legend, where it finds itself great and lifts its eyelids so as not to see itself so small.
> [Este país de obispos gordos, de generales tontos, de políticos usureros, enredadores y
> «analfabetos», no quiere verse en esas yermas llanuras sin árboles, de suelo arenoso, en el
> que apenas si se destacan cabañas de barro, donde viven vida animal doce millones de guzanos, que doblan el cuerpo, al surcar la tierra con aquel arado ... en esas Universidades de profesores interinos; en este Madrid hambriento; en esa prensa de palabras huecas; mírase siempre en la leyenda, donde se encuentra grande y aprieta los párpados para no verse tan pequeña.] (Maeztu, 1899, pp. 85-86).

In particular, the young Maeztu attacks Castile, the heart of Spain, as being a wasteland, as opposed to the "peripheral" areas of the nation, which had developed thriving, modern industries. In the chapter "The Castilian Plateau" ["*La meseta castellana*"], the writer argues that Castile itself must be "colonized" by the economically vibrant areas of the periphery, such as Barcelona, Valencia, Almería, Bilbao, Málaga, Huelva, and Vigo, if the nation is to be salvaged from the rubble of the disintegrated empire. Maeztu argues that bereft of its colonies, the flourishing industrial areas of Spain must now look to Castile as both the breadbasket of the nation and a vibrant market for the products of the rest of the nation (1899, p. 161).

This must be done, or dire consequences will follow: "Blind are those who do not see that if this industrialization of the Castilian soil is not brought about by the periphery, it will in any case be realized, but not by Spanish hands!" [¡Ciegos los que no vean que si esta industrialización del suelo castellano no acierta a realizarla el litoral, se verificará de todos modos, mas no por manos españolas!] (Maeztu, 1899, p. 166). Maeztu, like the other writers of the Generation of '98, saw only too clearly that what was destroying Spain was coming from within, not from without, and that if the rest of Europe reviled Spain for its lack of development, Spaniards only had themselves to blame, not the rest of the world. Yet, how could Castile recover from centuries of self-sacrifice for the cause of the ideals of empire? "And how is Castile going to offer it (a vibrant market), depopulated by a thousand wars, ruined by usury and the treasury, backwards because of the hateful legends of dead ages that still survive in her?" [¿Y cómo va á ofrecerlo Castilla, despoblada por mil guerras, arruinada por usura y el fisco, atrasada porque en ella perviven las odiosas leyendas de los tiempos muertos?"] (Maeztu, 1899, p. 161).

Between 1899, when the youthful and fiery Maeztu had written *Hacia otra España* [*Towards Another Spain*], and the maturity of 1934, when he wrote *In Defense of Spanishness* [*Defensa de la hispanidad*], Maeztu's spirit had calmed, he had become a fervent Roman Catholic and had embraced a profound nationalism. Propounding a renewed sense of "*hispanidad*," Maeztu now preached that the historic destiny of Spain was to bring all the peoples of the world to religious salvation, and to unite them all under the banner of that "*hispanidad*." He now called for Spaniards to go forth as "*caballeros de la hispanidad*" ["knights of Spanishness"] to undertake this mission throughout the world, and to share the Catholic faith and Spanish values, which, as past colonial endeavours had shown, were not exclusive and were "universalist" (Maeztu, 1941, p. 300). Yet, it must be remembered that this entire project, which was both a new vision for Spain and also a return to the nation's traditional ideals, had its foundation in the need to integrate the productiveness of the peripheral regions of Spain with its moribund core, "*la meseta castellana*" ["the Castilian Plateau"]. Maeztu was never to witness the implementation of his new vision for Spain, for he was executed by leftist militiamen in 1936, one of the first victims of the savage fratricide that was overshadowing the land.

The semi-autobiographical protagonist Azorín in the novel The Will [La voluntad] (1902) by the author of the same name, has gone from a town to Madrid, and now finds that neither satisfies him. As protagonist Azorín himself recognizes, perhaps the dystopia of the Spanish landscape has little or nothing to do with the geography of where he lives, but rather with his mental landscape, which is far more complex and variegated than what lies before the eyes:

> In the end, Azorín decides to leave Madrid. Where is he going? Geographically, Azorín knows where he is directing his feet; but about his intellectual and ethical direction, his confusion is greater every day. Azorín is almost a symbol; his perplexities, his anxieties, and his grief, very well might represent an entire generation without will, without energy, indecisive, irresolute, a generation that has neither the audacity of the Romantic generation nor the faith of the Naturalist generation to affirm.
>
> [Al fin, Azorín se decide á marcharse de Madrid. ¿Dónde va? Geográficamente, Azorín sabe dónde encamina sus pasos; pero en cuanto á la orientación intelectual y ética, su desconcierto es mayor cada día. Azorín es casi un símbolo; sus perplejidades, sus ansias, sus desconsuelos, bien pueden representar toda una generación sin volutand, sin energía, indecisa, irresoluta, una generación que no tiene ni la audacia de la generación romántica, ni la fe de afirmar de la generación naturalista.] (Azorín, 1968, p. 255)

Might this not have been the problem that the writers of the Generation of '98 were pointing to, Spain's apparent lack of desire to make the changes it needed to make?

Sadly, inattention to the national ills ended in the Civil War (1936-1939) and the deaths of some three million people in a country the size of Ohio. The writers of the Generation of '98 had blasted the clarion call of reform and had warned of the impending dystopian doom in both the town and the city; unfortunately, divisions within Spain were too deep and too longstanding to avoid the horrific bloodletting that followed shortly after the defeat, loss, and humiliation of the "Disaster of '98.". Historians William D. Phillips, Jr. and Carla Rahn Phillips explain the breadth of the tragedy:

> It is not an exaggeration to say that all of the anger, frustration, class antagonism, and other corrosive forces that had eaten away at Spanish society for at least a century spilled over into the conflict, making the Spanish Civil War one of the worst internal confrontations in European history. Individuals defined their true loyalties based on religious adherence or rejection, political ideology, economic class, occupation, family history, or a combination of factors ... Neighbors turned on each other through sincere conviction, fear, personal animosity, ambition, cowardice, or any number of other motives. Alongside the suppressed resentments and hatreds of the past, the Civil War created a new set of horrors to remember. (Phillips and Phillips, 2017, p. 337)

Maeztu was not the only member of the generation of writers associated with the "Disaster of '98" to foresee and forewarn his countrymen of the mortal threat of the hatred of Spaniards for fellow Spaniards. The problem so concerned Unamuno that he dedicated an entire novel to the theme, *Abel Sánchez* (1917), subtitled *"The Story of a Passion"* [*"Historia de una pasión"*], which tells the tale of a deadly rivalry and passive aggression between two best friends throughout their entire lives, affecting not only them but their families through several generations. Following the lines of the biblical story of Cain and Abel, "Joaquín," a physician who is a hardened, jealous, practical, and exacting man, eventually kills "Abel," his lifetime friend and rival, who is a painter, a free spirit, and beloved by all. At the end of the tale, Joaquín confesses to killing his friend and questions why he has been filled with jealousy throughout his life:

> Why have I been so envious, so bad? What did I do to be this way? What milk did I drink? Was it a potion of hatred? Has it been a potion of blood? Why was I born in a land of hatred? In a land in which the commandment seems to be: "Hate your neighbour as you hate yourself." Because I have lived hating myself; because here we all live hating ourselves.
> [¿Por qué he sido tan envidioso, tan malo? ¿Qué hice para ser así? ¿Qué leche mamé?

>¿Era un bebedizo de odio? ¿Ha sido un bebedizo de sangre? ¿Por qué nací en tierra de odios? ¿En tierra en que el precepto parece ser: "Odia a tu prójimo como a ti mismo."
>Porque he vivido odiándome; porque aquí todos vivimos odiándonos.]
>(Unamuno, 1980, p. 150)

Unamuno was to witness the first bitter months of the Civil War before he was given the relief of death. Perhaps one aspect of his work sums up the thought of all the members of the Generation of '98. In his essay entitled "*¡Adentro!*" ("Go Within!"), the great scholar argued that what the Spanish people needed to do more than anything was to develop an originality and a uniqueness that could be put to the service of all people. To discover this rich vein of "*hispanidad*," Unamuno insisted that his countrymen look critically within themselves to identify the best of the Spanish character, what he termed the search for the "intra-man" ["*intrahombre*"] (Nozick, 1971, p. 87). Had this not been the project of all of the writers of the Generation of '98? Had the nation taken greater heed of their warnings, their portrayals of Spanish life, and their suggestions for renewal, perhaps Spain could have begun a process of reforming and healing the dystopian landscape that the illusions of empire had wreaked upon every aspect of Spanish life, in time to avoid the tragedy of over some 800,000 victims and the sectional and internecine strife that continue to plague the nation to this day (Thomas, 1977, p. 927).

Works Cited

Azorín. (1967) *Una hora de España*, Austral, Madrid.

Azorín. (1984) *La voluntad*, E. Iman Fox (ed), Castalia, Madrid.

Baroja, P. (1968) *El árbol de la ciencia*, Las Américas Publishing Company, New York.

Baroja, P. (1974). *The Tree of Knowledge*, translated by Aubrey F.G. Bell, Howard Fertig, New York.

Chandler, R. and K. Schwartz. (1961) *A New History of Spanish Literature*, Louisiana State University Press, Baton Rouge.

Davies, R.T. (1964) *The Golden Century of Spain: 1501-1621*, Macmillan & Co. Ltd., New York.

Defourneaux, M. (1970) *Daily Life in Spain in the Golden Age*, translated by Newton Branch, Praeger, New York.

Elliott, J.H. (2002) *Imperial Spain, 1469-1716*, Penguin Books, London.

Gaztambide, J. (1958) *Historia de la bula de la cruzada en España*, Editorial del Seminario, Vitoria

Guevara, A. (1984) *Menosprecio de corte y alabanza de aldea / Arte de marear*, Asunción Rallo (ed), Cátedra, Madrid.

Kamen, H. (2008) *Imagining Spain: Historical Myths & National Identity*, Yale University Press, New Haven.

Laín Entralgo, P. (1997) *La Generación del 98*, Espasa-Calpe, Madrid.

Machado, A. (1997) *Campos de Castilla*. Robert Havard (ed), Bristol Classical Press, London.

Maeztu, R. (1941) *Defensa de la hispanidad*, Gráfica Universal, Madrid.

Maeztu, R. (1899) *Hacia otra España*, Imprenta y Encuadernación de Andrés P. Cardenal, Bilbao.

More, C. (2014) *Understanding the Industrial Revolution*, Routledge, New York.

Nozick, M. (1971) *Miguel de Unamuno: The Agony of Belief*, Princeton University Press, Princeton.

Patt, B. (1971) *Pío Baroja*, Twayne, New York.

Payne, S. (1973) *A History of Spain and Portugal*, 2 vols., University of Wisconsin Press, Madison.

Phillips, W. & C. Rahn Phillips. (2017) *A Concise History of Spain*, Cambridge University Press, Cambridge and New York.

Thomas, H. (1977) *The Spanish Civil War*, Harper and Row, New York.

Unamuno, M. (1980) *Abel Sánchez*, Espasa-Calpe, Madrid.

Unamuno, M. (1898) '¡Muera Don Quijote', *Vida Nueva* [Madrid], 26 junio, n/p.
https://gredos.usal.es/bitstream/handle/10366/84028/CMU_1-130.pdf?sequence=1&isAllowed=y. Accessed 26 August 2021.
Valle-Inclán, R. (1970) *Divinas palabras*, Espasa-Calpe, Madrid.
Valle-Inclán, R. (1976) *Luces de Bohemia / Bohemian Lights*, translated by Anthony N. Zahareas, University of Texas Press, Austin.
Valle-Inclán, R. (1993) *Three Plays. Divine Words; Bohemian Lights; Silver Face*, translated by Maria M. Delgado, Methuen Drama, London.
Vicens Vives, J. (1969) *An Economic History of Spain*, translated by Frances M. López-Morillas, Princeton University Press, Princeton.

Between Retreats and Returns: The Elusive Homeland in Temsula Ao's *These Hills Called Home*

This chapter examined the construction of the homeland as a conflicting combination of a lost and longed rurality and a misplaced urbanity in a short story by Temsula Ao, one of the noted Anglophone writers of Nagaland and Northeast India. The story taken up for review here, namely- 'A New Chapter' comes from Ao's short story collection *These Hills Called Home: Stories from a War Zone* (2006). Emerging from a region from not only the territorial fringe of the postcolonial Indian State but also from the fringe of mainstream Indian imagination, this narrative offers an uncommon yet underexplored model of pastoral discourse. Their literary discreetness and appeal, as argued in this paper, derive largely from the unusual way they adapt the pastoral device of the rural-urban dualism as an oblique but decisive spatial trope to point up the difficulties and dilemmas encountered in a troubled ethnic homeland. Quite understandably, as literature produced in a postcolonial conflict zone, this narrative bears unmistakable reflections of conflict and crisis that continue to overshadow the region's political climate. However, the present paper focuses mainly on the way the narrative seeks to negotiate the shifty and difficult issues of Naga national/collective identity, that is—negotiating crisis and the eventual de/re-arrangement of Individual and collective selves—by foregrounding and juxtaposing the vision of a more peaceable/agreeable rural Naga homeland to that of a distressingly urbanized landscape. The pastoral/textual tropes of retreat and return, the paper argues, despite reinforcing nostalgic visions of a more agreeable rural homeland, eventually bring to the fore the impossibility of a definitive return to such a missing homeland. To this extent, the Naga homeland emerges in these stories as an in-between or midway between a space of nostalgic retreat and a more immediate yet alarming everyday reality.

Before moving on, it will be useful to briefly look at the poetics and politics of the pastoral as a discourse of retreat and return. Terry Gifford's well-known definition of pastoral in the book *Pastoral* (2009), throws more light on this. The three key meanings of 'pastoral' according to Gifford are- first, as a genre- that is, a historical form with a long tradition which began in poetry and morphed into other genres; second, as an area of content—that is, any literature that describes the country with an implicit or explicit contrast to the urban and; third, as a pejorative or critical-discursive frame to view nature, rurality and its representation (Gifford 2009, p. 1). Whereas the first two views identify a certain kind of celebratory attitude towards nature as the hallmark of pastoral writing, the third view, that is—pastoral as a critical frame—is underscored by a stronger emphasis on the ideological orientation of any potential pastoral narrative. Significantly, Gifford repeatedly emphasizes the point that pastoral writings always rely on some form of movement between retreat and return. Interestingly, the retreat to a utopian or at least more agreeable location and a return therefrom, in most pastoral literature, is a transformative act. To this extent, the pastoral movement, in a text, may happen in two ways- either intra-textually, or in the sense that the pastoral retreat 'returns' some insights to the urban audience (p. 2). The critical-epistemic legitimacy or import of most contemporary pastoral literature corresponds to their embeddedness in issues of immediate times rather than that of a long-lost time and space.

It is significant that Gifford, throughout his book, reiterates the need to shift towards a more extensive, dynamic and inclusive view of pastoral from one that identifies the pastoral with a set of thematic and stylistic conventions. This largely corresponds to the pastoral's mutation into apparently non-pastoral literary-cultural modes. This paper derives from this imperative to move towards a renewed notion of pastoral and also the need to explore its potential feasibility as a critical frame in apparently unseeing contexts. It seeks to re-situate the idea of pastoral in a context, often perceived as exceptional by those situated outside it. As already suggested, the immediate historical-spatial context is that of Nagaland or so to say, the northeast of India. It is important to note that Nagaland or the Northeast continue to be at the margins of Indian territory as well as of the average Indian imagination. As is discussed later, the postcolonial history of Nagaland is marked by a regular shadow of violence and counter-violence keeping the region in a perpetual state of unease. Search for a homeland, in such a context, becomes an unavoidable yet difficult exercise. Quite understandably, Writings from such a war zone resonate with the nostalgic retreat to memories of a lost homeland. Temsula Ao's writings, instead of offering themselves as a site of aesthetic-emotional retreat, emerge as a certain kind of critical contact zone to engage with an immediate but disagreeable, urbanised homeland. It is from this perspective that the 'pastoral' emerges as a useful epistemic frame to understand the construction of Nagaland as a real and imagined ethnic homeland in her writings.

In his book, Gifford highlights the ways the 'pastoral' has evolved through a series of mutations, and transformations (p. 4) to adapt to apparently unseeming contexts and considerations. It is this generic elasticity that largely underlies the extensive appeal of the pastoral as literary and critical discourse. To reiterate Gifford, the widespread literary and critical import of contemporary pastoral writings comes from its ability to effectively bypass the limitations of generic protocols and priorities of the classical pastoral and regularly renew itself into emerging forms (pp. 4-5). Some of the usual pastoral protocols are- a celebration of life in the country and the life of the shepherd (p. 1); the trope of retreat and return (p. 1); celebration of nature; highlighting the tension between the country and the town (p. 15) etc. Contemporary pastorals, despite retaining most of these attributes, have substantially transformed themselves to emerge as a powerful critical genre negotiating complex social issues. This transformation has been poignantly captured by Leo Marx's distinction between the 'complex' and the 'sentimental' pastoral (p. 25) or between the 'pastoral of sentiment' and the 'pastoral of mind' (p. 32).

Set in the backdrop of violence-ridden Naga Hills of the post-independence times the stories in *These Hills Called Home* capture the uncertainties and trauma prevailing in these times. The narratives of conflict, unrest and victimization could be viewed as a certain kind of resistance to amnesia, or collective memory, and hence, as allegories of the postcolonial Naga politics and history. However, one important but underexplored dimension of this peculiar body of writing is the way they construct the Naga homeland as an uneasy midway between recently lost but more agreeable rurality and an un-desirable/avoidable and misplaced urbaneness. Given the centrality of identity as an issue in the lives and writings of postcolonial Nagaland, marked by a constant shadow of violence till recent times, it becomes important to relate this rural-urban spatial paradox, as they surface in Temsula Ao's writing, to larger debates and politics of postcolonial Naga identity. Ao's precursory comments offer a useful entry point into this. She writes: "It was though a great cataclysmic upheaval threw up many realities for the Nagas within which they are still struggling to settle for a legitimate identity (Ao, 2006, p. x)." Understandably, the construction of space in the narratives is entrenched in this politics of identity construction.

The short story 'A New Chapter' reconstructs the complexities and confusion in the social, political and psychological landscape of the conflict-ridden Naga Hills in the last decades of the twentieth century. The remaining sections of this paper examine the centrality of a certain kind of rural/urban divide to these emerging dynamics of Naga identity and focus on instances which give obvious clues into the actuality of such a literal/literary spatiality. It is important to look at the ways Temsula Ao reconstructs the strife-torn Naga Hills as an uneasy coincidence between an increasingly overwrought rurality and a pervasive-cum-insidious urbanism.

As suggested, what makes the narrative under review, a pastoral text is a clearly perceptible and artfully constructed literal-metaphoric dualism of the rural and the urban that underlie it and which is in no way separable from the major issue of (un)-becoming of identities in a violent Homeland. Like their other counterparts in the volume *These Hills Called Home*, 'A New Chapter' corresponds to the "turbulent years of bloodshed and tears that make up the history of the Nagas from the early fifties of the last century, and their demand for independence from the Indian State (Ao, p. x)." Hence, it will be useful to briefly revisit the context—the historical and otherwise—forming the backdrop of this narrative. The post-colonial history of what is viewed as the Northeast of India has been marked by a perennial shadow of violence and conflict between ethnic groups, ethnically backed militias, and more importantly between independentist ethnic groups and the Indian state. The Naga Hills (which largely corresponds to the present Indian state of Nagaland) are often viewed as the birthplace of this series of sub-nationalist insurrections in the region and as South Asia's longest-running guerrilla campaign (Bhaumik 2009, p. 91). The imagination of a Naga nationhood, that has sustained the demand of, and struggles initially for a Naga ethnic homeland, and subsequently for a Greater Nagaland goes back to the formation of the Naga Club after the First World War and its stated position before the Simon Commission in 1929 that the Nagas were a united and unconquered people (Baruah 2005, p. 107). However, a fuller and more concrete Naga claim for independence could be traced back to the delegation led by Angami Zapu Phizo (1913-1990), the legendary chief of the Naga underground movement, in 1947 to Delhi to meet Mahatma Gandhi and place the Naga claim for Independence (Hazarika 1995, p. 97). The indifference of the colonial and postcolonial Indian State to the demand for an independent and sovereign Naga territory, despite a series of agitation and protests, led to the declaration of Naga Independence in 1956, leading to decades-long armed conflicts between the Naga rebels and the Indian state. Despite peace accords, negotiations and the grant of full statehood, the Naga imbroglio remains unresolved even today.

Quite understandably, as a narrative emerging from a troubled homeland, Ao's short story 'A New Chapter' is marked by an unavoidable engagement with the difficulties and problems of negotiating identities in such a crisis zone. Ao's view that these stories are nothing but attempts to "re-visit the lives of those people whose pain has gone unmentioned (Ao 2006, p. ix)", highlights the centrality of dislocation as a theme in this narrative. Interestingly, it is the human cost of conflicts that remains the focus of these narratives. "What the stories are trying to say is that in such conflicts, there are no winners, only victims, and the results can be measured only in human terms. For the victims, the trauma goes beyond the realm of just the physical maiming and the loss of life- their very humanity is assaulted and violated, and the onslaught leaves the survivors scarred both in mind and soul (Ao 2006, p. x)." This prefatory comment, in interesting ways, foreshadows the series of retreats and returns that the narratives in the volume fictionalize. It is important to note that these narratives always rely on constructing multiple spatial-temporal juxtapositions to fictionalize, or so to say, to retreat into a lost and longed Naga homeland. These retreats, in individual stories, correspond to a more general and obligatory process of retreat Temsula Ao takes as a committed Naga writer. Given the view of the pastoral retreat as a borderland location or space to critique/interrogate disturbing social realities (Gifford 2009, p. 23), Ao's engagement with the tricky shades of a newly arriving urban life in Nagaland in antithesis to an overwrought rural lifeway transforms the stories under review into justified pastoral writing. The writer's view that these stories are a) a literary resistance to the "sudden displacement of the young from a placid existence in rural habitats to a world of conflict and confusion in urban settlements" consequent to an atmosphere of crisis (Ao, p. x); and b) attempts to capture the ambience of the traditional Naga way of life challenged and upset by a fixation for unwholesome urbanism, corroborates this thesis.

Given the transformative orientation and effect of real and imagined 'retreat' in pastoral texts (Gifford 2009, p. 1), that is— the view that the trope of retreating into pastoral settings must return some insights to the urbanized readership— it is important to examine potential insights Ao's writings aim to return to the potential reader. In keeping with the critical and restorative role attributed to pastoral discourse, these narratives celebrate a more intimate, integrated and meaningful living in co-existence with nature. They extol "the virtue of human beings living at peace with themselves and in harmony with nature and with neighbours (Ao, p. xi)." Both the rhetoric and vision foregrounding/celebrating nature, in these stories, transform them into unmistakable instances of celebratory-critical pastoral discourse in a disquiet landscape.

The short story 'A New Chapter' deals with the fascinating story of Bendangnugsang or Nungsang, the useless but ambitious son of a prestigious Naga family. In the narrative, Temsula Ao recounts how this college-dropout young boy, from a family of government servants and bureaucrats, dreams of becoming the moneymaker of the family (p. 123), becomes a corrupt army contractor (p. 125), turns to double-deal to make a quick buck (pp. 127-132), and finally succeeds in winning a seat to the state assembly by hoodwinking people with sentimentalizing tricks. Apparently, like most other stories included in the volume *These Hills Called Home: Stories from A War Zone,* this is also a narrative of shifting loyalties, changing equations that mark social, political and other landscapes in the conflict-stricken Naga Hills of the Nineteen Sixties and thereafter. However, what makes this narrative important from the p literary-critical point of view of the pastoral is an imperceptible but overriding duality of the rural and the urban as spaces of socio-cultural and ethical-emotional transactions.

While dealing with the almost incredible journey of Bendangnungsang or Nungsang from that of an unimpressive jobless life to that of a member of the Legislative Assembly 'A New Chapter' foregrounds the disarranging climate of the Naga homeland. The story, we are told, begins somewhere in the mid-sixties in Nagaland, a time of 'uneasy surface calm' (p. 122), a time that overturned the quiet lives of the Nagas and changed every single man and woman in the land forever. "Slowly and painfully, Nagas were beginning to look at themselves through new prisms, some self-created and some thrust upon them. Those who survived learned to adapt to the new trends and new lifestyles (122)." Calling attention to the overhauling upshots of conflict and confrontation with the Indian state, Ao writes:

> Old loyalties became suspect as new players emerged and forged makeshift alliances in unfamiliar political spaces. But the battle lines remained the same; the forces merely shifted their vantage points and re-invented their strategies to accommodate the new equations. While the underground forces retreated further into their jungle hideouts, the occupying army ensconced itself in prime locations in towns and villages and built new fortified homes away from home (122).

It is these contradictions and dilemmas that form the backdrop to 'A New Chapter'. Interestingly and paradoxically, this climate of indeterminacy that unsettles the ordinary man offers the breeding ground for a new class of Nagas more into fortune-seeking and co-optation. "They came to be known as army contractors who now entered the space between the opposing factions and were poised to make their fortunes from the spoils of the war (p. 123)." As Ao writes, "These contractors were a new class of Nagas, who emerged as the third force in the power equation between the two warring armies. Both sides recognised their utility in their game and used them unscrupulously (p. 123)." The story of Nungsang, offers a succinct illustration of these uneasy trade-offs amongst factions of self-seekers as well as between these and the state, eventually betraying the interest of their co-mates. Significantly, the betrayed co-mate, in the narratives under review, not only comes from rural hinterlands but represents the rural values of trust and bonhomie. In the story, it is Merenla, a widowed lady farmer and a distant cousin of Nungsang who is lured into a business agreement with Nungsang and eventually finds herself being scapegoated to the rapacity of Nungsang whom she considers as her kindred. As the narrative reveals, Nungsang is the youngest but frustrated child of a well-off Naga family. "He came from a good family; all his brothers and sisters held high government posts and he decided that if he could not be a 'sahib' like his siblings, he would be the money-maker of the family (p. 123)." Interestingly, his overambitious but exaggerated dreams of being a figure lack any practical sense of how to be rich. He begins as an ordinary supplier supplying vegetables and meat to military outposts. Several times he had to go to his village to procure vegetables and livestock to supply to outposts near the village. It is during one of such business trips, that Nungsang is 'reacquainted' with Merenla (p. 124), his poor yet self-esteemed, widowed cousin with her field of vegetables as her sole means of livelihood. As Nungsang comes to her village looking for supplies, Merenla finds a new market for her produce and is more than happy. As life gets easier for Merenla and her two small children with the flow of cash from Nungsang, Nungsang suddenly realizes that he is not making any profit at all out of his contracts. Disappointed and desperate, Nungsang approaches Bhandari, a dishonest and cunning contractor for a way out. Bhandari enables him to manipulate the supply contracts by substituting genuine items with cheap ones. "Bhandari merely gave him a pitying look and brought out a pen and paper. He made two columns and began to write. Parallel to the approved items, he put the names of alternatives; for example, in the place of meat-on-hoof he wrote pumpkins, squash and gourd (p. 126)." A different phase of business begins and the wheels of fortune turn in Nungsang's favour. He begins to make a good profit through this network of fraudulent substitution and gradually turns into a common bully of the town. He not only refuses to pay those small vendors supplying him meat, fish and vegetables but threatens them with 'veiled threats of dire consequence' (p. 128). He even succeeds in arranging a government job for the son of an underground leader cum childhood friend by emotionally blackmailing his parents and brothers, to bargain for his fraudulent deals. However, as the years roll along, an increasingly irritated Nungsang gets frustrated with his job. Ao writes:

> Though the business was now 'picking up', thanks to the various manipulations he had become an expert at, the years of being a mere contractor were beginning to take a toll on Nungsang. Though he still hobnobbed with people like Bhandari, he had always harboured notions of his superiority over people like him who come from nondescript backgrounds. He began to dream of a new future (p. 133).

The new dream that Nungsang is chasing is a seat in the state assembly in the forthcoming election. With Bhandari's support, Nungsang succeeds in wooing his family and co-contractors to support him. However, things prove to be much more challenging than his expectations as on the fourth last day of the campaign they are caught unaware by a huge and vibrant procession. "The whole town came out to watch the seemingly endless vehicles carrying hundreds of supporters of the rival candidate (p. 137)." Headed by Bhandari, Nungsang's camp plans out an immediate counter-move to this crisis. "What Imrong planned was to paint symbols and slogans on the white cloth and decorate each truck with a number of these, while smaller pieces would be made into flags. All would carry Nungsang's election symbol: a beautiful hornbill (p. 139)." The next day, Nungsang's camp takes out a procession not only predominated by flags and banners of the legendary and ancestral bird of the community but also by the disciplined disposition of its participants. Bhandari recalled, "how the riders in the trucks had been seen drinking and behaving rowdily and decided that their procession would project a sober and civilized image instead... no drunken and disorderly behaviour was to be tolerated (p. 139)." As expected, this orchestrated and manipulated politicization of the racial-cultural heritage managed to win the election for Nungsang.

> Even years later, older people recalled that the sight of the legendary bird stirred something elemental in their racial memory and they fancied that the birds had descended from their loft parches in the deep and dark jungles and had come to participate in the political parade with a clear message for the people. They claimed that their votes were swayed by the impact made by the sight of this ancestral symbol (p.140).

Eventually, Nungsang's camp succeeds in winning the election by corruption and coercion but the impressive journey of Nungsang comes at the cost of many casualties. The most immediate of these is the petty suppliers of the market who were "left licking their wounds while the newly elected Member made preparations to go to Kohima for the oath-taking (p. 142)." However, it is the poor village widow Merenla who emerges as the worst of all causalities. Like his other creditors, Nungsang also forgets Merenla and the promises made to her. Nobody comes to buy her pumpkins and they are left to be rotten in her courtyard. "She had begun to worry, for, unlike other years, this season, she not only planted pumpkin seeds in her field but she even leased a portion of her neighbour's land to do the same (p. 143)." Despite the grave sense of foreboding that overtakes her, Merenla still retains faith in her distant cousin Nungsang but not before much long, her trust is shattered. "But there was no word from either Nungsang or his friend. This poor woman who had innocently believed that she had found an easier way of earning a livelihood through this arrangement with her cousin, now found herself abandoned. She felt quite betrayed (p. 143)." Interestingly, it is not the loss of her labour that hurts Merenla, but the breach of the faith and trust she put on someone who posed as her cousin:

> This, she thought, was cruel because she was brought up on the tradition that the family ties were more sacrosanct than any others and besides, he did have a business obligation to her as well. Slowly and painfully she began to see that people who go away from villages think and act differently even if they are relatives. She said to herself over and over again that a fellow villager would never have treated her in this manner (p.144).

What reiterates Merenla's rural gullibility or innocuousness is the fact in all these years she never realizes the role played by her pumpkins in her cousin's "unscrupulous scramble for money and power and how she had been used in his scheme of dark dealing (p. 143)." Raising pigs and pumpkins and collaborating with her cousin, for her, is nothing but "a good and honest way" to earn a living for her sons and herself (p. 143)." This corroborates the attributes of rustic simplicity and honesty which marks Merenla's rustic self and to this extent foregrounds her as an effective antithesis to the corrupt, complex and misguided urbanites such as Nungsang and Bhandari.

What further reinforces the rural-urban contradiction that underlies the narrative is Merenla's unusual response to the crisis that leaves her shattered. As an increasingly crippling sense of being betrayed unsettles her, Merenla decides to act. She invites her relatives to her cottage and gives away to them as many pumpkins as they want. "Yet many more remained, threatening once more to engulf Merenla and her sons with their rotting odour symbolising the great debacle of this simple woman's venture as a 'supplier' (p. 145)." Unable to free herself from the memories of betrayal and mistrust, Merenla next performs something unusual. "Wearing a red scarf on her head, Merenla Began to shout 'Vote for' loudly and with every shout she would hurl a pumpkin to the ground below (p. 145)." Interestingly, to the co-villagers, this was almost like re-performing a strange ritual performed in the old days to get rid of something unclean. It is important to note the way the ethnic heritage or rituals are (mis)-appropriated by Merenla as well as Nungsang. Whereas Nungsang's camp objectifies the ancestral bird and by extension the Naga ethnic heritage, for Merenla, the village widow, re-performing the ritual is a way to regain her lost sense of integrity. The symbolic re-performance of a cleansing or purifying ritual is a spontaneous and selfless act rather than a self-seeking one. This whole episode, thus, brings to the fore the conflict between an essentially organic, simple and hence preferable rustic/rural consciousness and an unthinking, uncaring and distorted urbanism making slow inroads into Ao's ethnic homeland. In the story, Merenla emerges as the symbol of that vanishing but preferred time and space that is Naga Hills, an extraordinary epic made of a cluster of village republics, founded on and sustained through a tradition of trust and loyalty. In that homeland, honour and honesty still win the day, unlike the one of Nungsang and Bhandari.

It is important to take note of the use of 'cleansing' as a central trope towards the last part of the story. Merenla's act of hurling away the rotten pumpkins at the village street is not aimed at clearing only her home, but more importantly, her mind. "Tired, as she was, she was determined to rid her home and her life of all the reminders of her earlier association with her kinsman, and as soon as she felt rested, she resumed the task of 'cleansing' (p. 147)." As desired, Merenla succeeds in absolving herself from the enticing associations with her distant and designing, urbanised cousin. What reinforces the pastoral appeal of the text is the construction of not only the poor widow farmer Merenla but the collective response of her co-villagers in general. The care and compassion that underscore their reaction to her crisis as well as attempts to conciliation is another effective antithesis to the disruption and dislocations in the urbane centres. The villagers immediately recognize "the message that she conveyed to them through her very vociferous and public rejection of this identity on the day that she had 'cleansed' her house and herself of something that had 'wounded' her both in the material and psychological sense (p. 147)." From the day of material-symbolic cleansing, the village people stopped calling her

'Pumpkin Merenla', a name which they gave to her during the period of her association with Nungsang. The narrative ends on a happy and carefree note that marks the restoration of rustic regularity and rhythm. "Life in the village went on as before and this simple woman, now called Merenla as before, unobtrusively merged into the rhythm of age-old village life, far away from the political permutations and combinations forming and re-forming elsewhere in the land (p. 147)." Thus, the final part of the narrative reiterates the unmissable disparity between the rural and the urbanised Naga homeland. It will be useful, at this point, to recall Temsula Ao's view on the writerly obligations she feels to her homeland. She writes:

> The inheritors of such a history have a tremendous responsibility to sift through the collective experience and make sense of the impact left by the struggle on their lives. *Our social wisdom has always extolled the virtue of human beings living at peace with themselves and in harmony with nature and with our neighbours*. It is only when the Nagas re-embrace and re-write this vision into the fabric of their lives despite the compulsions of a fast-changing world, can we say that the memories of the turbulent years have served us well (p. Xi: emphasis added).

It is not insignificant that despite being set in the backdrop of trouble and unease, Ao's narrative celebrates the collective heritage of resilience, peace, harmony and solidarity symbolised by the distressed and deceived yet determined village women Merenla, her co-mates and their rural world. It will not be incorrect to view, to this extent, the different layers of transactions— material, emotional and ethical— as symbolic constructions of juxtaposed rurality and town-culture. The villages, despite the onrush of misshaped and deviant urban priorities with surreptitious implications, continue to be places of respite and resort or so to say, of retreat. Merenla's encounter with Nungsang and his eventual disillusionment, from this perspective, is best viewed as an unusual and interesting example of the pastoral passage of retreat and return. From the perspective of the pastoral discourse, the rural hinterland of Merenla could be viewed as an important critical space to engage with the rural/urban problem in a fast-fluctuating ethnic homeland, namely the Naga Hills of northeast India.

Temsula Ao's short story 'A New Chapter' illustrates not only the ways contemporary pastorals depart from the hackneyed frames and focus of the conventional pastoral but also how the genre has effectively adapted itself to emerging socio-spatial dynamics and contexts. Situated in the borderlines of India, the postcolonial Naga Hills continue to be in a state of unease and fluctuation. The question/ imagination of a homeland continues to be central to the rhetoric and reality of nation-building in troubled postcolonial sites such as Nagaland. Ao's narrative emerges as an important creative-critical site to look at this key theme of post-colonial politics in the northeast and while doing so foregrounds the role of the pastoral as a potential alternative perspective.

Works Cited

Ao, T. (2006) 'A New Chapter', *These Hills Called Home: Stories from A War-Zone,* New Delhi, Zubaan. Pp.121-147.

Ao, T. (2006) 'The Night', *These Hills Called Home: Stories from A War-Zone,* New Delhi, Zubaan, Pp. 44-56.

Baruah, S. (2005) *Durable Disorder: Understanding the Politics of Northeast India.* New Delhi, OUP.

Bhaumik, S. (2009) *Troubled Periphery: Crisis of India's North-East,* New Delhi, Sage.

Gifford, T. (2009) *Pastoral,* New York, Routledge.

Hazarika, S. (1995) *Strangers of the Mist: Tales of war & Peace from India's Northeast,* New Delhi, Penguin.

Marx, L. (1964) *The Machine in the Garden: Technology and the Pastoral Ideal in America,* New York, OUP.

The Pastoral as History and Myth: 'Professorial' Travail in Freya Stark's Ionian Quest

Pastoral literature and lifestyle are often a reaction to 'modernity' and an escape to the nostalgia of a largely imagined past. Romantic evocations of rural bucolicity in the wake of urbanisation usually accompany the binaries of city and village life, and this idea of the nostalgic pastoral is usually produced for the consumption of the Western urban subject, alienated by modern life seeking refuge in the idea of simpler times and pleasures. 'Literary Travel Writing', the notoriously mutable genre of literature, evokes an idea of the pastoral in its aspiration of ascendance and escape from the Cartesian one-dimensionality of modern life. The Modern Travel Book, much like the predominant movement of its time, Modernism — one of whose variants produced the definitive Modern Travel Book in the form of Robert Byron's *The Road to Oxiana* (1937) — was a reaction to capitalist modernity in the 20th century that was commodifying the idea of travel to the extent that it was now nearly indistinguishable from its antithesis, tourism. The genre of pastoral literature is almost as hazy as travel writing. Fredrick Garber writes in *Pastoral Spaces*; "Pastoral is not, it seems, a genre in the sense that tragedy and comedy have come to be defined" (Garber, 1988, p. 431). The pastoral, with its evocation of nostalgia, is more of a mode than a genre, as distinguished by Paul Alpers. The objective of this paper is to extend the idea of pastoral beyond Terry Gifford's three main definitions of the Pastoral — depiction of the life of rural folk (shepherds), a contrast of the countryside with the urban and the derogatory depiction of country life — to a foray into myth and history in the wake of industrial capitalism's transformation of human mobility and travel in the 20th century.

Paul Fussell, while identifying the genre of the Travel Book in *Abroad: British Literary Travelling Between the Wars*, refused to include Freya Stark's writing in his study. Although he applauds Stark's laborious efforts in undertaking her journeys, he feels that her writing lacks "the dimension of delight in language and disposition, in all the literary contrivances" (Fussell, 1982, p. 197). He also takes offence at the various awards that Stark received from the British government, including medals and grants from the Royal Geographical Society. Fussell seems to believe that Freya Stark represented the establishment, unlike the rebellious subversions of Robert Byron's Gentleman persona.

In this chapter, I, however, seek to argue that Dame Freya Madeline Stark's (1893-1993) scholarly quest to Ionia was a further subversion of the contentious 'Gentlemanly persona' in literary travel writing, primarily by her being a woman; in fact, she was the first white woman to have explored parts of the 'Middle East' and a pioneering legend of modern travel literature. Her works epitomize the quality of erudition that has historically set the scholarly benchmark for the Modern Travel Book, as identified by Fussell. Stark was of Polish-German descent and spent a childhood of solitude in the shadow of illness and her parents' troubled marriage. Confined at home, she took recourse to reading and learned French and Latin on her own. On her ninth birthday, receiving a copy of *One Thousand and One Nights* led to a permanent fascination with the Orient (The theme of Orientalism is one of the foundational themes of travel writing which has drawn much flak from postcolonial critics such as Mary Louise Pratt). That she could travel to these faraway places as a woman was also a result of defiance against her initial years of ill health and a tragic factory accident at the age of 13 that permanently disfigured her face despite many skin grafting surgeries. As she grew up, she studied Arabic and Persian and attended the School of Oriental and African Studies (SOAS) and Bedford College in London.

Stark broke stereotypes of her privileged class and education by registering as a nurse at the brink of the First World War. During the late 1920s and 1930s, she travelled through Eastern Persia, where she explored and located the 'Valleys of Assassins' in the mountains between Iraq and Iran. In 1935, she travelled to *Hadramaut* in modern-day Yemen and chronicled her journeys in her Arabian trilogy, for which she was awarded the Founder's Medal of the Royal Geographical Society — which seems to have contributed to

Paul Fussell's displeasure, and subsequent refusal to include her works in his study of literary travelling.

Extending the Genre of the Pastoral and Travel Writing

According to Terry Gifford, the term 'pastoral' has gone beyond Leo Marx's definition of "no shepherd, no pastoral" (Gifford, 2020, p. 1) to beyond the "artifice of the specific literary form" (Gifford, 2020, p. 1). In recent times, the term has come to mean a broader retreat into a notion of the 'country', which in different ways contrasts with the notion of the 'urban'. Here, if we are to equate this notion of the urban with Western liberal modernity, the equivalent of 'country' would be the nostalgia of myth and history. This is how the chapter seeks to reinterpret the 'pastoral' as a retreat into myth and history, in the genre of 'travel writing' with the explicit intention of retreating from the alienation of an increasingly 'urban' condition of modernity.

Travel writing often exhibits a prominent phenomenological motif, emphasizing the subjective experience of the world as perceived by the traveller and the intricate relationship between the traveller and their surroundings. How the traveller relates to it is either through a residue of experience left by an earlier traveller or an experience gleaned through some other source. The fictional aspect of travel writing is, therefore, the 'perspective', the 'point of view' which brings any literary text into being. Both Travel and Travel Writing are about leaving home, the *oikos* (which means 'home' and everything that entails being at home in the Greek philosophical tradition), and going into the unfamiliar. The places change with time, but the accounts of the journeys remain frozen in time. Since travel writing is, in a sense, both fiction and non-fiction given the way it is crafted and also the subject position of the author-persona, the aspects of time and narrative are important for this discussion. The French philosopher Paul Ricœur, distinguishes between historical and fictional narratives, as Elina Theodorou Staikou argues in *Metaphors of Travel and Writing:*

> The Deconstruction of the "At-Home" and the Promise of the Other: "The phenomenological motif of travel writing by definition roots

it in the experience of the present, nevertheless a present that bears the imprints of a past (the traveller's cultural past, the historical past of the culture visited, the span or division of time between and throughout perception and inscription) and of a future (the impending return and integration to the home culture, which is at once a past and a future). These can never consist of successive episodes in a journey; they are far more complex and implicated with one another. (Staikou, 2002, p. 161)

Paul Fussell's *Abroad: British Literary Travelling Between the Wars* has given us the first model to read Travel Writing, where he looks back at travel in the 20th century and identifies figures such as T.E. Lawrence's *Seven Pillars of Wisdom* as the vanguard of the British Literary Diaspora in the 1920s and 30s. Fussell distinguishes the *Travel Book* from the *Guide Book*, which is prescriptive, not autobiographical or dependent on a narrative which sustains itself with elements of fiction. Trying to define what a travel book is, writes Fussell, is more akin to exploration than travel. Fussell writes:

> A guidebook is addressed to those who plan to follow the traveller, doing what he has done, but more selectively. A travel book, at its 'purest', is addressed to those who do not plan to follow the traveller at all, but who require the exotic or comic anomalies, wonders, and scandals of the literary form romance which their place or time cannot entirely supply. "Travel books are a sub-species of memoir in which the autobiographical narrative arises from the speaker's encounter with distant or unfamiliar data, and in which the narrative—unlike that in a novel or a romance- claims literal validity by constant reference to actuality. (Fussell, 1982, p. 203)

This seems to go against the grain of phenomenological thought. Fussell's claim of reference to 'actuality' is merely the classic realist device of verisimilitude of first-person narrative, and this is what this chapter seeks to contest by considering Fussell's attempt at this nomenclature and expanding it by including writers he consciously rejected such as Freya Stark; while also extending the idea of the pastoral to the escapist realms of history and myth.

Ionia: Cradle of Civilization as the Pastoral

Freya Stark's unique professorial travel in *Ionia: A Quest* was published in 1951, at the age of 61, in the backdrop of a lifetime of engagement with travel and travel writing during the golden age of travel between the Wars. (Ionia is a region in ancient Greece, on the eastern coast of the Aegean Sea. Many prominent Greek city-states-including Miletus, Ephesus, and Priene, were based in this region-which shaped the growth of Western philosophy, science and literature. The region was a transcultural melting point between Greece and the Near East.) This was her first book in a trilogy of Turkish travel books published through the 1950s, the others being: *The Lycian Shore* (1956) and *Alexander's Path: From Caria to Cilicia* (1958). *Ionia: A Quest* is a journey through time and history, where Stark transcends the realm of physical travel and forays into an ancient world of culture and civilization that resonates, yet is seemingly drifting far from the realities of modern life. Written in lyrical prose, Stark complements descriptions of her present world with evocatively long digressions into ancient history that is, paradoxically, both alien and yet intimately familiar to the modern reader, evoking a sense of the Freudian uncanny.

Ionia begins with an epigram that denounces tourism, "The reader he has in mind is the tourist, who visited Greece for pleasure" (Stark, 1954, Epigram to *Ionia: A Quest*). In the Autumn of 1952, Stark travelled about the Western coasts of Asia Minor, and among the 55 sites of historic ruins that she visited, she found only one tourist, in Pergamum — a great city in ancient Ionia, whose ruins are located in modern-day Turkey — who was sightseeing, ostensibly just like Stark. However, Freya Stark was no ordinary 'tourist', merely sightseeing. Her quest is an attempt to recover from the fragments of history that remained neglected like broken columns and walls that were often hidden away under foliage and trees that had grown over them "like a manuscript whose words have ebbed away" (Stark, 1954, p. xiii).

From there, she attempts to construct a record of these times that have come "trickling down through the slopes of time towards us through devious tunnels" (Stark, 1954, p xiii). These form a part of the history of the origins of both Eastern and Western civilizations. Her quest is to fill in historical gaps, and also to discover what elements from that original breeding ground of civilization could be recovered and adapted in the mid-20th century emerging modernity. This is the 'double search' of this book, it's not a touristic exercise in consumption, but a conscious and intellectually laborious dive into the past to excavate meaning from myth and history by travelling through the present. This quest is to serve as a guidebook—which, in turn, manifests itself as a bridge between Fussell's distinction between a Travel Book and a guidebook— among the ruins, and Stark forewarns that it would require as much patience for the reader to read, as it took for the writer to write it, which is 'travail' at its purest form, which even Paul Fussell attests to. Stark's quest aims to ask far-reaching questions, and she asserts that her results lie upon a groundwork of historical facts as much as her means allow. As Stark is not a historian or a scholar, she reveals that she began this erudite project with a similar level of ignorance that the first-time readers of the book could be expected to have.

Before embarking on the journey to see the ruins of this city, Stark decides that she needs a guide. As she was limiting her travel to Ionia, she realizes that the difficulties therefore lie not in space, but in the mysteries of time, and chooses to use Herodotus, the ancient Greek Historian and author of *The Histories* (written around 450 BC) as her travelling companion. Justifying her odd choice of a guide from so far back in antiquity, Stark writes:

> I would be led to the world I desired: and as for not finding things standing—I am one of those who prefer neglected ruins, places untouched even by the archaeologist, where one's thoughts can build their palaces, and the past, draped and veiled in its garment of earth, lies like the sleeping beauty undiscovered and undisturbed (Stark, 1954, p. 17).

Herodotus is regarded as the father of scholarship in history, whose famous treatise *The Persian Wars*, in addition to chronicling dates, different characters and battle strategies, also attempted to analyse the events behind the battles and the larger narrative of the war. Herodotus has, however, been criticised by subsequent 'professional' historians for taking liberties with 'facts' and including dialogues in his books of characters that never interacted in real life, even while Herodotus himself strives to remind his readers that his account, just like much of travel writing, is coloured with his interpretations and opinions. Through this declaration of her intention of using Herodotus as her guide, Stark reminds the readers that her authorities for the sources of myth and history are not conventionally academic, and would mostly be rejected by a historian. This emphasises the fictional nature of this seemingly non-fictional project. *Ionia: A Quest*, as an eclectic blend of myth and history, is therefore, as much fiction, as it is a work of non-fiction.

"An Innocent and Authentic Curiosity" and the "Pastoral"

Ionia: A Quest begins with a description of dawn in Ionia in ornate prose where Stark describes sunrise in Ionia in imagistic literary language, as she writes of the sun that "she slipped along evenly, and split the smooth surface of the sea as if it were silk. From the horizon, darkening not in a sharp line but definitely like blotting paper, a colour of violets deepened and encompassed our world (Stark, 1954, p. 3)." Descriptions like these abound throughout the book, emphasising the languorous literariness of her writing. As she immerses herself into alterity, Stark observes the quiet pride of the Turkish, who seem respectful, but never appear servile, and comes to recognize this quality as the charm of Turkish manners. Her lyrical prose is laced with biting humour, which would probably be deemed offensive in the 21st century, such as the line "Two middle-aged women moved about like battleships, so square and broad below: they were built in the Doric order and made everything look fragile around them" (Stark, 1954, p. 3). This description, however, is one of her first impressions of the people and the place, and her insights into the plight of women in ancient Greece get more sympathetic and insightful during the book.

Travellers in the middle of the 20th century, when they were still pioneers in journeys, they undertook always laid out a philosophy of travel. Stark, too is full of this self-consciousness, as she wonders what she is travelling to find and what her real motivations for such a journey could be. With some soul-searching, Stark concludes that her motivation for travel, far from being an exercise in consumption, is "pure, disinterested curiosity, the human thrust in time (Stark, 1954, p. 4)." It is a curiosity that is its end and not a means to some specific goal. Stark observes that the British are to be criticised for the lack of this virtue of authentic and innocent curiosity. She writes: "Curiosity ought to increase as one gets older. The Earth grows bigger, it ceases to contain itself, it laps beyond its sphere; and Time comes less and less to be confined in this tangible air (Stark, 1954, p. 4)".

While Enlightenment rationality insists on the creation of knowledge and accumulation of data, Stark prefers to ponder on the unknown—what cannot be known through primary perception—much like Alphonso Lingis, whose travels and philosophy of travel I discuss in "Existential Alterity in Alphonso Lingis's Abuses" — for example, the elemental sensations of the night about her, with its distinctive sounds and silences, or the mysterious music of the islands to which she has no frame of reference. Stark argues that education neglected the pursuit of disinterested curiosity in the dark and middle-ages of Europe because of ignorance of scientific ideas, and also because of the hold of religion on the people. However, in Classical Greece, education was aligned towards this pursuit where the observation of natural phenomena—like sunrise and sunset—generates a lot of scientific speculation, in addition to a sense of genuine delight. Stark argues that this Ionian curiosity was not because the world or human civilization was new. She writes that this 'disinterested curiosity' does not arise from a sense of security — which the ancient Ionians certainly did not enjoy — but was something which seems ineffable in modern times, as its meaning does not seem to have any referent in the contemporary world.

Freya Stark's notion of 'disinterested curiosity' also finds resonance in William Empson's definition of the pastoral as the "process of putting the complex into the simple" (Empson, 1935, p. 23). Empson, therefore, justifies the inclusion of "non-rural" texts as versions of the pastoral since "the essential trick of the old pastoral, which was felt to imply a beautiful relationship between rich and poor, was to make simple people express strong feelings (felt as the most universal subject, something fundamentally true about everybody) in learned and fashionable language" (Empson, 1935, p. 11). Analysing the nature of this 'innocent curiosity' and its elusiveness in the modern world, Stark writes that it exists outside the symbolic limits of the structure of language. Even though — through writing and speech — language, to an extent, can seek to reconstruct the geographical landscape and the thoughts they generated among the people at the time, this 'innocent curiosity' is evoked through encounters with material vestiges of the past such as simple ruins of pottery and items of quotidian use from millennia ago.

Just like Robert Byron's *The Road to Oxiana*, Stark's account is interspersed with photographs of Ionia such as The Agora in Smyrna and The Amphorae of Clazomenae. As Stark reaches Smyrna, she observes that it is "the first civilized state ever planted on the west coast of Asia Minor" (Stark, 1954, p.9). It is from here that the Phrygians reportedly drove Pelops, cites Stark. By referencing Pelops' encounter with the Phrygians, the text incorporates a mythical element into the historical discourse. This blending of myth and history is a common feature in ancient narratives, as it adds a layer of symbolic meaning and cultural significance to the events being described. Stark, too, lyrically describes the scenes of the places coupled with history and mythology and feels that "the Ionian scenery, keyed to a perfection so delicate and unobtrusive that, like the more elusive woman, it needs both devotion and time" (Stark, 1954, p. 11). Dwelling on the history of Clazomenae, she touches upon the story of the philosopher Anaxogoras, whose teachings were handed on to Pericles and Euripides. Observing that the early Ionian philosophers had a passionate interest in weather, Stark disagrees with the notion that ancient writers had no feeling for scenery, and writes that this could apply if we look at static backgrounds, which are passive and meant to be looked at and admired; such as the landscapes of towns where the notion of the 'picturesque' was conceived. The Ionians, however, were treated to views of an animated horizon, always dynamic. It is not scenery but vision, "the eyes of men who live with an open country around them and look at what they see (Stark, 1954, p. 22)." It was a world, Stark reiterates, where curiosity — a trait increasingly diminishing in the 20th century — reigned supreme. Freya Stark's narrative, thus, fits with Roger Sale's argument about the essentially escapist nature of the pastoral, where the escape is not only in seeking refuge in the countryside but also in the past.

Freya Stark had a complicated relationship with British imperialism as she was staunchly British, though having been raised out of England in Italy. Many critics have identified Stark as an imperialist, and in *Ionia: A Quest*, Stark unironically devotes a section to her reflections on imperialism. Dwelling on the commercial and cultural homogenisation brought about by the construction of highway networks, she writes about how the *Hittite* sculptures that trace the routes of Anatolia are on the cliff of the Hermus valley and can be seen from a road being widened by American bulldozers. The same road was described by Herodotus, and its system of posts instituted by the Persians survived into the modern age of the railway system. This Trans-Anatolian highway was also the first instance of a road that saw the use of coined money authorized by government stamps. The Greek cities, though they were repeatedly conquered, were treated with care because of their geographic location by every nation that ran the Asiatic Road. Stark sees the formula of colonialism in this light where an enterprising maritime fringe dominates a producing but more primitive mainland. She writes that "Imperialism is simply the use of inland productiveness for the benefit of the power at the sea-end or other commercial outlet of a trade route" (Stark, 1954, p. 47). As many of the ancient Greek colonies were established close to the sea by the Ionian coast, the colonies had a profound cultural impact on what we now recognise as ancient Greek culture; including the formation of the Greek alphabet and art, which bear close resemblance to the civilizations of the ancient Near-East. As Stark passes through Greece, she thinks of all the English Gentlemen travellers who have passed through this place. Stark believes that the 19th century was the best time for travel books as a lot of quintessential British gentlemen travellers passed through Turkey: "a variety of tough and cultivated people were about there, and if it is true that every country gets the Englishmen it deserves — the deservings of Turkey rank high" (Stark 1954, p. 98). Stark describes 'pure' travellers like W.M. Leake in

1880 and amateurs like Sir Charles Fellows, to erudite clergymen, to engineers like Mr Wood who discovered the Artemisium in Ephesus. We see here that Stark is very conscious of the Gentleman's dominance over travel, but feels very much at home taking her place within the category and considers herself a part of this tradition. Her account is thus a rare perspective of a woman in the tradition of Gentlemanly travel.

Stark's account falls in a liminal space between history and mythology, as she reconstructs the violence and turbulence of the Ionian era from a time before Christ to a few centuries into the first millennium. It seems as though history before the industrial age was very different and almost stable and thousands of years of a way of life is suddenly in the process of vanishing with large-scale excavation projects and the impending modernity even in the 1950s. As she travels towards the centre of Ionia, Stark writes that she leaves history, both medieval and modern behind. Stark writes that one of the questions she would ask Herodotus if she had an hour's conversation with him would be his opinion about foreigners. She suspects that his opinions would be much like an English gentleman of her times:

> He would be interested in what is remote and pleased with its variety, and safe in the consciousness that his own was best. If one's lot is not best, one has altered it long ago: and as the Greeks spent so much time and energy in discovering the good life, it would be depressing for them to think that other people, with less mental effort, had succeeded in finding a better. (Stark, 1954, p. 141)

Underlying her philosophy of travel, Stark writes that the respect which curiosity inspires makes it more welcome than charity for it makes us not only in love with, but also interested in the 'other'.

Conclusion

Raymond Williams observes in *The Country and the City* (1973) that the pastoral celebrates an idyllic past: "An idealization, based on a temporary situation and a deep desire for stability, served to evade the actual and bitter contradictions of the time" (Williams, 1975, p. 60). This chapter has sought to demonstrate how Freya Stark, too, in a similar vein reacts to the end of the golden age of travel between the two World Wars, to construct Ionia as a pastoral other to encroaching modernity and mass tourism.

In her final thoughts on her travels, Stark reflects on how the legacy of millennia of civilization is carried forward through generations and can perhaps only be accessed by this kind of erudite travail that evokes history and myth in the mould of the pastoral to provide an escape into time from postcolonial industrial modernity. The primary element in the Pastoral is nostalgia, but in this instance, nostalgia transcends its emotional component to become a performance. As Fredrick Garber observes: "Nostalgia is more than a feeling because, in its pastoral form, it is also the creator of an act. It is an impulse, energy, force, and a thrust…what nostalgia performs or causes to be performed, is the *nostos*, the act of return, the homecoming (in its pastoral version a seeking for return or homecoming) that appears in all pastorals and is essential to the workings of the mode (Garber, 1988, p. 458)." This mode of the pastoral, which makes us imagine radical alternatives to the problems of the present, projects a "being-in-world" as well as a "being-in-history". This kind of erudite travel, travel writing, and even reading these kinds of travel books is something of a lost art. Colin Thubron, one of the last living "Gentleman travellers", has famously said that reading *Ionia: A Quest* inspired him to travel, and counts it among his favourite books of all time. This chapter has examined this escapist, yet erudite "travel of the mind" as an evocation of a romantic pastoral that seeks an alternative to the emerging commercial tourism. The cerebral travail in this kind of travel is the severe intellectual labour that Stark undertakes as the purpose of her journey, making digressions into history, philosophy, art and the nostalgia of ancient cultures. She defies the idea of the British gentleman in various rebellious ways, all the while embodying the erudite persona and indulging in nostalgic musings among the ruins of past civilizations.

Works Cited

Alpers, P. J. (1979) 'What is pastoral?', ELH, 46(1), pp. 1-23.

Bernard, J. (1996) 'Recent Studies In Renaissance Pastoral', English Literary Renaissance, 26(2), pp. 356-84. Available at: http://www.jstor.org/stable/43447524

Byron, R. (1982) *The Road to Oxiana*. Oxford University Press.

Chatterjee, A. (2019) 'Existential Alterity in Alphonso Lingis's Abuses', Critical Quarterly, 61(3), pp. 92-106. doi: 10.1111/criq.12494.

Fussell, P. (1982) *Abroad: British Literary Travelling between the Wars*. Oxford University Press.

Garber, F. (1988) 'Pastoral Spaces', Texas Studies in Literature and Language, 30(3), pp. 431-60. Available at: http://www.jstor.org/stable/40754867

Gifford, T. (2020) *Pastoral*. Routledge.

Lawrence, T. E. (1992). *Lawrence of Arabia: Seven Pillars of Wisdom*. Easton Press.

Herodotus. (1998). *The Histories*. Translated by Robin Waterfield. Oxford University Press.

"One Thousand and One Nights." (2010). Translated by Malcolm C. Lyons. Penguin Classics.

Williams, R. (1975) *The Country and the City*. London: Chatto & Windus.

Sales, R. (1983) *English Literature in History 1780-1830: Pastoral and Politics*. London: Hutchinson.

Staikou, E. T. (2002) '*Metaphors of Travel and Writing: Deconstruction of the "at-Home" and the Promise of the Other*', PhD thesis, University of Warwick.

Stark, F. (1954). *Ionia: A Quest*. John Murray.

Stark, F. (1956). *The Lycian Shore*. John Murray.

Stark, F. (1958). *Alexander's Path: From Caria to Cilicia*. John Murray.

Todorov, T. (1990) *Genres in Discourse*. Cambridge University Press.

ibidem.eu